To Mr. Bernard Feinman
with my compliments
and kind regards

H. Leon Merlin.

9/10/1980.

THE OLD AGE STORY

THE OLD AGE STORY

by

LEON MERKIN, M.D.

VANTAGE PRESS

NEW YORK   WASHINGTON   HOLLYWOOD

FIRST EDITION

All rights reserved, including the right of reproduction in whole or in part in any form.

Copyright, © 1971, by Leon Merkin.

Published by Vantage Press, Inc.
516 West 34th Street, New York, N.Y. 10001

Manufactured in the United States of America.

Standard Book No. 533-00003-3

Dedicated to my beloved wife

ROZA KIZIA

Motto

(*From a Prayer*)

"O, God, our Lord,
Cast us not off
When we are old,
Forsake us not
When our strength
Faileth."

CONTENTS

Introduction   xi

PART I

The Organic Diseases of Old Age

CHAPTER		PAGE
I.	Who Is Old?	17
II.	The Anatomy of Old Age	20
III.	The Physiology of Old Age	24
IV.	The Pathology of Old Age	28
V.	Arteriosclerosis, or Hardening of the Arteries	31
VI.	Arteriosclerosis of the Heart (a) Coronary Artery Disease (b) Coronary Artery Occlusion	36
VII.	Arteriosclerotic Hypertension, or High Blood Pressure and Stroke Due to Hardening of the Arteries	48
VIII.	Little Strokes	59
IX.	Other Old-Age Diseases of the Heart	64
X.	The Brain in Old Age	68
XI.	The Diseases of the Peripheral Circulation in Old Age	81
XII.	The Eyes and the Ears in Old Age	90
XIII.	Lung Diseases in Old Age	97
XIV.	Diseases of Digestion in Old Age	106
XV.	Constipation and Diarrhea	113
XVI.	Gas and Gas Pain	124

XVII.	Diabetes in Old Age	129
XVIII.	Diseases of the Muscles, Joints and Bones	135

    (a) Rheumatism
    (b) Arthritis
    (c) Gout
    (d) Osteoporosis
    (e) Low Back Pain

XIX.	Diseases of the Prostate	147
XX.	Women's Change of Life and Women's Old-Age Diseases	155
XXI.	Old Age and Obesity	166
XXII.	Lack of Appetite in Old Age	178
XXIII.	Anemia and Other Blood Diseases	181
XXIV.	Allergies in Old Age	186
XXV.	Accidents, Fractures and Surgery in Aged Patients	189
XXVI.	Alcoholism in Old Age	195
XXVII.	Sex Life in Old Age	203

    (a) Sex in Men
    (b) Sex in Women

PART II

Mental Health in Old Age

XXVIII.	Mental Diseases in Old Age	219

    (a) Progressive Paralysis
    (b) Senile Depression
    (c) Paranoia (Persecution Mania)
    (d) Physical Defects Causing Mental Disturbances

        (e) Memory Defects
        (f) Senility

XXIX.	Suicide in Old Age	233
XXX.	Death and Dying in Old Age	237
XXXI.	Sleep in Old Age (Dreams)	244

PART III

Life in The "Golden" Old Age

XXXII.	Occupations in Old Age	255
XXXIII.	Hobbies in Old Age	261
XXXIV.	Sport and Physical Activities in Old Age	266
XXXV.	Marriage and Re-marriage, Separation and Divorce in Old Age	274
XXXVI.	Children, Grandchildren and Relatives in Old Age	283
XXXVII.	Life Expectancy and Longevity in Old Age	291
XXXVIII.	The Problem of Retirement	304
XXXIX.	Where to Live in Old Age?	312

        (a) Nursing Homes
        (b) Homes for the Aged
        (c) Residences for Old-Age People

Postscript	329
Acknowledgments	332
Notes about the Author	333

INTRODUCTION

Our population is aging. Thanks to penicillin, streptomycin and other antibiotics we are able to cure pneumonia, tuberculosis and other infectious diseases which shortened the life of people and kept longevity on a low level. Many other diseases which killed people at younger ages are now manageable and allow the patients to attain old age—to give only the example of pernicious anemia, or subacute endocarditis (inflammation of the lining of the heart), or heart failure. The great advances in prevention of children's diseases; the vaccinations against polio, measles, diphtheria, etc.; the knowledge of the cause of diseases and their treatment—all this pushed life expectancy up, and increased the number of older people. The medical advances in the last 50 years were greater than in the preceding 500 years. And, last but not least, economic progress, industrialization, the new methods of agriculture and of preservation of food, the care for the purity of it and of the water, the much higher standard of living which allowed people to be fed well, to be housed adequately, to be dressed more appropriately to changes of climate, the possibility of more rest, more vacations, more participation in sports—all this gave people a greater chance to survive, to live a longer span of life, and under better conditions.

If we accept the fact of an older age of our population, then we have to ask ourselves at which age are we old? And the second question is, What should be our span of life? Both questions cannot be answered definitely, because one can be old at the age of 45, while another is still young in body and soul at the age of 80 or more. Then comes also the problem—Do we speak about external appearances or about the medical findings for the determination of aging? A person can look old and be just the same completely healthy. On the other hand, people can look very well and youngish and still suffer from diseases which have to be attributed to the ravages of age. The calendar age is in this respect completely irrelevant. From the medical point of view it is the function of the organs which determines the actual age of a person, in other words—the aging process of the body and its organs. In short, the question at which age we are old is a moot question and completely individual.

Of course, there are certain accepted norms which are neither medical nor corresponding to realities of daily life. Social Security considers 65 as the beginning of old age. For women they consider, just as arbitrarily, 62 as the turning point. In many institutions, corporations, military establishments, etc., 65 is the age of compulsory retirement. It means literally that, one day before your 65th birthday you are still full of vigor and capable of working full-time with zeal and competence; on the day of your birthday you are suddenly considered old, decrepit, no good, not to be trusted to make a proper decision as would be expected from a young man, say, of 64. It sounds and it is ridiculous, but such is life. Of course, there are plenty of men of 65 or women of 62 who would gladly retire at that age, who look forward to that fateful birthday because they are just tired. On the average, they have worked already 40 years—that is enough. They are too tired to go to the "salt mines," tired of the daily routine. They want to live a more gracious, more relaxed life which will allow them to get engrossed in hobbies, to travel, to play, to sleep—in short, what they call enjoying life to the full.

We should also be not so selfish. Younger people want a promotion, more responsibility and more acceptance of their abilities. So the old people have to make room for the younger generation and to become onlookers, to watch on the sidelines how the youngsters are doing. This is, in a nutshell, the answer to the question at which age are we old. The second question, What should be our ideal span of life? is just as difficult to answer. The Bible fixed it at three score and ten, measuring 70. This is arbitrary, of course; it happens to be the age at which King David died. But even in the Bible there are differences of opinion. So, in the "Ethics of the Fathers," it says, "At sixty a man attains old age, at seventy his head is heavy, at eighty he has the gift of 'special strength,' at ninety he bends beneath the weight of years, at a hundred he is as if he were already dead and has passed away from the world." Of course everybody knows about the age of Methuselah, who lived over 900 years; but we don't know how the years were calculated at the time when the Bible was written. In our times, the span of life differed and still differs all over the world. One hundred years ago 45 was the average age in civilized countries, though there were a lot of people who attained 80 or more. At 30 one belonged to middle age. The girls married at 16 or 15; at 30 they were already middle-aged matrons with 6, 7 or more children of all ages. Now, with improvement of health and economic conditions in the affluent societies, thirty is young, 40 to 50 middle-aged, 60-70 older age or elderly, 80 very old. At the same time the life-span in underdeveloped countries is still very low; and forty years is advanced age, if not old.

One has, however, to make in the calculation of the life-span in the U.S.A. and Western European countries, one basic observation. Longevity, on the average, as statistics show, is not due solely to attaining older age by the average person, but by the fact that, due to vaccinations and better treatment, the children do not die as much as, say, 50 years ago. They used to die from children's diseases; the infantile mortality was high, what with summer diarrheas, unhygienic milk and other food, infections, etc.—all things which now do not exist. The result is that, because of the highly-diminished infantile mortality, longevity in those developed countries went up to the level of about 65-68 on the average.

Of course, the grown-ups also profited from the better health and hygienic conditions. They do not die from pneumonias and other infections such as typhoid fever, typhus, or as they used to in older times from the plague or cholera. They are better fed, clad and housed, so that poverty diseases such as tuberculosis, for instance, do not play such havoc with their life and health. So the life span of grown-ups is also increased.

Theoretically, there is no reason why a human being should

not go "Back to Methuselah" as Bernard Shaw wrote it. There are daily advances in health, in conquest of diseases, in understanding of the function of the human body; there is a continuous improvement of living conditions, of the economic standard of life. All this enhances the prospect of a long and good life.

There are, however, hindrances to a progressive advancement of the life-span of a human being. As the proverb says, "There is a reason why trees should not grow to heaven." In short—the aging process of the body. When we buy a car, we expect it to grow old; and when it gets to that shape, we just discard it—throw it in the junkyard. But the engine of the body, though it can be repaired, has to go on and on with hardly any replacement, and cannot be exchanged for a new one. So, there is a limit how long and how often we can repair the "old car" which suffers from the ravages of the daily wear and tear of life. And here is the main reason why we have to accept a limit to a possibility of attaining of a very, very old age of say, hundreds of years; and Methuselah has to remain an unobtainable dream.

Within the framework of such a scope of life, let us consider what is old age: what are the limitations, which are the possibilities, in which way it differs from young age, what can be done to live a happy and satisfactory old age, how to improve what an older man has, and how to husband the existing capabilities, talents and strength of the aging body and soul . . . in plain English, how to live a healthy, happy and gracious old age.

This shall be the task of this book.

Part I

THE ORGANIC DISEASES OF OLD AGE

CHAPTER I

WHO IS OLD?

As it was said in the introduction, the calendar age does not play any role in the determination of the question of age or, rather, of aging. One can be 45 years and really old, another person can be 70 and still youngish. The evaluation whether a person is old and has to be considered as old depends on many factors. Apart from sicknesses which are due to aging and about which we shall talk in following chapters, the primary decision as to whether one should be considered old or elderly depends on two factors: (a) slowing down, (b) mental attitude.

There are plenty of young and middle-aged people who are slow: slow in movement, slow to decide, slow to speak, even slow to eat. However, such slowness is either inborn or brought about by environmental influences—the latter from the example or admonition of parents and teachers who do not like the children to be hasty. Therefore, they teach them to eat slowly, to move deliberately, not to rush with decisions which may be fateful or bad for their career or for their position within their environment, even if it is only school and schoolmates. Children and teenagers are susceptible to tuition, advice and admonition. Contrary to the general opinion, they want to be taught, they want to be advised, they even want to be punished for disobedience to parents. Also, even when the parents or teachers do not tell them to slow down, the urge to imitate causes them to become slow if the parents are slow.

But if somebody is by nature fast, can make up his or her mind at once; if a person usually walks fast, eats fast, talks fast, if there is no disease which causes a change, and if such a person slows down, this is the first sign of old age. It might be connected with hardening of arteries or with slowing down of reflexes, but if the slowing down does not correspond to the usual behavior of a person, then it is a signal of diminution of vigor and of youthful urge to do, to achieve things in a jiffy.

Another signal is the mental attitude. There is an old saying that young people tend to be revolutionary in every respect. They do not accept the ideological or social values of their parents; they do not want even to dress in the same way; their music, their art, their taste, their behavior have to be different from that of their parents, even if it is only as a protest, not due to a deep conviction. The same applies to the attitude towards religion and tradition, towards the social structure. It is normal behavior. Of course, there are young people who are never young, who imitate their parents and follow exactly in the footsteps of their elders. But they belong to a small minority; the majority wants an innovation, something new, something which belongs to their generation, not to the old one.

Now, the first sign, not necessarily of maturity, but of aging, is the retreat from the new positions and the return to the old values. That does not mean that conservatism is a sign of old age. Sometimes conservatism is revolutionary, if the preceding generation was revolutionary. One can see it, for instance, in Russia, where the new younger generation of Communist leaders is more conservative, more bourgeois, less idealistic, more down to earth than the old Bolsheviks, the fire-eaters who wanted to incite revolution all over the world in a hurry.

However, retreat is not the same as maturity which compels the young people to reconsider, to go away from extremes and to take the middle road. This is not a sign of old age; this is middle age, which brings understanding for another point of view, a realization that even a new idea has to overcome obstacles of daily life—in a word, that one has to compromise and to make the best of it. Still, it does not mean giving up certain preconceived ideas. It is only adjustment as a sign of maturity.

It is different if and when there is a radical turn-about, so to say from one day to another. An agnostic who suddenly becomes deeply religious, a religious man who suddenly violently opposes any kind of religion or religious thought; a known leftist who suddenly becomes an ultra-rightist with violent opposition to any change, and complete uncompromising return to old values of the ancestors without consideration of the new times and of new conditions.

Very typical as sign of a change of mental attitude due to the aging process is the wish to return to everything which was in his or her childhood. The childhood is glorified; that time was wonderful, contrary to the present times. That applies to food, with a sudden remembrance of dishes made by mother 50 years ago; by dress which shall approximate the dresses as worn by parents in the distant past; by language which becomes simplified in order to approach the simple language of childhood and maybe adolescence. It is especially striking in people whose native tongue was not that of maturity and old age—in immigrants, a sudden return to the long-forgotten language as spoken in the old country decades before; a longing and sudden decision to revisit the places where one was born and brought up as a child, to see places which one believed one did not remember any more.

These are not signs of sentimentality and romantic feelings. If they occur in people over 50 and persist, they show the beginning of old age. Another very typical sign is the attitude towards dressing. A person who is aging becomes either too clean, too meticulous in dressing habits, too particular; or on the contrary, too neglectful, too sloppy in dressing, without consideration of propriety. A woman suddenly starts to go down by elevator to pick up the mail in a dressing gown, though she never did it before. A man forgets to close his fly, or does not care whether he has the tie on or not. The same applies to eating habits, to the ritual of the use of cutlery, of plates, of eating on a tablecloth and the use of clean napkins. In short, whatever can be interpreted as neglect, as lackadaisical behavior or as change of habits—if not due to a disease—can be considered as a sign of aging. Such a person is old, and it does *not* matter what age the birth certificate shows.

CHAPTER II

THE ANATOMY OF OLD AGE

At old age we have the same organs as at birth; however, as we get older, certain anatomical changes occur. I would like to stress that these changes of which we are talking are changes due to the aging process, even if the person had or has no diseases which cause changes. The best comparison would be to compare the human body to a tree. An old tree is not a sick tree, but still it cannot be compared to a young tree. The trunk gets bigger—one can even calculate the age of a tree by the rings of the trunk. Now, the human body or the limbs do not develop rings; however, the bones of an adult are different from those of a child or adolescent. Again, the bones of an aging person are different from those of a mature adult. Take, for instance, a fracture. A child or adolescent breaks a bone—it is often what is called a green branch fracture, just like a soft breaking of a young branch of a tree. The bones of an adult are more resistant; they break by violence, by impact of force. In aging, the bones become brittle, more fragile. They break at a slight provocation, without application of great force or violence. This is the reason why, for instance, a so-called hip fracture is rare in young or middle-aged people, but very common in the aged.

But the same applies to other parts of the body. The arteries contain elastic fibres; they can best be compared with a rubber hose or a pipe. A simple rubber hose, as we use for watering of the lawn, can be stretched in its length, and even in its width; it can sustain a lot of water pressure without any damage. But if the hose is a few years old, it gets hard; if you try to stretch or bend it, it breaks. Well, our arteries get also harder. They also lose their elasticity and, by increased pressure (blood pressure or stress) they break with disastrous results. The veins also undergo changes with age. They are not exposed to such a stress and pressure as the arteries, but they cannot stand much strain, either. If one stands a lot, his veins on the legs become wider—and he gets varicose veins. The widening of the veins in old age is visible also in other places. Very common are widened veins on the side of the face—what is called in medicine "temporal"—between the eyes and the ears. The veins become more visible also on the hands or on the neck. The internal organs too show signs of aging. Take the ovaries of a woman: everybody knows about "change of life." The menstruation flow stops because the ovaries undergo changes; they, so to say, dry up. They are not diseased, but the aging process causes a stoppage of production of the hormones which are needed for a normal function. Correspondingly, in the man the prostate gland gets harder, bigger and produces less of the juice which mingles normally with the semen.

The heart and the lungs, if they are not sick, show few signs of aging. The elasticity is also diminished. The heart and the lungs also have normally elastic fibers, and these change in their consistency just as the arteries do; but the basic anatomical structure of these two most important life-giving organs does not change with age, as it should be. Otherwise, people could not attain very old age as some do.

The brain, however, does undergo changes, and that causes what we call senility. The stomach usually slows down its production of juices, but not always. Just the same, the diminution of the production of stomach juices brings about a smaller number of ulcers in old age. As for the bowels, their function, which is proverbially slow in old age—who of old people does not complain about constipation?—is connected with aging anatomical changes; again, loss of elastic fibers and weakening muscles in their structure. This slackening of the strength of the muscles and of their vigor causes external changes of the face, wrinkles, folding of the belly skin and muscles. Hernias occur more often in old age because of the lack of strength of the abdominal muscles, which give in at a slight strain such as lifting a suitcase or a chair or overbending by picking up something from the floor. Generally speaking, there is at old age a lessening of the strength of the muscles, especially of people who are not used to walking. Because of the diminution of muscle strength in the legs, they walk slowly, just "like an old person." However, if a person is used to daily walking, he or she can be as vigorous in old age as a young person. A prime example is our ex-President Truman who, at the age of almost 80, walked very well, like a person of much younger age.

The nerves are tributaries of the brain. Apart from diseases, they show aging processes only as much as they are governed by the brain, which ages, sometimes, rapidly. Otherwise, they are not affected by age. If people are nervous, excitable or apathetic at old age, this has no connection with aging of the nerves—at least not from the point of view of anatomical changes.

The skin ages and shows the ravages of age more than any other organ. Wrinkles, dryness, changes in pigmentation, warts, dark spots on face or hands (people call them liver spots), or, on the contrary, loss of pigmentation—white spots on a dark skin—are such obvious signs of age that they are accepted as characteristics of old age. Of course, one of the main characteristics by which people point out old age is the gray hair to which the blond, red, or black hair of a person changes. People get gray hair occasionally also in young age, but usually it is the very first sign of approaching old age. The hair is not diseased; some men and women have beautiful white or gray hair to the end of their life, and some are even proud of it. Just the same, gray hair (which is, by the way, the same old hair which has only lost its pigment) is a stigma of old age and is shunned by the female sex, even by very old women; hence the dyeing of the hair in order to look "younger," as if the color of the hair would conceal all other signs of aging. In some cases, if the gray hair were the only sign of age, the dyeing of the hair might help the person to look younger; in most cases it only accentuates the real age of the woman. Whatever it may be, gray hair is considered by people as a sure sign of at least an elderly lady, and in man as a sign of no more a young man.

Teeth can remain healthy and good in some cases, even in very old age. Generally speaking, however, though one can lose teeth in a very young age by neglect, wrong food, disease, etc., with age usually comes a decay of the teeth. Very often the teeth fall out by shrinking of the gums, by changes in the sockets of the teeth, or by deficiency in the minerals of the teeth themselves. Superficially seen, a person is considered old by his or her appearance: white or gray hair, wrinkles in the face, dentures or missing teeth—all the wear and tear of the passage of time.

Changes of the eye axis causes presbyopia—which is an old-age change—and causes the need for eyeglasses for reading. And, if you hear stories about the grandma who could read without glasses at the age of 80, you have to know that she was nearsighted; and nearsighted people cannot see far, whether young or old. But they read well without glasses, especially when they get older, and the older they become the better they read without glasses.

The ears too do not escape old-age changes, though less than the eyes. Normal eyes always become presbyopic—that is, aged—and require glasses for reading, while the hearing is often hard in old age but does not have to be a rule. Many old people hear very well. Regarding the eyes, one has to mention also the "senile arch"—*arcus senilis*—a gray ring around the iris of the eye, which occurs only in old age; and which is, medically speaking, completely harmless.

In order to complete the list, one has to mention the liver, the gall bladder and the spleen. Unless affected by diseases, they do not change by aging. Any changes in them are self-inflicted by bad habits, such as alcohol consumption and/or faulty food habits.

In general, the anatomical changes which occur in old age are by themselves not decisive in regard to the problem of longevity. More important are the physiological changes of which we shall talk in the next chapter.

CHAPTER III

THE PHYSIOLOGY OF OLD AGE

Everybody knows now what anatomy means, if only because of the films *"Anatomy of A Murder"* and *"Anatomy of Love,"* and of other anatomies which are actually not anatomies at all. In plain English, anatomy means the structure of the body. Physiology, which is less known and understood by the layman, is in fact more important than anatomy. Physiology means the normal function of the body, of its organs and of their correlation one to another. Why physiology is more important than anatomy can be easily explained by the following instances. You can cut off a leg or an arm, and perform most of daily routine work just the same. You can function. But, even if one possesses both legs and both arms, but if they are paralyzed by a stroke or by polio, one is grossly handicapped and practically an invalid. Why? Because the normal function of the limbs is disturbed.

In the consideration of the physiology of old age, we are interested to find out in which way old age interferes with the normal function of the body.

The function of the body depends on the normal performance of the organs—primarily of the glands, of the nerves and of the brain. We have to understand that we have two systems of glands. They produce a juice. Some of the juices are visible. The salivary glands produce saliva—we spit it out. The stomach produces stomach juice; if we have too much of it, it comes up to the chest and causes heartburn. The liver produces bile, and via the stomach it comes up and causes a bitter taste in the mouth; and if we vomit, it can stain the vomit yellow. It can even come up as pure bile.

On the other hand, some of the glands produce juices which go into the blood circulation, and therefore they are not visible. Such glands we call *endocrine* glands—so to say, inner glands. They are in a way even more important for life and well-being than the outer glands, because they govern the most functions of our body. Insulin, which is so important for diabetics, is a product, a juice of an endocrine gland—the pancreas, called "sweetbreads" by a butcher. In the stomach there is also a production of endocrine juices which are not excreted but which also help in the digestion of food. They are called enzymes, and their function is to split the protein in the meat, the fat and the starches into particles which can be absorbed by the body and deposited where they are needed for normal function of the organs. The insulin, of which we talked, helps to digest the sugar and the starch of the food; and if it is lacking, we become diabetics. There are many more endocrine glands which play a most important role in the function of the body. There are adrenal glands which are located above the kidneys. They produce a juice called adrenalin which controls, among other things, the blood pressure, and circulates in the blood vessels. The women have ovaries which produce hormones—that is, juices which regulate menstruation. There is the thyroid gland in the neck which controls our metabolism; another gland—the parathyroid—controls the absorption and distribution of calcium which we take with our food. And, last but not least, there is a gland in the brain called the pituitary which is the master gland which directs all the above endocrine glands—how and how much, and when they should produce the inner juices, and where and how much to ship to each organ—just as a central office of a corporation directs the production of a factory and the distribution of its products.

Now, this short description of the function of our glands with their visible and invisible juices is necessary for the evaluation of the impact of old age on the glands. The impact is such that in almost all cases the production of these juices is slowed down, and in some cases it is stopped altogether; in other cases, the production is maintained, but on a smaller scale. In some cases the production is stepped up, even to frenzy. In all cases of old age there is a re-organization of the function of the body. Nature is very economical; waste is eliminated and not approved. For instance: the ovaries are needed for reproduction of the human species; an elderly woman is not supposed to have children any more. Therefore, the cessation of menstruation and of production of eggs—otherwise it would be a waste of energy. The other juices—hormones—are also produced in smaller quantities according to the diminished activities of an older person. On the other hand, if an older person remains active, whatever normal function exists, the body produces as much as necessary. This, by the way, is a medical problem of retirement, of which we shall have to speak later.

The problem of the aging body, with its loss of elasticity, springiness and acuity, is the adaptation to the environment. Practically, an old person can perform physically as well as a younger person. But after about 50% of such an activity, tiredness sets in, contrary to a young individual. This is due to slowing down of the function of the above-described glands. In the case of a person who works with his brain, again the mental abilities may remain the same in an aging person, but the reflexes are slowed down. He or she is not as alert as when they were younger, and correspondingly the performance in their mental task is smaller, or possibly even inadequate. Here we come to the aging processes of the nerves and of the brain. Even in manual work, if it is not menial work, you need a certain amount of mental alertness if only for time-saving approaches to the work on hand—apart from the need of a skill which also requires some mental abilities.

Now, the aging process causes a slowdown, not only of the production of hormones or any other juices, but also of reflexes. There may be a delay of only a split second; but, considering that our mental processes are of the speed of a lightning if not faster, a slowing down of reflexes can sometimes have even fatal results. You can observe it on the street when an old person stands on the crossing of two streets and has to decide when to cross according to the light-change. Not infrequently he or she chooses to cross just when the light starts to change. Combined with slower walking, this can bring the old person under the wheels of a car. It is even more dangerous if such a person is in the driver's seat of a car. The slowing down of nervous reflexes can easily cause an accident just because he or she is aware of the handicap and drives at a maddening rush in the hustle and bustle of a busy highway. This is one of the reasons why there are so many suggestions to take away driver's licenses from old people, or at least to order them to have yearly driving tests. The same applies to old persons who work on an assembly line or at any other split-second performance on a job. In short, the slowing down of reflexes and mental processes do not play a role if in old age you can take it easy and conserve your strength and energy.

In summary, one can say that in old age the physiological function of the body deteriorates only in so far as all activities of the organism are slower but intact—with the exception of activities which are not needed any more, such as childbearing with the shutoff of ovarial function. The slowing down of the function of the body should lead to adjustment of the mode of life of an aging person in regard to work and in regard to food intake. Unfortunately, this adjustment is not done with pleasant consequences. However, there are exceptions to the rule. The chronological age does not necessarily apply to the body age, and some personalities in our time are examples of the exception—for instance ex-Presidents Truman and the late Eisenhower, the late German Chancellor Adenauer, the ex-premier of Israel, Ben-Gurion, or the late Winston Churchill. But, they are the exceptions; let us preferably stick to the rule.

CHAPTER IV

THE PATHOLOGY OF OLD AGE

The word "pathology," contrary to physiology and anatomy, means the changes which occur in the body due to diseases; or, to be more exact, due to changing *conditions* in which the body organs have to operate and to function. In other words, pathology is the disturbed structure or function of the organs which constitute the body. In the majority of cases the pathological condition is created by diseases; but especially in old age many of those conditions are the result of ordinary wear and tear, just like an old suit or an old dress or an old pair of shoes become old because a person wore them, and after a while they are not new any more. If we substitute the word "new" for "young" we come to the same result: the body and its organs, at least some of them, or all of them, are not young any more; they show the effects of wear and tear. It is surprising how well our body is built. A dress, a suit, a pair of shoes will be discarded after a while when it shows its age, but none of the organs will be discarded (unless not needed, like an appendix, an ovary or a womb) though they have to work from birth to death without a moment's respite. We also usually have some changes—several dresses or suits or shoes—and do not have to wear them day and night without interruption; thus we give them time to rest from the wear and tear. We can give them to the cleaners and repair shops to restore as much as possible their previous condition of comparative newness. Of course, in a way, many of us try to do the same with our bodies. We take a vacation to rest from the daily hustle and bustle; we keep to a diet in order to improve or to restore the ordinary function of the organs which, in our so-called civilized world, are abused by our mode of life; we take vitamins or medicine to cure the diseased organs, to give them or our whole body more vigor. And we look for thousands of years for the fountain of youth, seeking desperately to catch the vanishing youthful appearance and drive, or at least to let it stay—in other words, we would like to stop the unrelenting progress of age and its effect on the body. How futile it is, one can see when observing nature, with its change from one season to another, from spring and bloom to fall, winter and decay. As the old sages said, "A generation goes and a generation comes." In order for a new generation to come and to build, the previous generation has to go and to vanish.

However, notwithstanding the wise sayings and observations, human beings have always tried to stop the decay, to eradicate diseases—all this in order to prolong life. Even if they were smart enough to realize the futility of achieving it for the whole of mankind, they have tried and still try to achieve the prolongation of life for themselves or for a selected group of people. The whole history of medicine is one long chain of the endeavors to fight diseases and the ravages of age—to find out also the reason for aging and how to stop or at least to delay the aging process. Pathology is the science of diseases and their effect on the body. From a general point of view, there should be nothing which distinguishes diseases in regard to age. But that is not so; we have diseases which occur primarily in children and in very young people—for instance in adolescents; and if one is beyond that age, one can say with a feeling of relief, "Thanks to God, that cannot happen to me!" On the other hand we have diseases which hardly ever occur in children and adolescents, and they (if they care, and they usually don't) can say proudly, "That cannot happen to me." And that applies not only to pathological changes which occur due to wear and tear, but even to infectious diseases. It looks as if the germs would also make a selection of their victims. Some prefer young, juicy bodies, as in children; some prefer dried-up, worn-out bodies with little resistance left. That is the general explanation of the fact that we make categories of diseases—children's diseases, old-age diseases, etc. That is a general rule with, of course, exceptions. An adult or an old person can catch an infectious disease of childhood. I remember vividly a friend of mine whose wife developed measles a few days after the wedding—and he, being a pediatrician just out of college and hospital training, had as his first patient his own bride with measles; just as I remember an old grandma to whom I was called for a case of chickenpox which she had primarily in the mouth and which she acquired by frequent and ardent kissing of her grandchild.

On the other hand, to the surprise of some investigators, arteriosclerosis—or, as it is commonly called, hardening of the arteries, a disease of old age or a condition of the aging process—was found on autopsies of children, adolescents and young adults. Usually it was just the beginning of arteriosclerosis, but in young adults, such as soldiers of 19-21 years of age, not infrequently it was in advanced stage which was occasionally even the underlying cause of the disease which led to death. One can say that the aging process starts at birth, and every day of our life brings us nearer to the grave: only, in some people the process is accelerated, in some delayed; and that is the main reason for the difference in the longevity of people.

In the following chapters we shall deal with the details of the pathological changes which occur in the body at old age. It is not the purpose of this book to deal with diseases and body changes as such. In other words, whatever is common to all ages shall be omitted, unless it is more common, more frequent at old age. Primarily we want to discuss what is important to older people; what is characteristic for old age; what disturbs them, and how it affects their daily life; and what to do about the sicknesses—how to fight them and how to adjust oneself physically, mentally and spiritually.

CHAPTER V

ARTERIOSCLEROSIS, OR HARDENING OF THE ARTERIES

Arteriosclerosis, or hardening of the arteries, as it is commonly called, is *the* disease of old age. As I mentioned in the previous chapter, it occurs also in younger people, but only rarely; and it plays no role in the life of the younger generation, of children and even of middle-aged people. Just as the external signs of gray hair, wrinkles and general appearance are the features of aging, so also arteriosclerosis characterizes old age from the medical point of view. Why is arteriosclerosis so important? Because it involves the whole body. Everywhere we have arteries, and where there are arteries there can be a change—a sclerosis, a hardening of the blood vessels—and accordingly a disturbance of their function up to development of a disease. One has to understand that the arteries are the distributors of all the vital material which is needed for the functioning of the body. They convey the oxygen which we need for breathing and for the function of all parts of the body. They convey the final particles of food, which is split in the stomach and the other digestive organs, to every spot in the body where it is needed. They bring the blood from the heart through the net of arteries up to the smallest capillaries (they are the minute arteries by which the artery branches end) starting with the scalp and ending with the tip of the little toes. The internal organs are, of course, just as involved in the distribution of the blood, and they need the construction material for their cells and the oxygen brought to them by the arteries, just as much the blood is needed for the muscles, the ligaments, the joints and the skin. In short, where is life there are arteries, big or small, long or short, thick or thin. And vice versa—where there are no arteries there is no life. In order for the smallest cell to live it needs oxygen and food—all this conveyed by the arteries.

Therefore, the proper functioning of this arterial system is of utmost importance for health and life. Ordinarily, we accept the functioning of the arteries as a matter of course; we do not pay any attention to the arteries because we assume that they are doing their job as they should. It is different when we get older. We are conscious of a possible breakdown of the system, of faults in the distribution of the blood. The hardening of the arteries became the curse of modern civilization, with all the diseases, discomforts and malfunctionings of the body which stem from arteriosclerosis.

And what is arteriosclerosis? Why should arteries suddenly harden, and why in older age? We do not have a complete and final answer to this question. We have a lot of evidence which points to the culprit which causes this curse of modern times; but the evidence, as in court, is only circumstantial, though very convincing.

To understand arteriosclerosis, it is best to compare arteries to rubber tubes, hoses or pipes. The arteries are elastic, can be stretched to a certain degree, have a different width and length according to the size and needs of a part of the body; but this width is constant in a given artery as long as it is not changed by disease or by any other pathological occurrence. Now, if we compare the artery with a rubber hose, we also know that with age the rubber hose gets harder, less elastic, can be stretched less easily—and if we overdo it, the hose breaks. On the other hand, if we compare the artery with a water-pipe which conveys and distributes water from the water-tank to all the apartments of a house, we find that a water-pipe when it gets old becomes rusty. There are accumulations of calcium and other debris in the pipe which make the lumen—the width—of the pipe more narrow, with the result that we do not get as much water coming through as in a new pipe. The same applies to an artery. With age it becomes by the accumulation of debris more narrow, and the blood supply to this or that organ diminishes.

So, we have two characteristic signs of arteriosclerosis. The artery is less elastic and cannot stretch itself when the body needs it; and it breaks if it is overstretched or too hard, and loses its elasticity. It gets all the characteristics of an old rubber hose and of an old water-pipe.

Why it becomes like that can be surmised, though there are many answers to that problem. The fact is that, on autopsy of people who have arteriosclerosis, one finds regularly the same changes in the structure of the arteries—namely, a deposit of a specific fat, called cholesterol, and also a deposit of fibrin, which is a tough tissue (as seen easily in scars), and later on the deposit of calcium. All this together causes hardening of the arteries or arteriosclerosis.

It starts with the deposition of cholesterol. The cholesterol (together with some other fatty substances) is a normal component of the blood serum, which is the liquid part of the blood. It is partly formed by the body itself; and to a greater part it is in our food, namely, in the fat which we digest in butter, in cream, in fatty meat, and some other foods of lesser importance in this respect. Now, if we eat more of the cholesterol food than is good for us, the body cannot eliminate the cholesterol and deposits it in some favorite spots. It is the main ingredient, for instance, of gallstones; however, primarily it is being deposited in the wall of the arteries, where it causes a narrowing of the width of the artery. Thus it impedes the flow of the blood, just like rust in the water-pipe. This by itself is a disturbance; and to the cholesterol layer which changes the smoothness of the wall, there comes an addition of fibrin, of calcium, and the whole structure of the artery is changed for the worst. That the cholesterol plays a very important role in the production of arteriosclerosis was proven already 50 years ago by Dr. Anitchkov, who produced arteriosclerosis spots in rabbits with cholesterol dissolved in sunflower oil. The same result can be obtained with saturated fatty acids. Therefore came the outcry for reduction of cholesterol in the food, avoidance in older age of butter, cream, fatty meat and eggs, and preferring unsaturated fat, such as certain margarines and oils which do not contain cholesterol.

If we accept that in the beginning of arteriosclerosis there is the accumulation of cholesterol in the arteries, there still remains the question of why this happens in older people, not in younger ones or children. After all, they also eat food containing cholesterol, sometimes even more than older people. The answer to it can be found in the better metabolism of young people. The metabolism of older people is generally slower; they also have less physical activities, and they are prone to more eating without sufficient exercise. There are, according to Dr. Keys of Minneapolis, two general groups of persons. In the first group, the cholesterol in the blood rises continuously from puberty to the fifties; after this, the level continues to rise in women but tends to fall in men. The diet of these individuals is characterized by a high level of saturated fatty acids (butter, cream, eggs, etc.) and there is a high incidence of diseases connected with arteriosclerosis. In the other population group these trends are less marked. The intake of such fat is less, and cases of obesity, coronary and other arteriosclerotic diseases are also less common. Where there is a low standard of living, there can be established a correlation between obesity and cholesterol level. Therefore, also in younger people you can find cholesterol in the blood, high in obesity cases. There is no coincidence that fat children or adolescents are found in families where the parents and/or grandparents are obese. It is not only inheritance of a poor metabolism which leads to obesity, but also the eating habits of parents who insist that their children should eat as they do.

There are many additional reasons for the development of arteriosclerosis. I have already mentioned low metabolism. It is known that, for instance, people with a thyroid condition which causes high metabolism have a low cholesterol content of the blood. And vice versa—if the thyroid function is slow, as in the disease of myxedema, the cholesterol is also high. Cholesterol is also high in diabetic persons who get arteriosclerotic changes sooner than anybody else; cholesterol is also high in certain kidney diseases. All these disturbances in the function of certain glands precipitate the formation of arteriosclerotic patches in the arteries, up to complete transformation of an artery into a rusty, clogged pipe. A certain role is also played by the disturbance of the regulation of the fat transport through the artery. This disturbance of the regulation of transportation is often caused by a disturbance of the nervous system, especially of the so-called autonomic nervous system which influences the function of our internal organs—stomach, intestines, glands etc. Lack of oxygen in the blood, any long-standing blood changes, deposition of foreign material in the arteries, such as fibrin or crystals formed from the intake of certain foods—all this causes an untoward reaction in the arteries and their blood flow, with resulting arterioclerosis.

To fight arteriosclerosis is not easy, and practically impossible if the changes in the arteries are long-standing and fixed: especially if there is in the arteries not only a deposit of cholesterol but also of calcium, which causes the ultimate hardening of the arteries. If that is the case, the only thing which can be done is to stop further deterioration, or further formation of arteriosclerotic changes. It is worthwhile because a narrowed artery still allows a certain, if diminished, blood flow. If arteriosclerosis is left alone, if nothing is being done, the process of hardening, of obliteration of the lumen, of the clogging goes inexorably on until the artery is completely closed and lost for any function. If it is an important one, there is disease; if it is a vital one, death follows.

Of course, it is easier to fight arteriosclerosis in its early stages, and that means in earlier age—say, in the beginning of the fifties, and not in the sixties or seventies. The cholesterol accumulation can usually be reversed by diet, by change of the mode of life, by exercise, by medicine. And the same regime applies in older age, even in well-established cases of arteriosclerosis, just in order to stop the further development of arteriosclerotic changes.

These are the general remarks about the general arteriosclerosis. In the following chapters we shall discuss how arteriosclerosis influences individual organs of the body.

CHAPTER VI

ARTERIOSCLEROSIS OF THE HEART

(a) Coronary Arteries Disease

As the word arteriosclerosis signifies it, the arteriosclerosis of the heart means actually only the arteriosclerosis of the arteries of the heart. This has very little to do with other parts of the heart, such as the heart muscle or the heart valves; each of them can have old age diseases, but that has nothing to do with hardening of the arteries, or at least only indirectly.

The arteries of the heart can be divided in two distinct groups. The big arteries which originate in the heart and from there go like branches of a tree in all directions of the body are: the aorta—the main artery of the body—and the pulmonary arteries which supply the lungs with blood. The other group are the coronary arteries; these are the arteries which are needed for the feeding or the maintenance of the heart itself. They are called coronary arteries because they go around the heart like a crown (from the Latin word *corona* which means a crown).

Because of its vital importance and frequency of occurrence in our world of modern civilization, let us have a look at the *coronary arteries disease*. It represents a narrowing or an occlusion of the coronary arteries and is usually due to arteriosclerosis. In the chapter about general arteriosclerosis we explained already how the arteriosclerosis causes a narrowing of an artery, with the result of a lack of balance between blood supply and the demands of the organ which needs the blood. In coronary artery disease this imbalance results in a damage to the heart muscle which needs the blood for proper functioning. We all know that the heart is a pump which has to work all our life without interruption; otherwise we would be dead. The pump works by rhythmic contraction of the heart muscle which, for proper function, has to be supplied with sufficient amount of blood. If that is not the case, we have a coronary artery disease. If the blood comes through, though in insufficient amounts, it results in angina pectoris. If there is no supply whatsoever, if there is obstruction, we deal with an infarction, or what is commonly known as a heart attack.

What is angina pectoris? It is a chest pain usually located in the center of the chest behind the breast bone. Only rarely, the location is in the left chest side; occasionally it goes to the neck, the shoulder or the pit of the stomach. It is not always a real pain; very often it is only a discomfort or a feeling of distress or pressure. The pain is not sharp but rather squeezing, like having somebody sitting on the chest. The pain may be very severe, almost up to a fainting feeling, and sometimes it is just a mild discomfort, a feeling that one has a chest. Normally the pain lasts only a few minutes. If it lasts longer, an hour or more, and/or does not get relieved by medicine, there is suspicion of a heart attack.

The reason for the attack of angina pectoris is the inability of the coronary arteries to supply sufficient blood containing oxygen to the heart muscle. It occurs when there is either a greater demand for blood or when there is a lesser blood flow in the coronaries. That happens in cases of exercise, emotion or after a heavy meal. Of course, the basic condition is a pre-existing arteriosclerosis with a narrowing of the coronary arteries. This restricted blood circulation can cause an attack even after a mild exertion by an increased demand for oxygen in the blood. And even if this narrowing is only slight, an unusually heavy exertion can also precipitate an angina attack by an excessive demand of oxygen for heart function.

One can have coronary arteries disease without angina pectoris attacks, if he just takes it easy, does not have emotional upsets, does not exert himself physically, does not eat too much, and so on. However, if he does have arteriosclerotic coronary arteries, any unusual exertion or any additional strain, such as physical exertion to which a person is not used—for instance grass-mowing at a summer bungalow, walking against the wind, climbing stairs, lifting of heavy suitcases, excitement, eating a heavy meal—all this can cause an attack of anginal pain. It is true that many times an attack of angina pectoris occurs at rest and even during sleep. The explanation for this is manifold. Some investigators believe that people get the attacks 3 to 4 hours after a heavy meal not only because of an excessive demand for oxygen but for two additional reasons—hyperlipemia, which means too much fat in the blood entering it from the fat in the food; and deficiency of blood in the coronary circulation due to need of more blood in the stomach circulation for the digestion of the heavy meal. Also, a neurotic person can get tense by some harmless remark or incident which can cause a cramp in the coronary arteries and thus prevent regular blood circulation. Unpleasant dreams or nightmares can also cause attacks of angina, and even a heart attack —the more so that, during sleep, there is generally a slowing down of the blood circulation all over the body. There are also a few organic diseases which may play the role of a trigger in the incidence of anginal attacks. I would like to stress the word "trigger." It is known that a gall-bladder disease, gallstones and/or a gall-bladder inflammation can cause anginal pain. The same applies in a lesser degree to a hiatus hernia, which is a frequent occurrence in older age, and which means an entrance of a part of the stomach into the chest cavity near the heart. In my experience I have found that sometimes the physician believed that the removal of the gall-bladder and/or the repair of the stomach hernia will eliminate the angina pectoris. The coincidence of arteriosclerosis with accompanying coronary arteries disease and a gall-bladder disease with or without hiatus hernia is very frequent in older age. However, the removal of these latter diseases does not change the existing arteriosclerosis with the concommitant angina pectoris. Therefore, one can expect that even after these operations—which, by the way, are not so simple in older people, who easily get complications after an operation—a person suffering from anginal attacks will continue having them. However, if one considers the gall-bladder disease and/or the hiatus hernia as "triggers," then one can say that some of the existing triggers will be eliminated—not less but no more.

Whatever may be the reason for the occurrence of the attacks of angina pectoris, the fact remains that even the mildest attack can become severe and occasionally cause, in the end effect, a heart attack. It is clear that, if we cannot change the fact of existing arteriosclerosis of the coronary arteries we can at least do something to avoid a too great demand on the heart. That means change of mode of life: do not exert yourself too much; especially avoid an exertion to which you are not used. If you never mow the lawn, don't start doing it at an older age. The same applies to any other similar exertion to which you are not accustomed. And even if one is used to that kind of work, one has to be reminded of what was said in previous chapters, namely, that though an older person can do the same work as a younger, he or she cannot do more than 50% of the capacity of a younger person. In plain English—take it easy and you'll be all right. The same applies to emotional stress and unnecessary excitement (if it can be avoided). Do not eat heavy meals and fatty, difficult-to-digest food. If you already have a coronary arteries disease and anginal attacks, don't climb stairs; change to a bus ride if you used to go by subway; if you live in a walk-up apartment and have to climb stairs, change the apartment to one on the ground floor or in an elevator apartment house. If you cannot do it because of a shortage of housing or for financial reasons, make every day a list of things to be bought or to be accomplished. Walk slowly up the stairs; take your time, and avoid going up the stairs more than once daily.

Apart from the change of life-habits, remember that we have medicine to help victims of angina pectoris. Sedatives and tranquilizers will prevent you from becoming too emotional about petty grievances and upsets. That will eliminate many "triggers." We also have wonderful remedies to widen the coronary arteries for prevention as well as for treatment.

All these precautions will considerably diminish the frequency of attacks. They will cut down the duration of an attack and make your life, if you are suffering from angina, more pleasant and comfortable; and in the long run this will prolong your span of life.

One word more about alcohol in case of an anginal attack. It is well known that many physicians recommend a shot of whisky in case of chest pain. Some even recommend liquor as a medicine for prevention of anginal pain. The truth is that alcohol is not a vasodilator; that is, it does not widen the arteries, and consequently it does not bring more blood to the heart or more oxygen into the blood. What liquor really does —in small amounts it is a tranquilizer and quietens an excited person. Either the pain is triggered by excitement, or the excitement is there because of the pain—especially if one knows that he has a coronary arteries disease and knows about its implications. In short, there is no harm in taking a small quantity of liquor; but it is not a substitute for a medicine which widens the arteries and brings a better blood flow to the heart.

(b) *Coronary Artery Occlusion (Heart Attack—Myocardial Infarction)*

A heart attack differs from angina pectoris attack by the fact that there is not only a temporary deficiency of the blood supply to the heart through the coronary arteries, but that there is an occlusion of a coronary artery. The blood does not flow at all. There is a clot which works like a cork in a bottle; it stops the circulation in this particular heart artery. Usually it happens in an artery which has already an impediment of the blood circulation by arteriosclerotic changes, as described previously. This is the mechanism of the coronary occlusion, of the heart attack. And the signs are similar to those of angina pectoris, only much worse. The pain is crushing, almost deadly —one has the feeling of impending death. The person with the heart attack gets pale and has cold sweats; the pulse is hardly possible to feel; the blood pressure falls rapidly, and the pain in the chest does not stop. It continues for hours, sometimes even for days, and can be only partly relieved by narcotics, such as morphine. There is a lack of oxygen in the whole circulation because of the clot and its effect on the function of the heart. That is the reason why people who have suffered a heart attack are given oxygen either through a tube or in an oxygen tent. In any case, if one gets a heart attack, he or she is a hospital case and has to count on a stay there for 3 to 6 weeks, depending on the rate of recovery, on complications, and so on.

The fate of a person who has a heart attack depends on its severity, and the severity depends on the location of the blood clot. The coronary arteries have branches. If the clot is located in a small branch which supplies a small and not vital part of the heart muscle, all the described signs and symptoms of the heart attack occur in a very much milder form. The pain is less severe and does not last that long; sometimes there is even hardly any need for oxygen because the circulation is not much impeded. There are even plenty of cases when a person suffers a heart attack without realizing that he or she had one; it is found by examination of an electrocardiogram which shows definite signs of a heart attack, sometimes even months and years after the attack. There is not even a must for chest pain in the meaning of angina pectoris after such a mild attack, and the history of it is found on a routine electrocardiogram, done in the course of a general checkup—as it should be done in an older person anyway.

On the other hand, if the clot occurs in a large main coronary artery, it can lead to immediate death, or to a prolonged period of sickness. Sometimes it still ends in death; sometimes it leaves the patient as an invalid for the rest of his or her life; and sometimes, even after a most severe attack, a person can recover completely—to give only the example of President Johnson, who had a most severe heart attack in 1956 and recovered completely to continue his work as Senator, Vice-President and President.

The usual medical name for a heart attack is myocardial infarction. The reason for it is that the stoppage of circulation in a coronary artery branch by a clot causes stoppage of blood supply to a part of the heart muscle which cannot function—that is, to contract and pump. The area of the damage to the heart muscle can be small or large. The muscle gets inflamed and frequently necrotic, which means this part of the muscle dies and finally it stays on as a scar which, like any other scar, has no blood circulation and takes no part in the life of the rest of the muscle. Therefore, if the area of the damaged heart muscle is very large, the muscle cannot function or cannot pump; and it ends in death or in such a weakening of the heart that it becomes flabby. Its action is such that we get the picture of heart failure, which means that the heart cannot work more than just to maintain life, and such a person becomes a complete invalid. On the other hand, the damaged muscle area can be very small—the size of a dime—and the scar does not impede the action of the heart. On autopsy of people who die from an accident or any disease not connected with the heart, one often finds such small scars, and the history of the patient does not reveal any previous heart attack or any other heart condition, though it might reveal knowledge of pre-existing arteriosclerosis.

Here it is necessary to dispel some persistent stories which every doctor hears in his office, namely, of people who suddenly die from a heart attack—and the story goes on that the deceased saw a doctor only a day or two before his death, and an electrocardiogram was taken and found to be normal. How to explain that the doctor did not find anything, gave his patient A-1 for health, and just the same the man died from a heart attack on the day of the examination or 1 to 2 days later? The answer is simple. First, why did the man go to the doctor for a complete checkup if he was so perfectly well? Apparently, he did have some complaints which led him to go for the checkup; especially if he was given an electrocardiogram, either at his own request or by the suspicion of his physician that his complaints were connected with a possible heart condition.

Secondly, there are many *men* who do not like to tell their wife or family that they had chest pain, even if they are worried about the pain and therefore go for a checkup to their doctor without knowledge of the wife. I say deliberately *men*, because women go sooner for their complaints to a doctor than men. In an average office of a doctor you'll find a disproportion of women patients compared with men. The likely ratio is 8:2— eight women to two men. Men go for a checkup either if the wife pesters them because she is worried about the health of the husband, or if they are worried themselves—that is, they do not feel well. Of course, if the men get a clean bill of health from their doctor after the checkup, they will be very happy to tell their wife or any other member of the family that they had a checkup and were found in good health.

And finally, one has to know that an electrocardiogram is not a final and decisive proof of a good condition of the heart. It will show the scar of a previous heart attack (though not always, if the attack was mild); it will show a strain of the heart muscle. But all this means that it will be a record of the *past* history of the patient. Even at the beginning of a heart attack, while all symptoms and blood tests are indicative of a heart attack, the electrocardiogram may be negative for a day or two. The more it happens, when the patient has only a fleeting chest pain or chest discomfort, may be from an angina pectoris. If the attacks of angina are frequent and very pronounced, you can expect to find the signs of it in the electrocardiogram. But it is well known that frequently the angina pectoris signs in the electrocardiogram are visible only after the patient is undergoing artificial exertion at the doctor's office, if the cardiogram is done again after the so-called Master's two-step exercise test. In other words, as mentioned before, a person sometimes gets an attack of angina pectoris after exertion to which he is not used. If the doctor exposes him to such an exertion and then takes a cardiogram, then there is a likelihood that it will show a pattern indicating a heart condition. But, how often is such a Master's test done? Once in a blue moon in so-called doubtful cases. Normally, a doctor and his patient are satisfied if the electrocardiogram proves to be normal, and that ends the examination for a heart condition.

This is the explanation of the so-called sudden death from a massive heart attack. It is sudden to the family and friends; it is not so sudden to the family physician, if he knew that the deceased suffered from hardening of the arteries. General arteriosclerosis as such is not a fatal disease. One can be bold in saying that in civilized countries 95% of all people above 50 years have more or less arteriosclerotic changes; and if they have them, the chances that the arteriosclerosis involves also the coronary arteries are extremely high. Therefore, the bill of health given by the physician pertains only to the moment of the checkup and means only that at that particular time the doctor did not find any acute condition or any condition which requires immediate attention. And that's all. The later heart attack can be due to any cause which I described previously, and of which the doctor could not know in advance.

Regarding distribution of heart attacks according to age and sex, one can say: we find nowadays more and more younger people getting a heart attack. It goes down already to the end of the twenties; gets more frequent at the age of 30 to 40. But prevalent are heart attacks between 50 and 65, though we get plenty with aging; in other words, because heart attacks are primarily connected with arteriosclerosis, therefore the aging process is the main factor in developing coronary arteries diseases, and the occurrence of heart attacks. There are a few diseases which can also lead to premature heart attacks, such as syphilis, diabetes, inborn high cholesterol in the blood, low metabolism due to malfunction of the thyroid gland, and some other diseases. But all these diseases constitute only a small percentage of the causes of a heart attack. Even in a younger person who has none of the above-mentioned diseases, one can assume that it is a case of a premature arteriosclerosis which led to the heart attack.

Women are protected from a heart attack by the hormones of their ovaries. It is very unusual for a woman who still has a normal menstrual period to get a heart attack, unless she suffers from one of the above-mentioned diseases. It happens that a woman gets a heart attack without diabetes, syphilis or thyroid condition, while she still has a normal menstrual period; but it is extremely rare and demands further investigation of the cause of the heart attack in that particular case. This fact of the protective influence of the female hormones is so well known that one of the cardiological investigators suggested giving men injections of female hormones in order to protect them against heart attacks. Theoretically, he may have some point; but practically it would mean to acquire female characteristics, possible loss of potency and of other signs of virility. Even knowing the danger of a heart attack, you will hardly find men who would be willing to give up their virility in exchange for a *possible* protection against a heart attack. (It is not 100% sure that such a treatment would work in men.)

However, this protection by the female hormones is lost as soon as the change of life occurs. If the ratio of women before the change of life to men of the same age was in regard to frequency of heart attacks 1:10 (one woman to ten men), there is equality regarding the frequency of heart attacks after the cessation of menstruation—namely, as many women as men. Why and how the female hormones protect the women, we don't know. We have only to accept the facts.

The treatment of the heart attack lies outside the scope of this book. This is a matter for doctors, not for patients. The prevention of heart attacks (as far as one can prevent them; it is neither easy nor certain that a heart attack can be prevented by any means) lies in the same direction as the prevention of coronary arteries disease, which was discussed in previous chapters. The difficulty with the prevention lies with our way of life. Supposing we know that the checkup shows a likelihood of an occurrence of a heart attack in a person; we still would not know when a heart attack will take place—maybe in a day, in a month, in a year, or maybe never. We can only say that such a person is prone to a heart attack. Shall we then tell the patient to give up his or her job or type of work? The risk goes in both directions: should the patient get a heart attack without being told by the doctor to take it easy, or to take a vacation, or to retire, the doctor will be blamed and accused of incompetence. If, on the other hand, the doctor would insist on retirement or change of way of life and his patient will not get a heart attack, the doctor will be accused of making an invalid of an active, happy person—maybe even of crippling him or her psychologically by making of the patient a hypochondriac who lives only for his health.

Therefore, the policy of medicine, which is an art and a science but not astrology or any other type of prophecy, is to warn the prone patient to take it *easier,* to rest more, to take more vacations, to work less hours, to eat less, to avoid anything in excess. But we don't have to disrupt the whole life of such a person—the more so since, on the one hand, an active person who is full of pep will not follow the advice of a doctor anyway and will continue doing what he or she did as before, even with all the warning of the doctor; and on the other hand, in the majority of such cases we deal with elderly people who, if they are employees, will be retired compulsorily in a few years whether they like it or not; or, if they are self-employed, they will notice later, if not sooner, that they have some failings either of the heart or of their mind or of memory, which will force them to slow down.

There is also another motive for not stressing this point of prevention too much. People are scared of heart attacks; they know one can die from a heart attack suddenly or become an invalid from one minute to another. On the other hand, the attitude of medicine towards the post-effects of a heart attack has changed in the last 15 years. Return to normal life and normal activity is allowed much earlier than before; there is even more leniency during the period of treatment of a heart attack. There is also the example of prominent personalities who have had a heart attack and returned to normal and often-strenuous life, such an ex-President Eisenhower, and ex-President Johnson, and several well-known politicians and Hollywood and Broadway actors. Therefore, the public vacillates between fear and hope. Being human beings, they prefer to hope for the best. And such an attitude is welcomed by doctors; it helps in the recovery and in the prevention. The final advice in regard to prevention is summarized in one sentence: Don't do anything in excess, and you'll prolong your life.

CHAPTER VII

ARTERIOSCLEROTIC HYPERTENSION, OR HIGH BLOOD PRESSURE AND STROKE DUE TO HARDENING OF THE ARTERIES

Everybody knows about blood pressure, and everyone who goes to the doctor is curious about his or her blood pressure when it is taken. You can see the satisfaction on the face of the patient when he or she is told that the blood pressure was normal, and you can see also the fear of the verdict. Who knows? Maybe the blood pressure is too high or too low. There is so much knowledge of the dangers of the blood pressure that this topic is a favorite at card parties, or golfing, or any other congregation of a few people who know each other comparatively well.

It is necessary to declare bluntly: low blood pressure is not dangerous and requires no treatment. A person can have all his life a pressure of 100 and live happily ever after. My own father at the age of 87 still had a blood pressure of 110, underwent two serious operations with it and came through with flying colors. With that blood pressure he was very healthy, and he died from an accident. Low blood pressure is welcomed by doctors and insurance companies when they give a life-insurance policy. It gives them a reasonable expectation that the policyholder will live to a ripe age and will pay premiums for many, many years. The significance of low blood pressure lies only in a sudden *drop* of it. If a person has normally, let us say, a blood pressure of 130 or 140, and suddenly it drops to 100 or less, then one can say "something is wrong in the Kingdom of Denmark"—there is some sickness going on. Not necessarily a heart attack, but some disease which involves the blood circulation and causes the drop in the blood pressure. It can be any disease, infectious or otherwise. Usually such a drop in the blood pressure is only temporary, and the pressure comes back to normal after recuperation. Because both types of low blood pressure are not a disease by itself, it is worth only to mention it for the benefit of such readers who have experienced either a temporary blood-pressure lowering or have always a low blood pressure. They can be assured that they have nothing to worry about.

A completely different story is the problem of high blood pressure, or, as it is called, hypertension. First of all, it is necessary to point out that hypertension can occur just as well in young people as in old ones, though for different reasons. Secondly, hypertension can run in families. The tendency can be inherited, and you can find families where grandparents, parents and children suffer from high blood pressure. But it is not the task of this book to discuss all possible reasons for the cause of hypertension—only in so far as it relates to old age.

One has to know that there are two figures for blood pressure—high and low. The high figure is called systolic, the low, diastolic blood pressure. For instance, one has a blood pressure of 120/80. That means systolic 120, diastolic pressure 80. The systolic pressure is the figure when the heart pump compresses, the diastolic when the pump relaxes. Now, when the blood pressure rises, very frequently both figures rise; for instance, one can have a high blood pressure of 180 or 200 over 100-110-120. But that is not always the case. There are cases when a person has 180 or 200 over only 80, in which case the high figure is much too high and the low figure stays normal. There are also cases when it is opposite: a person has a blood pressure of 140 and over 100. Here comes the question—What is normal in blood pressure?

There are no fixed figures for that. However, by comparing thousands and millions of readings, certain averages were found for the age of a person. There are no differences regarding sex or race, though there are differences in regard to mode of life, habits and food. For the low diastolic pressure, 80 is considered as a normal average for an adult. It can go down to 70 and still be normal; it can go up to 90 with age, though it is not necessarily so. A person can be 70 or 85 years old and still have a diastolic pressure of 80. For the systolic pressure there was for a very long period of time a rule: it should normally be 100 plus age. That is, at the age of 20—120, at 30—130, at 60—160, and so on. Then it was revised downwards. It is considered normal if one has 100 plus age less 10. That is: normal would be, at the age of 50—140, at age 70—160, and so on. Just the same, if one keeps his blood pressure within the limits of the old rule, he or she is still all right and does not have to worry about blood pressure.

As said before, there are many reasons for the increase of the blood pressure. Even a person with a normal blood pressure has occasionally a higher blood pressure; for instance, after intake of alcohol, or with fever or when excited. But these increases disappear after a short while. Hypertension, however, exists when a person has a higher-than-normal blood pressure in all circumstances, at any time of the year, in any climate or season. The increased blood pressure can go up under unfavorable circumstances, or go down with proper treatment or way of life. But, basically, hypertension means permanent high blood pressure and has to be considered as a disease. It is something which accompanies certain diseases, but then it is only a symptom, as in a case of a tumor of the so-called adrenal glands. But apart from diseases which strike people of all ages, it is a very prominent disease, especially of old age. And the cause of it is just, again, arteriosclerosis.

From the purely mechanical point of view, high blood pressure is due just to the increase of the pressure in the whole blood-circulation system. It starts with hardening of the main artery of the body—the aorta—which arises from the heart, forms an arch and then descends down the chest, passes into the cavity of the abdomen and forms the abdominal aorta. It gives up branches on its way down to all organs—not forgetting to send up branches to the arms, to the neck and to the head, including the brain; and after sending branches to both kidneys, it splits into two mighty branches which are the main supply source for the lower abdomen and both legs up to the little toes. Now, any narrowing of the width of this mighty blood river with its flow increases the pressure all over; and that applies primarily to the brain, and just as well to the kidneys. Just like a rusty pipe has a more narrow width, and the water comes out from the faucet in a thinner stream but under more pressure, the same happens to the human body in case of arteriosclerosis. One has to emphasize that a person can have extensive arteriosclerosis and *no* hypertension. This is due to two reasons: one, it is due to action and counteraction which go on all the time in the body; it is also due to the fact that even in extensive arteriosclerosis this mechanical narrowing of the arteries does not take place. And, two, hypertension is not simply a mechanical defect. We have hormones which increases the blood pressure if they are produced more than necessary for normal function, and we have hormones which counteract that hypertensive action. We spoke of the adrenal glands which are located just above the kidneys, like little caps. They produce adrenalin—a powerful hormone which increases the blood pressure and which we need badly for any exertion, but which the glands often produce in too great abundance, causing the disease of hypertension. We have the little pituitary master gland in the brain which works like a telephone switchboard and directs the production of most hormones in all the glands; and any disturbance of the glands can play havoc with our whole endocrine system—in a word, with the distribution and production of almost all our juices or hormones which are needed for proper function of the body organs.

So we see that the formation of the permanent hypertension is a very complicated phenomenon. But it happens very often and causes a lot of trouble. One has to add that the arteries of the kidneys play a most important role in the genesis of hypertension. If they do not function properly, and this is frequently the case in arteriosclerosis, it most likely causes hypertension. We have to know that the kidneys are our garbage-removal apparatus (in addition to the bowels) which eliminates all poisonous stuff from the body via urine production. If that superfluous material is not removed because the kidneys do not function well, we get uremia, which means that the stuff, instead of being removed, poisons the whole system by staying and entering the blood. And if not uremia, which is an acute and fatal disease, if the condition is not remedied we get a so-called sub-uremic condition; that is, a more chronic condition of too much residual material in the blood, similar to a condition when a person takes every day a little bit of a poison—not enough to kill, but enough to make sick. And hypertension comes along with other signs and symptoms when the kidneys do not function well.

In older age, at the beginning of hypertension we have arteriosclerosis. It may be generalized in all arteries; it may be localized in the arteries of the kidneys or of the brain. If we speak of high blood pressure of older people, we can almost forget all other causes of hypertension and concentrate on arteriosclerosis; if only for the reason that other causes of high blood pressure can happen in all ages, including old age, but they manifest themselves much earlier, and therefore they do not belong to the scope of this book.

So, we have high blood pressure as a post-effect of arteriosclerosis; and it is prevalent in older people. What does it cause? If people are lucky, as ironical as it may sound, they suffer from headache and from spells of dizziness. One can have even extreme high blood pressure, let us say 230/120 or even more, and have no complaints. Others can have 10 or 12 points above normal and have already the two typical symptoms of blood pressure. If I say the lucky people get headaches and dizziness, it is because such complaints bring them sooner to the doctor, who can do something to reduce the blood pressure and to remove the complaints. On the other hand, the people who do not have complaints are confronted with a possible catastrophe out of the blue sky, such as a stroke. A person whose headache and dizziness bring him to a doctor, will at least do something to prevent a stroke, even if he or she cannot get a guarantee that by treatment a possibility of a stroke can be excluded. Just the same, a decrease in the blood pressure gives better chances to avoid a stroke.

A stroke can occur also in a person with a high degree of arteriosclerosis, even without a high blood pressure, because a stroke is similar to a heart attack; it comes from a blood clot obstructing a main artery, usually in the brain or leading to the brain. And there is a further similarity to a heart attack: one can die on the spot after having gotten a stroke, one can remain an invalid for the rest of his or her life, and one can completely recover without any trace; and finally, one can partially recover with some remnant of the stroke still visible but maybe slowly improving. It all depends where the blood clot is located. If it obstructs a main artery centrally located, in the brain, the blood flow stops completely and the person dies immediately. If the obstruction is on one side, and on the other side the blood flow is not impeded, then the patient stays alive. Only his faculties are impeded, his ability to function is limited—namely, by the extent of the obstruction in the brain arteries, and depending on which part of the brain is involved in the stroke. The usual result of a stroke is paralysis, if not death. One side of the body can be paralyzed, arm and leg. If one is lucky and gets the stroke so that his left arm and leg are paralyzed, then the patient does not lose his ability to speak. The reason is simply that the speech center is located on the *left* side of the brain, and the function of the limbs and the other organs involved is opposite to that side of the brain. The left side of the brain governs the right side of the body, and vice versa. Generally speaking, a left-sided stroke is, I would say, more convenient if it has to happen. We are used to doing most of our work more with the right arm and right leg than with the left. Though many people write with the left hand, they are just the same not lefties—not southpaws. Most of their work is done with the right arm and hand. If the paralysis after a stroke remains, then such a patient has a hard time to relearn to use primarily his or her left arm, left hand and left leg. And what about the speech? In the first days after a stroke, usually there is a speech defect even if the left side is paralyzed. The reason is what is called edema—a swelling inside the brain caused by the sudden catastrophe. But this subsides after a short while, and the speech returns to normal. It is different with a paralysis on the right side. The lost speech sometimes does not return at all; sometimes it is improved after a very, very long period of speech therapy—retraining of the faculty to talk. Occasionally, very occasionally, the speech center is very little involved and the lucky patient can talk after a while, even if he or she cannot move the arm and leg.

The same applies to the paralysis of the arm and leg. Frequently the function of the limbs after a stroke returns to normal sooner or later; but not always, and the muscles which are needed for the movement of the limbs have to be retrained with heat, massage and exercises—by what is called physiotherapy. It depends not only on the skill of the physiotherapist, but first of all on the recovery power of the patient—that is, on what happened to the clot and the artery involved; whether there exists a good net of collateral circulation—that is, a net of small subsidiary arteries which widen and in due time take over the work of the damaged artery. If that is the case, if the damage to the brain tissue is minor and if the circulation is restored, one can expect that all traces of the stroke will disappear and the patient will be restored to normal life.

However, if one visits a nursing home or a home for the aged, one finds that a large proportion of the old people who spend the rest of their life in such homes are the victims of a stroke, with partial paralysis of the limbs and possibly with impairment of speech. This shows the danger of a stroke and the catastrophic results of it.

In recent years we have had some progress in the treatment of a stroke. First, the anti-coagulation treatment, if started after a small stroke (of which we shall talk later), helps to prevent a new and larger, catastrophic stroke. Secondly, there is a surgical approach to a stroke. It was found that many strokes occur due to a blood clot in the carotid (neck) arteries on the way to the brain. If the location is immediately diagnosed and the artery opened, it is possible to remove the clot and the impaired function of the limbs and speech will be restored. Even higher up in the more external part of the brain, such an operation is feasible and sometimes successful. One only has to have the good luck of a correct immediate localization diagnosis (usually by a nerve specialist, and special X-rays), the availability of a skilled special surgeon of the arteries, and—last but not least—to have the clot in an accessible position. Then the stroke with its post-effects is finished. If all these conditions do not exist, we have to go back to physiotherapy and rehabilitation.

The importance of a stroke in our whole population, not only in older people, can be gauged by the fact that approximately one million, five hundred thousand strokes occur in the United States each year. That means that one person in about 140 of all ages will get a stroke within a year. However, if we discard the persons who are not suffering from arteriosclerosis and in younger age without any of the few diseases which can cause a stroke also, we come to even a higher proportion of about 1:100. That means that at least one percent of our population will have a stroke sooner or later, if nothing is done to prevent it. There is no wonder that President Johnson created a committee to deal with some of the most important chronic and prevalent diseases; and arteriosclerosis with stroke has a high priority on the list. It is also not surprising that he made Dr. De Bakey the chairman of that committee; not because De Bakey happens to be a fellow Texan, but because De Bakey happens to be one of the outstanding surgeons, specializing in the surgery of the heart and of the vascular system.

Now, we spoke about strokes; what to do about them, apart from rehabilitation after the damage was done already? To sum up, it is: a dietary regime to reduce obesity and cholesterol content of the blood. We curb the intake of free sugar, which promotes a hidden inclination to diabetes and cuts down the formation of the so-called triglycerids—fat—which also play a role in the formation of the hardening of the arteries. We spoke already about a treatment with the female hormones which protect women against premature occurrence of arteriosclerosis. However, men consider the treatment with likely impotence and development of female characteristics as worse than the possibility of a heart attack or of a stroke.

Of course, one of the most important treatments for the prevention of strokes is the treatment of the high blood pressure which develops in the course of arteriosclerosis and is the main cause of a stroke.

Generally speaking, up to about 20 years ago, we had hardly an efficient treatment of hypertension. I remember, as a young doctor, that high blood pressure was treated more or less similarly to the treatment of 150 years ago—primarily by bloodletting. Only, instead of a scalpel as used by still older doctors, we had a thick needle by which we withdrew a pint of blood if the blood pressure was too high and threatened to cause a stroke. In addition, we thought that a patient with a high blood pressure should eat less meat (that was the only dietary restriction); and because most of the hypertensives had a flourishing face and often were excited, we gave them sedatives, primarily phenobarbital. That was more or less the whole medical armament in the fight against high blood pressure. Of course, if one got a stroke and remained alive, we withdrew even more blood, and more often. The other things remained the same: rest, protein-poor diet, and very few rehabilitation procedures—just massage and an attempt to teach walking.

Now, blood-letting as a treatment is practically discarded; we know that protein is not the culprit in the development either of arteriosclerosis or hypertension. Now the culprit is salt—or, rather, the sodium mineral in the salt. Therefore a salt-poor or even a salt-free diet for high blood pressure is used, up to the extreme of a rice diet a la Prof. Kempner. In addition, we learned from the Indians that the Rauwolfia plant contains a drug called Reserpine which lowers the blood pressure. This is being given under a multitude of brand names such as Raudixin, Serpasil, etc. Then came the idea to extract the superfluous salt from the body by giving drugs which cause diuresis—which means causing a profuse urination by which the sodium of the salt in the urine is eliminated. There is a tremendous amount of these drugs calls diuretics, and they all have one purpose—to remove the sodium and thus lower the blood pressure. In some cases the drug industry produces a combination of the Rauwolfia drug with the diuretic, thus trying to kill two birds with one stone. There are many reasons why the idea might be wrong; there are also many side-reactions to the Rauwolfia and the diuretic preparations. It would go too far to discuss the merits and the disadvantages of such treatment; it is up to the doctor to see what is good for that particular patient. On the whole, one can say that the new treatment with the Rauwolfia and salt-removing (diuretics) pills is very successful, and a far cry from the old-fashioned treatment of 25-30 years ago. One has to admit that one drug, the so-called mercurial, which is given by injection in order to eliminate urine and salt, was known also 40 years ago. However, it was given for persons with heart failure without knowledge that, by the same token, the injection eliminated not only water from the body but also salt—that is sodium—and lowered the blood pressure. This drug mercurial, is still one of the best for the elimination of the superfluous water and salt from the body.

We have more weapons in the fight against high blood pressure. It was found out that the cause of hypertension is also a preponderance of one nervous system compared with the function of the other. It is the so-called sympathetic nervous system which narrows the arteries by overfunction, and there are medicines which prevent this overfunction of the sympathetic nervous system. Those drugs also lower the blood pressure, sometimes even more than desired. By the same train of thought, the surgeon Dr. Smithwick came to the idea that high blood pressure can be reduced by cutting off the branches of the sympathetic nervous system which are primarily responsible for the development of the high blood pressure. And this operation also proved to be highly successful.

Like all branches of medicine, the one which deals with high blood pressure made great strides forward; though with all this armamentarium we are still far from conquering hypertension like we conquered smallpox or polio. There are still plenty of people who take all the new-fangled drugs, and just the same have high blood pressure and get strokes. So we return to the same problem—how to prevent a stroke? And the answer at present lies in the so-called little strokes.

CHAPTER VIII

LITTLE STROKES

Just as chest pain with angina pectoris is a warning of a possible heart attack, nature gives a warning of a possible real stroke with paralysis by the occurrence of little strokes. They are much more common than people think, and they are disregarded by their fleeting appearance—just as people disregard chest pain, which in the majority of cases is considered (falsely) as gas pain or indigestion.

What are the signs of a little stroke? As said before, the symptoms are fleeting; they disappear very soon. If a doctor looks for a possible little stroke, he can get some information from the patient, but it is advisable to talk to members of the family or colleagues who observed the patient during such an episode. One has to remember that on examination a few days after an attack of a little stroke, the result may be completely negative. Therefore it is necessary to reconstruct the whole episode as it was felt by the patient and observed by relatives and/or friends. The episode of the little stroke is most often the loss of the normal function of the brain; and even if that returns to normal in no time, very characteristically it recurs again, though each time possibly in a different degree, lasting shorter or lasting longer, being more poignant or less poignant in the signs of the change from normal.

There are two different little strokes and, accordingly, different signs of it. It depends on the localization of the insufficiency of circulation. Similar to angina pectoris pain, which results from insufficient blood circulation in the coronary arteries of the heart, here we have insufficiency in the blood circulation in the arteries—either those leading to the heart or in the arteries of the brain itself. The first type is called *carotid artery insufficiency,* which means that the big artery in the neck where you feel the pulse is disturbed in its function. Unfortunately, the experience has shown that this kind of insufficiency leads more often to a stroke than an insufficiency in the brain arteries themselves.

The carotid artery insufficiency or defect in its blood circulation usually causes weakness and numbness in the limbs of one side. Then, there is one-sided temporary blindness which occurs in about 1/3 of cases of the transient defects in the carotid blood circulation. There exists also a transient paralysis of arm and/or leg, a loss of feeling or difficulty of speech.

In the second type of a little stroke, which we call vertebrobasilar insufficiency, the symptoms are different. In the case of such a little stroke we deal with a temporarily insufficient blood supply—that is, a defect of circulation in the artery which leads from the spine; that is why it is called vertebral, because it supplies the vertebrae (the spinal column) and basilar: because from there it goes to the brain and supplies the central artery, which is called the basilary. In such an attack the back portions of the brain are involved. As in a brain concussion, the symptoms of such a little stroke are dizziness and nausea. We may find also weakness and/or numbness of the limbs, but these are additional, not quite characteristic for that type of little stroke. However, frequently we find numbness of the face, which is very important for the diagnosis of that second type of a little stroke. There is also usually speech difficulty, difficulty of swallowing, and double vision.

We have also to find out whether the patient gets his attacks if he turns his head and wears a tight collar. If he gets unconscious or weak under these circumstances, it is suspicious that he or she might have a kinking of one of the spine arteries which is being temporarily compressed by the tight collar or by violently turning the head.

An arthritis or disc disease of the neck spine can also involve a spine artery and lead to insufficiency of the blood circulation in the brain artery, by the arthritic outgrow of the spinal vertebra (which is called osteophyte) which presses upon the nerve and on the blood supply.

Sometimes, the little stroke involves only one arm's weakness, if there is a compression or diminution of the blood flow in the artery which is located under the collar bone (and therefore called subclavia).

The doctor has many ways to discover the danger of an impending big or little stroke. Among others, the difference in the blood pressure of 40 or 50 points between the figures for one arm and another is suspicious for a possible occurrence of a stroke. The difference in the strength of pulsation between the neck (carotid) arteries on both sides is also suspicious. Also in certain cases there is an unusual noise (called in French, *bruit*) over the neck's carotid artery. There are also changes in the eyegrounds which are suspicious for a pending danger of a stroke. Apart from temporary blindness, it happens that the patient notices blurring of the vision in one eye. People with high blood pressure usually have changes in the eyegrounds. But, if the changes are different in one eye from those in the other, there is also a suspicion of a possible little stroke which either already has occurred or can soon occur.

One has to understand that there is a great variety of little strokes. Some involve only an arm or only a leg; some are very transient, lasting only a few minutes or a few hours, and escape the attention of the doctor and of the patient, especially if they do not produce any degree of paralysis and cause only a temporary weakness of a limb. In such a case the patient decides that he has rheumatism or arthritis and does not consult a doctor at all. He is prone to take the most optimistic or most harmless view of his transient discomfort. In this lies the danger of the little stroke, namely, its neglect by the people who suffer from it.

There is no treatment of a little stroke, because it disappears before any treatment can be started. If it does not disappear that fast, then it is not a little stroke and has to be treated like a real stroke.

If the little stroke is recognized as such, then it has to be dealt with on a preventive basis. That is, we have to try to prevent another little stroke or a real stroke with its catastrophic consequences. We can prevent it in four ways. First, if we deal with a person who has high blood pressure, we have to reduce it by all means at our disposal. Secondly, if a person is obese, we have to reduce the weight because overweight increases the blood pressure and puts a heavier burden on the blood circulation. Thirdly, as mentioned in previous chapters regarding the real stroke, we have nowadays a possibility of removing, by surgery, the clot which obstructs the blood circulation. If the testing shows the exact spot of the obstruction, an operation and removal of the clot will prevent the development of a real stroke. Of course, not every patient can be operated on. He or she should not be too old; should not have additional serious chronic diseases; should not have a bad heart, either in the meaning of heart failure and damage, or in the meaning of an existing angina pectoris or a past heart attack. In other words, it should be a younger person with an impediment of the blood circulation, in otherwise comparatively good health. Then, there is a good prospect for a successful operation. Finally and fourthly, we have the prevention by anti-coagulation—which means that by chemical means (tablets) we can diminish the clotting readiness of the blood. The blood is more liquid and does not coagulate or clot as easily as it normally does, for instance, in a cut or wound. Unfortunately, this anti-coagulation method can be used only under supervision of a doctor, and by testing the blood at frequent intervals in order to prevent too much dilution of the blood (actually, though it is called so by laymen, the blood is not being diluted but prevented from clotting) or too little. If it is too little, there is no protection against clot formation; if it is too much, it can cause bleeding in the kidneys or the intestines or any other place in the body. The blood test, called prothrombin time, indicates the exact measure of anti-coagulation. In plain English, it means that such a prevention involves money for the doctor, for the tablets and for the frequent blood tests. However, it is done in thousands and millions of people who suffer either from coronary disease, or from large strokes or little strokes, or even clots in the veins (which is called the thrombophlebitis disease). Under skillful handling it can be done without too much discomfort for the patient.

The advantage of this kind of prevention is that it reduces the probability of clotting and thus the development of strokes, which after all are due to formation of clots in the arteries. It is not an absolute guarantee that the clots will not form just the same; but the risk is smaller, and this is the best which we can offer at present. After all, there is no treatment on earth in any disease which gives a 100% guarantee.

These four methods of prevention of little strokes, if religiously adhered to, are the best ways to avoid strokes, little or big, and to diminish the number of the hundreds of thousands of people who go every year, in this country alone, through the catastrophe of a stroke, with permanent paralysis, total disability, invalidism and dependence on other people. As the proverb says: "Better an ounce of prevention than a pound of treatment."

It might be worthwhile to stress again that big or little strokes are not necessarily the result of high blood pressure. There are plenty of people who have a normal blood pressure, but just the same an extensive arteriosclerosis which is even visible on X-rays. One sees calcification—that is, hardening of the arteries—in the aorta (the main artery of the body) sometimes all along its course. One can find the same hardening of the arteries in the legs or any other region of the body where the X-rays penetrate and the arteries can be visualized. Strokes occur more often in persons who have high blood pressure, but any other arteriosclerotic change which causes an obstruction in the blood flow in an artery, if it is supplying blood to the brain, can cause a stroke. In other words, our problem is not only fighting high blood pressure, but first of all to prevent arteriosclerosis—and if there is one already, to find ways and means to stop it from spreading and further developing. The research goes on to find out the final cause or causes of arteriosclerosis, which we don't know yet conclusively, and how to eliminate the existing hardening of the arteries. We have to declare frankly: we don't know at present yet, and have to accept the arteriosclerosis as a wear-and-tear disease—an unavoidable cause of aging of the body.

CHAPTER IX

OTHER OLD-AGE DISEASES OF THE HEART

Peculiarly enough, there are very few diseases of the heart which can be attributed to old age. Defects in the valves, what is commonly called a leak in the heart, is either inborn—congenital—or due to an acute rheumatic fever (by the way, a disease which has nothing to do with rheumatism or arthritis). This is a disease of adolescence, childhood or youth and hardly ever occurs in older people. Syphilis can cause changes in the aortic valve, in the meaning of aortic valve insufficiency or aortitis, which is an inflammation of the aorta. Syphilis infections are also common in young people by lack of prevention of veneral disease during sexual intercourse. However, the syphilitic changes of the heart are a late sign of a syphilis which one contracted in young age. In this way, one encounters a syphilitic change in the heart rather in older than in younger people.

More important from the general point of view is the condition of the heart muscle in older age. We mentioned already that, in a heart attack, apart from an obstruction of a coronary artery, there comes a myocardial infarction—which means a softening, weakening and scarring of the heart muscle within the area of the obstruction of the coronary artery. Now, this is, generally speaking, a heart-muscle damage. This damage can also occur independently of a heart attack, namely, by an overstrain of the strength of the heart. Theoretically, there should not exist such a condition. Our heart is an engine which should last forever. The main function of the heart is to pump incessantly day and night every second of our life. And this pumping is done by the heart muscle, which contracts and relaxes. Imagine a car the motor of which has to work day and night for years and years on end. How long can such an overstrained motor last? But our motor, the heart, can do it and does. It is built better than any conceived engine or motor.

If it gets spoiled, if it refuses to work normally, if it shows signs of strain, it is not due to any defect of construction but due to disease. As said in the beginning of this chapter, some people are born with a defective heart, just like some children are born with defective limbs or a defective brain, etc. But, normally, the heart is built to last forever. Now there are some diseases which do not affect the heart: for instance, cancer of the heart does not exist. On the other hand, the valves which regulate the blood flow within the heart are very delicate, and germs can attack them easily. We have, for instance, a so-called subacute bacterial endocarditis when the germs attack the lining of the heart inside and cause a disease which used to be fatal. Now it is curable, but it still is a very serious and protracted illness. This can occur at any age, young and old, though still more in younger than older people. Other infectious diseases can also damage the heart and cause a strain of the mechanism of the function of the heart. In most cases, however, the heart muscle is damaged by diseases which affect the heart not directly but indirectly by attacking other organs which require more work by the heart due to their illness, and thus strain the heart muscle. Such are, for example, lung and other respiratory diseases, whether pneumonia or bronchitis or asthma or emphysema or what-not. Difficulty of breathing in all these diseases causes a strain on the heart. If the respiratory disease is acute, the strain of the heart is temporary and its function returns to normal in short time. If there is a chronic disease of the lungs and of the bronchial tubes—in one word, of the respiratory system—the strain on the heart is also chronic or perpetual, resulting in constant changes which demand chronic treatment and cause a permanent damage to the heart. We have in the case of the chronic disease of the respiratory organs a condition called "cor pulmonale" which means a "lung heart"—that is, a heart the function of which depends on the condition of the lungs. And while we can treat the heart, we cannot restore it to normal as long as there is a chronic condition of the lungs.

The same applies to all other organs. We have to remember that the heart is the source of the blood supply everywhere in the body, and where there is any kind of disease or damage, it has a repercussion in the heart. If a person loses blood for whatever reason, or does not produce enough blood, the heart cannot pump enough blood and suffers itself by the deficiency of the blood amount. The quality of the blood also caused by disease has its effect on the heart. The condition of all other organs—liver, kidney, spleen, intestines, stomach—have in their turn an influence on the function of the heart.

There is also sometimes a mechanical damage to the heart. Apart from accidents, stabbing, shots, etc., there exists a possibility of an overstrain by physical activity. This applies specifically to old age. There is a limit to what a heart can do. Even if the heart can last indefinitely—as proven by the fact of people who are over 100 years old and whose heart functions, otherwise they would be dead and buried—there comes a time when even this wonderful motor has to take it easy. Because, after all, the older ones becomes, the more incidents of disease, work, stress and emotion he or she experiences, and they leave a scar or a stamp on the function of the body of which the heart is the most important part.

Therefore, if in older age there is too much physical activity, a damage to the heart muscle occurs. Too much lifting, too much carrying, too much exertion, too much sport (like golf or tennis), and an older person notices it and says, "I am apparently not as young as I used to be." If a person notices the limitations, and nevertheless continues to exert himself or herself in the same way, the result will be chronic damage, a myocardial damage with a following "cardiac failure." This means the inability to perform consequently even lighter work, such as bending or climbing stairs or hills without experiencing puffing, shortness of breath and so on. A chronic damage of the heart muscle with heart failure is a sign of the waning strength and function of the heart. In the last 15 to 20 years we have learned well how to combat such damage; and with the co-operation of the patient in regard to his mode of life, we can prolong the life for quite many years. Just the same, the damage to the heart muscle, whether by infection, disease or overstrain (physical and also emotional), is a very serious sign of shortening of the life expectancy. That means that a person with a damaged heart has to be doubly careful: not to catch infections or a cold, and to avoid exposure to heat and cold; not to exert himself or herself too much; to calculate when and how and where to travel—all this in order to conserve the strength of the damaged heart. With all these precautions and under careful observation and treatment by a doctor, one can, even with that kind of heart, live much, much longer than it was possible 50 or less years ago.

This is one of the reasons why people live nowadays longer than before.

CHAPTER X

THE BRAIN IN OLD AGE

Actually, we should speak about the changes in the blood circulation in the brain in old age as they affect the function of the brain. The brain itself, if it has a normal blood circulation, does not change much because of aging. If somebody is smart, if his or her brain cells and especially its rind—which is called "cortex," and is the seat of all our mental activity—are well developed and function well, they will continue to work well at the highest age. Even at ninety, one can be brilliant. Many of the works of famous writers were written and were even better when the writer was very old. We have plenty of statesmen of 70 to 80 who rule a country and do a good job of it. Greece had in our century a prime minister 90 years old. Churchill wrote his books of the Second World War when he was very old, and even his earlier books were written when he was not a youngster any more. Berenson, the famous art expert, wrote his books also in old age. We could give dozens of examples of how people do not lose their mental faculties because of aging; some become even more mature, more exquisite in their work when they get older, maybe because their work reflects the accumulation of the past experiences of the many years.

There comes something else which explains the good work of old people. Young people are in a hurry; everything should be done quickly—they have no time, no patience. Some good, mature work in any field of activity—poetry, fiction, statesmanship or carpentry—requires patience, deliberate doing, polishing of a piece of wood, of a tapestry, of a phrase, even of a word. It is peculiar that young people, who should think that they have all the time in the world on their hands all the forthcoming years, should be impatient and in a hurry, running from one task to another; while the old people on the brink, so to say, of death, with a few precious years of life remaining, should have the patience to do some work which requires years for accomplishment.

That reminds one of the story of the very old man who plants a sapling of a fruit tree in his garden. When asked why he does it, since he will be probably dead when the tree bears fruit, he answered that this may be true; but when he bought the garden as a young man, he found fruit trees bearing fruit, and he reaped the effort of people who planted the tree and left it to him—though they themselves could not reap the effort of their work.

To return from the philosophy of old age to the medical problems of the action of the brain in old age, the fact is that nerve cells in the brain cannot be substituted by any means; that their destruction is forever, that even a nerve in the periphery of the body, if cut or damaged, can regrow, but it is an extremely slow process—sometimes (if lucky) one inch in a month, but sometimes much, much longer, if ever. That is the reason why any operation which involves a cutting through skin nerves, leaves in that area a numbness which may last for months and years, and sometimes stays forever.

In the brain the destruction or damage of the cells is irreplaceable. Luckily enough, there are billions of cells and even of groups of such cells; and one cell or group of cells can take over the function of the damaged or destroyed cells with resulting minimal alteration of the function. If the damage or destruction is extensive, then the situation becomes hopeless. If it affects an area of mental abilities, the person becomes, if alive, a so-called "vegetable." He or she lives, eats, defecates, but without comprehension of what goes on around; in a way, less than a baby whose mental abilities grow and do not diminish.

In this book there is no reason to deal with brain diseases, such as tumors, cancer, etc., which occur in any age; they are not particular to old age, and one can refer such diseases to the proper authorities or books dealing with the matter. On the other hand, mental disorders, as far as they pertain to old age, will be dealt with in a special chapter. So, here we have to deal primarily with brain changes which occur in old age due to changes in blood circulation.

We spoke already about the havoc done to the body in the course of a stroke, which is due to occlusion of an artery in the brain and blockage of blood circulation in that area—with resulting disturbances of the activity of this or that part of the body, and especially of the limbs.

But there are plenty of changes in the function of the brain which are peculiar to old age and are not connected with strokes —big or little. One of the most important changes, which occurs very frequently, is *loss of memory*. That does not mean amnesia, which is so beloved by fiction writers and very rarely occurs— and, if at all, only for a short while (hours or days, hardly much longer). The loss of memory is usually partial: either loss of memory for certain occurrences or for names. The latter is very frequent; people forget names of people or cities or personalities which they usually know very well. It can, in more pronounced cases, be members of the family, even the name of one's own wife or husband or child. Sometimes they forget the date, the name of the President, or the name of the mother-in-law.

Of course, there is a Freudian theory that people forget what they do not want to remember. This theory is more than a theory; it is a fact and should be called psychological amnesia. In order to protect themselves, for self-preservation of their mind to avoid remembrance of unpleasant incidents, or incidents which burden their memory, people just put those incidents or those remembrances away in a kind of a drawer which is locked, not to be opened at all. This happens to almost everybody and is not a sign of disease or of an organic or mental change. And it differs from old-age loss of memory in that it happens in any age, even in children; I would even say, especially in children who do not want to remember unpleasant incidents, punishment, jeering of schoolmates, and so on.

The loss of memory can be, like a stroke, either permanent

or fleeting: fleeting like a little stroke is loss of memory which lasts only minutes, hours or days, and then returns to normal. Sometimes it is so fleeting as in a case of a patient of mine, a lady of 83, who phoned her girl friend, talked to her and, during the conversation, suddenly forgot the name of the girl friend and what they were talking about. While the girl still talked and talked and she only listened, trying furiously to remember, suddenly it came back to her; her friend on the other end even did not realize what had happened, and everything was all right. In another case a man to whom I talked over the telephone at 11 a.m. lost his memory one hour later; when I came to visit him two hours after our conversation, he did not even remember my first name, the name of his sister-in-law, the date, the number of his apartment, and so on. It has to be mentioned that in former years he had boasted with pride and justification of his excellent memory, by which he remembered the names of hundreds of people with whom he was in contact. In this case the loss of memory lasted 24 hours. The next day he was as before, and believed that I and his wife made a joke when we told him of his memory's behavior the day before.

This type of loss of memory belongs to the same category as the little stroke. It occurs through a cramp—a spasm in the blood circulation of the brain where the arteries supply the memory center. When the circulation, the oxygen and blood supply, is restored to normal, when the spasm disappears, the memory returns.

It is not the case with the more serious losses of memory. There is usually a permanent hardening of the arteries in this particular region of the brain which governs the memory. It can lead to a complete blockage with a total loss of memory, but it is rather rare. Frequent is the loss of memory for certain things and names, and preservation of it for others. In old age, when there is a permanent damage, people do not remember what happened yesterday but retain a good memory for things past. The older the incident, the better it is remembered in older age. Suddenly a person remembers vividly persons and incidents of early childhood which he or she has, as they believed, completely forgotten. The same happens with memory of languages. If it is a person of foreign extraction, living in the U.S.A., he or she tends to forget the English language which he or she may have used for 40 or 50 years, sometimes to the exclusion of any other language. The result of such a memory damage is that suddenly they well remember a word or an expression in their native tongue which they used as children, and do not remember the same word in English. This could be well proven in a patient of mine of over 80 who started suffering from loss of memory for daily occurrences and daily words. This man was born and lived in Russia until the revolution. In 1920 or so, he came from Russia to Germany where he lived for 20 years; and, of course, being a highly educated man, he learned German and spoke it very well. Then he emigrated to the U.S.A. When he was over 80 years old, he was in New York for about 25 years and again learned and spoke English perfectly well. When his memory started to wane, he used to forget the words for daily items in English. Occasionally he knew them in German, but with all his severe loss of memory, he always remembered the name of the item or of the expression in Russian.

Apparently, there were 3 layers in the memory deposit of the brain. The upper surface layer of English was not firmly anchored, and gave away as first; the German layer, which was deeper, stayed longer. But Russian, his childhood or early manhood tongue, he just could not forget; it was the foundation on which his intellect was built, and that remained stable like the Rock of Gibraltar.

The gradual or sudden loss of the memory for a language can sometimes be pathetic. I recollect a case of a German patient who came to this country in 1933 because of Nazi persecution. He was here for 32 years when he suddenly developed signs of arteriosclerosis in the heart, in various organs, and finally it affected his memory. His wife was American-born, his children and grandchildren were born here and they hardly ever spoke German, though they understood that language more or less.

The patient himself hardly ever spoke German because of his business connections and the family environment in which he lived. All of a sudden he had forgotten—not some words, but completely—his English, and started addressing everybody in German. The situation became even more difficult when he had to have a nurse for his heart condition; and the family had frantically to look for a German-speaking nurse, which was not so easy because he lived in a small town about 50 miles from New York where such nurses were unobtainable. The interesting part was that he had no deficit of words in German, and could converse freely and express his wishes to the nurse just like anybody else; only his good knowledge of English was completely gone.

There is another quirk to the problem of memory in older age. One can forget the word for "bread" or "napkin" but not words or expressions which are connected with the daily occupation, trade or profession. So the lawyer or the physician or engineer will maybe forget items of daily life but not the things for which he was trained—the laws, the diseases, the calculations; and especially, if he or she is devoted to their professional work, if they continue in it and are engrossed and eager to do what they always did. The same applies, of course, to women. If they were seamstresses or sewing-machine operators, or if they were just plain housewives, their daily work will not suffer from the loss of memory, nor will they have difficulty finding the words which they need for shopping, for instance. It may be that while in younger age they knew by heart what they wanted and needed in the supermarket, they might now need a written list of the intended shopping items. They might forget an appointment with a doctor or dentist. The reason may be more psychological than arteriosclerotic; but it is not likely that they will forget the appointment at the beauty parlor.

So, we get a picture of an older person who becomes forgetful. In some important jobs it may become an impossible situation, such as when a senior executive has to dictate a letter and cannot find the words or loses the train of his thoughts;

or a doctor who does not remember the name of a medical preparation or of the dosage which he has to prescribe. These instances can be multiplied and elaborated. In such a situation, the best possible solution would be a gracious retirement, and to take up a less responsible occupation where the loss of memory would be a minor matter.

Apart from a complete loss of memory, which occurs but rarely, this partial loss of memory is something which occurs quite often and frequently is not even observed or is hidden by smart people who suffer from it, so that it is not so obvious. On the whole, as in general arteriosclerosis, it is a progressive condition; the lapses of memory are getting more frequent and the extent of the loss of memory gets larger in scope. However, it is a very slow progress, and not infrequently it reaches a certain point at which the deterioration stops. Apparently, the hardening of the arteries in the memory center reaches a certain point beyond which it does not progress, or where it does not reach the deeper layers of the memory structure.

It is interesting to observe that the complaints about the loss of memory depend on the education of a person. An educated patient will complain bitterly about the loss of memory; he or she will also notice it earlier than a poorly educated person. Such a patient will be scared, afraid of loss of mental abilities, of getting out of the mind—and, if still working, of losing his or her position and having to retire; while the uneducated patient will notice it only when the loss of memory becomes very obvious and commented upon by relatives or neighbors. He or she in such a case will take it from the funny point of view; say, "Apparently old age is creeping upon me"; and that will be the end of it—unless the loss of memory obtains catastrophic proportions which force nursing care, such as if and when a patient plainly forgets to eat or to dress. The reason for the difference in the memory behavior of an educated and uneducated patient is the quantity of words which one requires in life. For daily life, shopping, small talk, etc., a simple, uneducated person requires only about 800 words. And again, here comes the peculiarity of not easily forgetting words or expressions which are constantly used—that is, the deeper layer which is firmly rooted in the mind—so that the words which an uneducated person forgets are lost in the conversation without being noticed much, unless the person forgets the name of an intimate friend or of a close relative.

In the case of an educated person the situation is different. His or her vocabulary may consist of 12,000 words, and the conversation turns around subjects of literature, arts, politics, etc., which one has used since the time of the education in high school or college. The daily objects do not belong to the sphere of the deep interest of the patient, with the result that in loss of memory he or she can forget the word "pencil" or "spoon" but not the word "geography" or "history" or "a poem." In other words, the less interested a person is in certain subjects or objects, the sooner they will be lost in the mind, because they belong to the superficial layer.

A completely different story is that of behavior in old age. Basically, we have to distinguish two different patterns. One is related to the loss of memory, the other to a general decline of personality. In the first case, people suddenly get more primitive table manners, if they were more formal before, because in such a case they return to the table manners which they had at their parents' home. It means that if they are children of a primitive home where the use of fork, knife or napkin was very superficial and the parents did not pay attention to the way the children ate as long as they ate, then with the advent of old-age changes in the brain, whether arteriosclerotic or otherwise, the patient, similar to the change of the language pattern, returns to the pattern of table manners behavior of childhood. The same would apply to clothing and other modalities of life. In other words, the so-called cultural and civilized behavior is only like paint on wood, and when it peels off you see the raw side underneath.

The other pattern in the change of behavior in old age is the decline of personality. Not in the meaning of a mental disease—such patients do not show mental deterioration in the form of delusions, hallucinations, etc., which point to a mental illness. They just change. The character of a person to which the environment is used becomes different. They may (very occasionally) change for the better; they may become more mellow, more pleasant, more understanding, softer in the approach to other people—like a good wine mellowing with age. However, this change is much rarer than the one when the character changes for the worse. People become more cantankerous, more aggressive; they fight everything and everybody, even close relatives and friends, and most of the time without any reason—or they make a mountain out of a molehill. Little by little they lose all their friends, who do not see any reason why they should tolerate such a behavior and expose themselves to an unwarranted aggression. Then such patients turn into themselves and start brooding; or worse, they turn their aggressive and unpleasant mood towards the wife or children, who have to suffer without knowing the reason. Such people are not only ungrateful but they are seeking for defects of behavior, mistakes or lack of respect in their relatives; they can easily convert a peaceful family life into a hell in which the relatives silently pray for the death of the member of the family who is afflicted with this kind of old-age brain change. The cause is usually arteriosclerosis of the brain arteries, which, as shown, can weave all kind of patterns in the life of an older person. In regard to this new pattern of behavior which suddenly becomes obvious, you can expect this obnoxious behavior rather from a person who *always* had these traits of character, only in a mild form—not so pronounced and not so obvious to everybody. By upbringing, training and education a person could suppress these characteristics. They usually were hidden to the outer world. Acquaintances were pleased by the behavior and considered such persons as charming and at least agreeable; while at home, behind the closed doors, such a person could behave outrageously towards members of his or her family, who noticed the difference of behavior externally and internally and learned to hate him or her.

In old age, due to arterosclerotic and other changes in the brain, the restraint exercised outwardly falls off, and the obnoxious behavior continues, so to say, in the street also towards comparative strangers, friends and acquaintances. It becomes accentuated at home. It can even lead to tragedies of violence with all consequences, if it is not early enough understood that this kind of behavior is sickness and should be taken care of by a doctor.

It should be understood that any change in the pattern of behavior, whether for better or worse, should be looked upon with suspicion of an underlying sickness, and should be reported to a doctor.

Parkinson's disease, so called by the name of the doctor who first described it in detail, is not necessarily a disease of old age. It is true, you can hardly find it in young people; but it happens. More often you can see this disease in middle age, but it is most frequently an affliction of old age. It is what people call "the shakes," which means that some parts of the body start shaking. It is a disease of one tiny part of the brain which does not involve the mental abilities of a person, not even the general health of a person, at least not in the beginning. It is a very slowly-progressing disease. It occurs in middle-aged people for unknown reasons; most researchers believe it is due to a virus which attacks this small portion of the brain. In old patients it is very common and considered as a disease connected with wear and tear, possibly hardening of the arteries in this particular brain area. The result in younger and older people is the same, whether due to a virus infection or to arteriosclerosis. The trembling or shaking is first confined to a hand or to a foot. Then it spreads to the whole arm or the whole leg. It is rare to have the trembling on both sides; it is usually left or right. If the shaking increases, it is impossible to hold anything in the hand; the cup or the spoon shakes and falls to the floor. In cases when only a leg is involved, the leg trembles and cannot stand still. The tremor (trembling) is not constant. It is called an intentional tremor, which means that as soon as the patient intends to do something, the tremor starts. Otherwise, the underlying disease is not visible. This is in the beginning. Later, there comes rigidity of the face muscles and the face looks masque-like—no expression, or, rather, no change of expression in the face, like we see it in a normal person. Simultaneously comes a change in the gait. A person with Parkinson's disease walks differently. He or she (both sexes are equally afflicted) walks with a propulsion. If you walk behind such a patient, you have the impression that somebody is pushing him or her, so that each step is separate, as it brought about by a winding mechanism which promotes the walking. These three symptoms—the shaking, the gait and the rigidity of the expression of the face—are so typical that they are sufficient for a diagnosis of Parkinson's disease.

However, a consolation in old age is the fact that the change in the gait and in the expression of the face—the rigidity—are more common in younger, middle-aged people whose Parkinson is caused by an infection, than in old-age Parkinson. The older people just shake—period. It is still very unpleasant and requires a lot of adaptation of daily life, such as eating, cleaning, shaving and so on, to the new circumstances, and especially if the trembling is very pronounced in the hand; and it becomes particularly difficult if it afflicts both hands, as it occasionally does. One has to learn to use cups and cutlery in order to be able to eat and not break china, not to let things fall to the floor, not to cut himself. People adjust themselves to the trembling. It takes more time, more effort and exertion; but because the mental function is not disturbed, patients learn what they can do and what not, and in which way to do it. It is interesting to see how Parkinson patients adjust themselves: a patient of mine who is a quite well-known painter, and whose right hand shakes, observed that his hand does not shake if he paints in a sitting position and has some support for his hand and the brush; in this way he continues in his occupation. One can also write if he or she continues writing; the first or second line will be all shaken up and impossible to decipher; afterwards, the hand becomes stable and the handwriting can even be very precise and legible.

The old-age Parkinson is, as said, an unpleasant disease;

but it is neither killing nor does it have a bad effect on the general health. Rather, psychologically it has a bad effect on the personality of the patient because he or she becomes awkward and a nuisance to the environment; notwithstanding all efforts, a cup or a dish breaks, food spills on the table or floor, and so on. There was some years ago on Broadway a play, *The Wooden Dish,* which shows what effect an old-age Parkinson can have on the patient and the relatives with whom the patient lives.

Another consolation is the interest shown by the medical profession in the finding of treatment for Parkinson. The result is that we have a multitude of remedies, some more, some less successful; but many of them greatly diminish the trembling. There is even a surgical treatment of Parkinson, discovered by Dr. Irving Cooper of the St. Barnabas Hospital in the Bronx, which abolishes, if the operation is successful, some of the worst features of Parkinson.

Here I have in conclusion to mention that Parkinson's disease does not always affect the arms or legs, or both. There are some cases—and I have the impression that they increase in quantity, at least as far as I can judge from my own experience—when what shakes are the vocal cords. It does not cause hoarseness. Very often no shaking of arms or legs accompanies the trembling of the vocal cords, but occasionally it does. The result of the Parkinson of the vocal cords is, on one hand, that the patient feels the faint trembling of the vocal cords, and it gives a kind of shaky quality to the voice which makes it difficult for the patient to converse; on the other hand, the Parkinson of the vocal cords makes the speech very often so blurred that it is difficult to understand it, unless as a relative one is used to that kind of speech and has the patience to distinguish the spoken words. As in the other types of old-age Parkinson, the usual medication is more or less successful. Typical for Parkinson is also the fluctuation in the intensity of the symptoms. The patient has good and bad days, or good or bad hours, depending on his or her emotions and nervous condition. Such a patient can shake more or almost not at all—with or without medication.

The same applies to vocal-cords Parkinson. Sometimes the words come out clear and absolutely understandable. Sometimes not one word is intelligible. As said, the whole business is a nuisance in old age, but without any danger to life or health. It is something you have to learn to live with.

During the last two or three years something tremendous occurred in the treatment of Parkinson's disease. Namely, for the first time a chemical treatment for this chronic disease was found. The name of the new medication is *Levodopa* and although new and although all side-reactions are not yet known, the Food and Drug Administration of the United States allowed the distribution under several brand names for treatment of Parkinson's disease under strict supervision of a doctor, and preferably at a hospital. Just the same, the results are often amazing, the disease in some cases practically disappeared, or at least greatly improved.

One has to emphasize that *Levodopa* is a new preparation, and it is much too early to say whether the improvement will be permanent or only transient; what kind of new side-reactions will be discovered in addition to those which are already known.

In any case, although the results are not uniform and although in many cases the results are not satisfactory at all, the discovery of the action of *Levodopa* on Parkinson's disease has to be considered as a considerable achievement of modern treatment of a disease of the nerves.

CHAPTER XI

THE DISEASES OF THE PERIPHERAL CIRCULATION IN OLD AGE

The peripheral circulation means the circulation of the blood in the arteries and veins in the arms and legs. Here we have to say in advance that the disturbances in the circulation of the blood in the *veins* are not particularly confined to old age; they can and do occur in all age groups. We have to deal in old age especially with arteriosclerosis, which, as the word implies, means a hardening of the *arteries,* not of veins—in which we do not find the sclerotic structural changes which cause the hardening. We do have in old age diseases of the veins; however, even if they are very often connected with slowing down of the circulation of the blood in the veins, nevertheless they are primarily due to inborn weakness of the walls of the veins. Such are, for instance, varicose veins, which are so often seen in old age, especially on the legs of women; but still, such women most often inherited the tendency to varicose veins from their mothers and had at least some varicose veins even as young women, and especially during pregnancy or shortly afterwards. It is true that the varicose veins, because of general loss of elasticity and weakness of the walls, give in in old age and widen, and therefore not only look unsightly, even ugly, but also impede walking. They are just full of blood which moves very slowly, without benefit to the blood circulation. It sometimes stagnates and clots, causing phlebitis, which is an inflammation of the veins. The clot inside the inflamed vein, if it moves, can cause an inflammation and clotting which moves upwards and can reach the veins in the abdomen. On has to understand that, while arteries bring the blood from the heart to the legs, the veins are supposed to return the blood to the heart; that means that the blood moves upwards. Now, the varicose veins are widened and absolutely useless for the blood, or to say the least, they are not needed; there are plenty of deep, well-functioning veins which perform the task. Therefore, the varicose veins can be removed surgically or by chemical obliteration without any damage. Because of the poor circulation in such veins, one sees often discoloration of the skin, especially above or below the ankles. It looks unpleasant; it distorts the natural beauty of a woman's leg, but it is not dangerous. Sometimes such a poor circulation causes an ulcer on the skin of the leg, called *ulcus cruris,* again mainly near the ankle. It heals poorly because of lack of circulation. With all the remedies on hand, it can persist for years. Some surgeons, if they are adventurous, cut them out. But even then, it is questionable whether the newly-created wound will heal; because, after all, the circulation remains poor.

Still, one has to remember that all the diseases of the veins —varicose veins, ulcers, clotting and phlebitis—though they occur most frequently in old age, are only secondary old-age diseases; they are not confined to old age only. You can find them in middle-aged people; and, apart from inheritance, the occupation plays a great role. The same woman or man with varicose veins will not get an exacerbation of them, with all the consequences, if he or she has a sedentary occupation or an occupation which demands walking and/or exertion. The varicose veins get bigger and bad when the person is a waiter or waitress or a salesman or saleswoman in a shop, or has any other occupation which requires *standing*—not walking—for hours on end. This causes a difficulty for the upward return of the blood to the heart, and can cause the worsening of the condition of the veins—in other words, it can become an occupational disease. In many of such cases the doctor has to tell the patient to change the occupation, if all the prescribed remedies do not help. For milder cases even the wearing of elastic stockings or of a support-hose can improve the condition, and the elevation of the legs at rest is also useful. But, in advanced cases, the only remedy is the change of the occupation from standing to walking or sitting; because, even if surgery should remove the existing varicose veins, there is no guarantee that new varicose veins will not develop in due time.

Of course, one has to stress that not everyone gets varicose veins with their unpleasant consequences, even as a waitress or saleswoman. (I emphasize the sex because men do get varicose veins, phlebitis, etc., but in much lesser degree and frequency than women; and there is more inheritance of the tendency from mother to daughter than from father to son.) You have to have an inborn tendency to a poor structure of the veins in order to get varicose veins of any importance (anyone can get small varicose veins), just as not everybody gets a hernia, regardless of occupation.

To sum up, disturbances of the blood circulation in the veins in old age are of minor importance and not particularly due to the aging process.

A completely different story is that of disturbances in the blood circulation in the peripheral arteries—that is, in the arteries of the arms and legs.

To begin with, the disturbances in the blood circulation of the arms are much less frequent and minor compared with the changes in the arteries of the legs. Basically, because the arms are near the heart and the great trunk artery—the aorta—they get an abundant blood supply from the main arteries. Changes in the arteries of the arms, including the hands, occur almost always when the main artery which branches out from the aorta becomes diseased and causes a lessening of the blood and oxygen supply to the arm and hand. Such disturbance occurs if the big artery gets clotted by a blood clot, which can come from other places in the body (what we call embolism) or emanates on the spot. Either causes a complete occlusion, with the danger of a gangrene and loss of an arm if nothing is done (usually one has to have an emergency operation to remove the clot); or the clot is smaller and still leaves some canal in the artery through which the blood flow continues. In such a case the deficiency of blood supply causes symptoms such as numbness, or "pins and needles" feeling, or plain pain—a condition similar to the angina pectoris which we described before, only the symptoms occur in the affected arm and not in the heart.

But, while the changes of the blood circulation in the arms and hands do not play a great role in the general picture of its changes in old age (I do not mention diseases like Raynaud's disease, which causes blanching of the hands, and some other diseases, because they do not necessarily occur in old age), there is a vast field of changes in the legs which appear primarily in older age. There are two reasons why we find them in the legs of older people. First, the legs are the most distant part of the body, if we take the heart as a central point. Secondly, the legs in a human being undergo a lot of wear and tear, whether by working with them, standing or walking. After all, we are two-legged creatures, and our legs are our main support in most of our activities. If hardening of the arteries appears —and it does appear in the greatest majority of human beings, at least in the so-called civilized world—then the legs are to be considered as the most likely victims, apart from the heart and the brain. When we get arteriosclerosis in the legs, we are in trouble, unless we do something to fight it. This arteriosclerosis of the legs is the main disease of the legs in older age, and cannot be compared in importance and severity to any other ailments, such as the previously-mentioned varicose veins, leg ulcers, or bunions or calluses on the soles, fallen arches, etc. All these ailments may be unpleasant and cause discomfort, but they are just unimportant from the point of view of general health and proper functioning of the body.

The main symptom of arteriosclerosis of the legs is what we call "claudication." Claudication is the condition when a person walks a few steps or a block or two or ten, and suddenly gets a pain in a leg or both legs which forces him or her to stop and to rest. Then, after some seconds or minutes the pain disappears and one can continue walking. This can happen all the way, after every block or after so many steps. It rarely happens at home, and there is a reason for it. In some milder cases such a condition arises only after walking a long distance, maybe half a mile; or it occurs sooner if one has to climb while walking, going up a hill or even a steeper incline of the street. The pain can be very sharp and can be light. It can last a second and also a minute. In any case, the condition of claudication makes a semi-invalid of the person because it forces him to use mechanical transportation even for short distances.

The cause of this disturbance is a deficiency of the blood circulation in the arteries of the leg due to narrowing of the width of the artery through which the blood, with its oxygen, has to flow. In almost all cases the narrowing is due to arteriosclerosis, and this type of arteriosclerosis does not differ from the others as described in previous chapters. It again depends on the importance of the artery in which the hardening and the narrowing occurs. If it is a small branch and the bigger ones are not affected, a person may have arteriosclerosis of the legs without even noticing it. Only when the arteriosclerosis spreads and reaches the larger branches does the patient notice that something is going wrong with his or her legs. I was always amazed that people constantlly considered the advice of a physician as the last resort. First, they try arch-supports; then they buy all kinds of foot-remedy stuff from a 5 and 10 cent store. Then they go to a chiropodist who cuts corns and puts something on the bunions, all with the patient's idea that the reason for the discomfort is external. Only, when the walking becomes a torture, they go to a doctor of medicine; and he finds the arteriosclerosis usually already well advanced, with diminished or absent pulses in the feet and the picture of a blooming hardening of the arteries in the most important arteries of the leg, and frequently in both legs—in one more, in another less; and accordingly, more claudication and pain in one and less in another.

There are plenty of cases when the artery in question is completely blocked by cholesterol, calcium, and other debris. There is no blood circulation anymore. If it is a small artery branch and there is plenty of what is called "collateral" circulation, then there occurs a detour; and the blood, like traffic, takes another route. If the damage occurs in a big vital branch, there is a danger of gangrene and loss of the leg. The leg, or maybe only the foot, becomes cold and gray, loses its pinkish color, is practically dead. Only instant surgery can sometimes save such a leg or foot. The surgeon has some surgical procedures which may restore the circulation. Often it is too late, and the foot or the leg has to be amputated.

However, this is not a frequent consequence of arteriosclerosis of the legs. More often there is the discomfort, only leading to semi-invalidism as described before. In order to understand what goes on and how to help, one has to know how the circulation works on walking. The blood comes from the heart, which pumps it, loaded with oxygen, into the leg. It returns to the heart after giving up the oxygen and all that is needed for the nutrition and well-being of the tissues via the venous system. Therefore, as previously described, the disturbance of the blood circulation in the veins is a separate entity and differs from that in the arteries. In any case, for the exercise of walking and contraction of the leg muscles which take part in the process of walking, you need new blood coming from the heart and returning to the heart, just the same as water coming from the tank and circulating in the pipes. If the arteries are narrowed and stay narrow, less blood comes through. When a person walks, and if the arteries are narrow, his or her leg muscles get a lesser blood supply and therefore cannot function as well as they should. This lack of blood or its deficiency causes pain which forces one to stop and to wait for the pain to go away. As soon as the person stops, the leg muscles are not strained. They can rest without exercise. And then, on the one hand, the pain due to exercise disappears; on the other hand, the heart sends a new supply of blood and the walking can re-start.

Now, a patient with this type of circulatory disturbance has a dilemma. Either he or she stops walking, and then the pain does not come up, or the patient walks and suffers from the pain. Which way is chosen depends on the person's character and economic situation, in a way similar to the attitude in a case of a stroke. If one is determined to get well, one can overcome many handicaps and return to good health. If one is weak of character, prone to self-pity, afraid of pain, too lazy to exercise even if it improves the health, then such a patient stays an invalid. Economically, it looks like that: if it is a rich patient, not determined to get well, who suffers from claudication, then he calls a taxi for the shortest distance, has a servant or other help, and thus avoids doing anything for himself. This type of patient relies on medicine to do the work for him. He will be willing to swallow any amount of pills, hoping that they will do the trick and put him back on his feet.

It is true, we have several medical remedies for peripheral arteries disease. We can even try, sometimes successfully, a surgical approach. There is a nervous system called the sympathetic nervous system which is responsible for the nervous stimulation of the arteries; this causes a tightening of the arteries and narrowing of their width (with the help of a hormone called adrenalin or epinephrine, which is produced by the adrenal glands and circulates in the blood). Now, if you cut the sympathetic nerves which lead to the legs, this type of stimulation plus tightening disappears, resulting in a widening of the arteries, more blood supply, and accordingly better motion—better walking with less pain. This surgery is applied in more desperate cases, especially when there is hardly any circulation and the blockage of the blood supply can and sometimes does cause a gangrene. Because the sympathetic nerves supply all arteries, it is not impossible that the cutting of those nerves could widen even small arteries. In this way, when the big arteries are blocked, then the blood supply is taken over by the collateral circulation—that is, by the net of small arteries which widen and get more blood. Such a possibility of improvement of peripheral arteries disease exists, though the results of such an operation are by no means guaranteed. In any case, an operation of that kind (sympathectomy) will be limited to more extreme cases when all medical approaches have failed.

The poor patient who cannot ride a taxi every few blocks,

and having claudication has still to walk to the job, just walks even if he has pain. What such a patient does is just what the doctor would order. Namely, the best treatment for the disease of the arteries of the legs is just walking. Walking causes a better flow of the blood to the arteries, strengthens the muscles of the legs, and invigorates the whole body. Now, what should a patient do if the pain occurs? He or she should stop until the pain disappears—which, as a rule, occurs after a few seconds or at the most after a minute—and should then continue walking. In the meantime, at rest, the heart sends new blood, and the walking can be resumed. If, as expected, the pain recurs, one has to stop again, has to wait for the disappearance of the pain and has to walk again. This is the best medicine because it represents a vigorous exercise of the arteries, which have to widen and contract—a kind of calisthenics or physical exercise. It was even found that exercise diminishes the cholesterol of the blood, which is the main cause of the narrowing of the arteries. This kind of exercise is even more important than the cholesterol-poor diet—though such a diet should not be neglected, because too much cholesterol in the food increases the content of cholesterol in the blood.

I often hear from my patients that they have walked enough at home or at the shop or at the factory. I said before that there is a reason to discount this kind of walking in the treatment of arteriosclerosis of the legs. The reason is simple. Whether it is a housewife or a shop attendant or a factory worker, all of them do not walk vigorously, or at least not continuously. If I say vigorously, I do not mean fast; because fast walking exhausts the amount of the blood in the leg arteries even faster. One has to walk, or try to walk energetically, even if slowly. And secondly, one has to walk continuously, even if one has to stop for a second because of the pain. In other words, the walking should be a task done with a purpose, not a by-product of another work like housekeeping or salesmanship, or laboring in the factory. Nobody walks continously at home or at any of the mentioned jobs. One walks a few steps and stops to look at something or to do something. It can be done 100 times and still it does not constitute an exercise, even if one becomes dog-tired by doing that kind of work. That type of walking does not produce an incentive to increase the blood supply, and therefore it is not an exercise of contraction and expansion of the artery. It was also found that the hard surface of the road and of the soil in walking in the streets, on the roads and in the fields has a better effect than walking on carpets, linoleum, etc., in the house or in the shops and factories.

To sum up—just walk half a mile, one mile, two miles and more, daily. And you will find that, as in all other exercises and sports, the more regularly you do it, the better is the performance; and in due time, the pain will disappear completely.

CHAPTER XII

THE EYES AND EARS IN OLD AGE

Everybody knows that one of the first signs of old age is the fact that you suddenly need glasses for reading. Just the same, even if such a condition of the eyes is called "presbyopia," which means "old-age change of eyes," it can actually start in much younger age than what we call old age. In very many cases the need for glasses for reading and any other work near the eyes occurs at the age of 45 or so, which, at least in our times, is not old age, but middle age. On the other hand, especially women, who consider the need of glasses for reading as a sign of approaching old age, are embarrassed that they need the glasses, and tell the doctor that they could not understand it because they remember vividly that Grandmother used to read or sew without glasses even at the age of 80.

Presbyopia as opposite to hyperopia or myopia *is* a change due to aging, even if it occurs in middle-aged people. A farsighted person (hyperopic) will need glasses for reading and near working—sewing, etc.—even as a youngster. A nearsighted one will need glasses for seeing from afar, and this condition can occur even in children. Far-sightedness and near-sightedness are hereditary; a child gets them from father or mother, or both. However, just a person with normal and even excellent vision becomes with age presbyopic and cannot read or write or sew without glasses. The old grandmother who could read or sew without glasses at the age of 80 was actually near-sighted and needed glasses all her life. However, as the saying goes, "Boys don't make passes at girls with glasses." Not so long ago, and even now, when glasses are omnipresent, there were and still are plenty of girls who prefer rather to walk nearly blind and not to recognize anybody in the street or in a hall than to wear glasses. The near-sighted person is perfectly all right without glasses at near distances, but not at a far distance. Now, even very near-sighted people, when they get older, suddenly notice that they can read, write or sew without glasses, even better than with glasses. The reason is that here comes a meeting of two conditions—myopia meets presbyopia, or minus meets plus—and the result is actually improvement of vision for the near distance but not much for the far distance. So, a person of 60 or 65 will be able to read, to write, to sew, and even to function as a surgeon without glasses, but will need them, say, for driving. And so is explained the mystery of the old lady who does not need glasses for reading even at the age of 80.

There is a sign of old age in the eyes which is definitely seen but preferred to be ignored by a patient, because it does not cause any disturbances; and in most cases, if not ignored, it is not known. It is a gray ring around the iris of the eye which is accordingly called *"arcus senilis"*—old-age arch. It is a definite sign of aging. It does not occur in younger or middle-aged people and is completely harmless—just like gray hair—with the difference that gray hair can occur in younger people, but not the "arch."

More important is another change which can occur at any age but preferably occurs in old age—namely, a cataract in one eye or both. A cataract is nothing but an increased density of the lens of the eye. Our eye is built like a photo camera and functions like a camera. A camera has a lens and the eye has a lens. If the lens of a camera is closed, you cannot take pictures; and the same happens to our eye if there is a clouding of the lens—a cataract. We just cannot see with a cloudy lens. Why some people get a cataract and some don't, we do not know, apart from knowing that a cataract occurs sooner in people suffering from certain diseases, or is due to an accident. We also know that in some families a cataract occurs in many members of the family which would point to some inheritance factors; but which—we do not know.

In any case the fact remains that, apart from certain illnesses, a cataract is something which develops very slowly but finally "ripens"—that is, completely covers the eye lens. In the beginning the patient notices some blurring of the vision, or the vision is better in one eye than on the other; or, better, in the middle or on the sides of the field of vision—which, of course, depends on the part of the lens where the cataract is more pronounced. We have no remedy to clear up the density of the lens—that is, to cure the cataract medically. We have only the consolation that it is a local change and a very slow one which can take many years for full development, and the patient in the meantime can see with a part of the affected lens. But finally the patient has to undergo surgery, consisting in the removal of the lens. The operation by itself is neither dangerous nor difficult in the skillful hands of an eye surgeon. As a matter of fact, it was done a couple of hundred years ago on a market or fair day in the country. A quack or a so-called surgeon or barber had a stand in the marketplace. The patient was sitting on a chair. The so-called surgeon took a small instrument, went through the pupil, and pushed the lens out of its place down to where it swam and later slowly deteriorated and disappeared. The lens namely is suspended in the middle of the eye by ligaments. When the quack cut the ligaments, the lens fell down on its own accord, and the patient could see at once—of course, not far; and his vision was not sharp because of the lack of a lens, but he was not blind anymore. Whether he got an infection or any other complication after such an operation is a different story. Nature being as it is, very often the patient survived and praised the Lord and the "surgeon" for the restoration of the vision.

The operation in our times consists in the complete removal of the lens. We give the patient a substitute lens; but we build it into the eyeglasses so that, after the operation, the patient has to wear glasses. Basically, it is a simple operation; however like any surgery, it can produce complications, such as profuse bleeding or detachment of the retina or glaucoma.

It is not within the scope of this book to go into all details regarding possible complications of a removal of a cataracted lens. It is enough to say that in 95% of cases the operation is successful and the vision is restored. I would like to emphasize that, though a cataract is primarily a disease of old age, nevertheless, even if a person has the wear-and-tear conditions which were mentioned in previous chapters, he or she can expect that the operation will be successful; and if there are complications, they can occur in younger people just as often as in older. Age is not a contra-indication to the removal of a cataract.

It might be useful to know that there is one disease which speeds up the formation of a cataract. This is diabetes mellitus, or sugar diabetes, so called in distinction to another diabetes —a rare disease when the patient also spills a lot of urine but not sugar. We shall talk more about diabetes later; it is an important disease of old age. But, in connection with cataract formation, it is necessary to stress the fact that diabetic patients not only more often get cataracts than others, but that there is some change in the metabolism of a diabetic patient which causes him or her to acquire a cataract much sooner, much more frequently, and at a younger age than other people. The method of removal of the cataract is the same as in non-diabetic persons. But, of course, you have to watch such a patient more carefully in order to avoid complications.

I mentioned that glaucoma of the eyes also occurs more frequently in old age. This is a disease in which the pressure inside the eyes, mostly in both eyes, is increased, and that sometimes causes pain and deterioration of vision up to blindness. It is necessary to emphasize that the pressure in the eyes, as it occurs in glaucoma, has nothing whatsoever to do with blood pressure. One can have a very normal or even a low blood pressure and the most severe glaucoma, and vice versa. Why the pressure inside the eyes increases, we don't know either. We distinguish between an acute and a chronic, a primary and secondary, glaucoma. An acute glaucoma occurs all of a sudden; out of the blue sky a patient gets a red eye with severe pain and is almost immediately in danger of losing the eyesight, if appropriate medical measures are not taken. In a chronic glaucoma the inside pressure rises slowly until it causes disturbances of the vision. We call a glaucoma a primary, if it comes by itself; it is called secondary when it comes as a complication of another disease, such as after an operation for a cataract.

In any case, a glaucoma is a serious disease and the cause of a large percentage of cases of blindness. It is, I would say, unfortunately not always connected with pain and redness of the eye. It is frequently discovered by chance, if and when a person is examined by an eye doctor who can check the eye pressure with a special instrument. An optometrist or optician and/or a general practitioner usually does not do it; it requires a special technique to check for glaucoma. Even the doctors themselves don't know when a glaucoma develops in their own eyes. At a convention of the American Medical Association a glaucoma test was offered to all participating doctors. To the surprise of some, it was shown that a certain number of the tested doctors had a high eye pressure and accordingly, a glaucoma of which they had not the slightest inkling.

The treatment in most cases is medical, by using certain drugs prescribed by a doctor. It has to be done daily and incessantly. In some cases an operation to relieve the pressure is performed by cutting, so to say, a window in the iris of the eye. But even after such an operation a patient has to be watched to avoid a new rise in the eye pressure which can occur after a while, even after years.

We have no way to prevent the occurrence of a glaucoma. The only way is to have the pressure in the eyes checked from time to time by an eye doctor or in an eye clinic; because, if detected early, glaucoma development and the deterioration of the vision can be stopped.

The other diseases of the aging eyes are connected with the hardening of the arteries. High blood pressure and arteriosclerosis leave their mark in the eyegrounds, where the eye arteries can be visualized by an instrument called an ophthalmoscope. The same instrument shows hemorrhages, blood clots, and changes in the optic (eye) nerve. Thus many diseases can be detected and treated; some of them are local, some are signs of an underlying general disease. In a way, one can say, the eye is a mirror of the soul; because the feelings of a person are often visible in the expression of the eyes. And very often a thorough examination of all parts of the eyes shows the condition of the body of a person as well.

It is terrible to lose the vision, to become blind. But there are as many disadvantages in the loss of hearing. It is necessary to know that many people do not realize that they do not hear well for the simple reason that one can be deaf in one ear, and have quite good hearing on the other—which compensates for the loss on one ear. The same, of course, can happen with the sight; and one who is blind in one eye can well compensate for the loss of the eyesight, if the other eye is all right. However, if not other people, the person in question can very well easily find out that his eye is blind just by covering the good eye. But it is not the same with hearing. Nobody closes the ear in order to find out how the other ear makes out. Then there is also bone conduction of the sound, which leads to the fact that some people hear well when they listen to the telephone, and don't hear when one talks to them, or only poorly. Loss of hearing can occur by a birth defect, by disease at any age. But very often the hearing deteriorates with age through nerve deafness when the hearing (auditory) nerve deteriorates by poor blood circulation and, accordingly, poor nutrition of it. The arteriosclerosis can also cause damage to the power of hearing; and it is a common view that the hearing gets worse with age. It is more or less expected in old age. It can be often remedied by a hearing aid; but often it is refused by older people, who are just as vain as young people and consider it as beneath their dignity to wear a visible sign—the hearing aid—of their defect. A hearing aid is still not acceptable as a natural remedy, contrary to glasses for poor vision, which are nowadays accepted. The result is that even when one can be helped, she or he refuses to be helped and prefers to lose a part of the conversation or wants to fake an understanding of what was said, not even knowing that the family or friends know that they do not hear well. On the other hand, deafness often causes mistrust. If a deaf person does not understand what is said, he or she can easily come to the conclusion that the talk was meant for him or her not to understand—that is directed against the deaf person. Such a situation can lead to a paranoid persecution—idea, with nervous tension or even a breakdown. It is interesting to observe that blind people are better adjusted to their defect than deaf ones; apparently the blind people do not have the feeling that they are excluded from participation in the life of their relatives or friends, while the deaf ones imagine that they lose a lot, that they live in a separate world, divided from the rest of humanity. This is especially the case in people who are not used to reading, which might compensate for listening; in such a case, seeing is not enough, and such people are not happy.

Treatment depends on the nature of the loss of hearing. There can be many reasons: the culprit may be the drum, the middle ear, the inner ear, the auditory nerve, or the condition of the arteries. Only a doctor can determine the cause. Sometimes the hearing aid can help and restore the hearing; sometimes there is no help, and one has to learn lip-reading in order to be able to participate in some way in the conversation. In any case, precaution is important, and a thorough examination by an ear specialist is of great help for diagnosis and prognosis of the outcome.

Loss of hearing does not diminish the longevity of a person and does not make him sick. Just the same, it can make a person plenty miserable.

CHAPTER XIII

LUNG DISEASES IN OLD AGE

Actually we should talk not about lung diseases but about the respiratory diseases; because then our discussion would involve all the parts of respiratory organs, starting with the mouth, down the larynx, then the important bronchial tree, and finally the lungs. However, there is little in the mouth, throat and larynx diseases which is specific for old age. Besides, the layman generally knows little about the classification of respiratory diseases. He is familiar with the most common lung diseases, and also with bronchitis. So let us stick to the nomenclature "lung diseases," and treat the respiratory diseases of the elderly one by one.

To start with the curse of centuries—tuberculosis of the lungs. It is, as everybody knows, common to all ages. I remember when I was a young doctor that it was considered primarily a disease of young people, starting with teenagers, very occasionally occurring even in children, and petering out in middle age, and rather rare in older people. Then it was considered as very mild, of little importance—a kind of a residual disease which originated when a person was young, or at best a flare-up.

It is recognized that, notwithstanding Koch's TB bacilli which cause tuberculosis, it is a social disease, depending on environment, on nutrition, on living quarters, on overcrowding, and on the social standard and earnings. Of course a rich person can get infected and have TB, in all forms. But the chances of infection are smaller, and the early detection and treatment are greater; so that tuberculosis just the same could be considered as a disease of the poor section of the population. With the advent of the new treatment with streptomycin, PAS and

Niazides, and with the improvement of the general social conditions in the civilized countries, there was such a tremendous progress in treatment and therefore diminution of contagiousness that tuberculosis was considered as doomed to complete eradication, similar to leprosy or to poliomyelitis.

However, it is not quite so. It is true, that the number of new infections diminished considerably. It is also true that, in most cases, TB can be cured without the previous methods of sanitaria in the mountains, and special nutrition and surgery—starting with an artificial pneumothorax and ending with the cutting out of the ribs and other surgery of the chest. However, we still have poor people and slum dwellings; we still have people who are poorly fed and live in overcrowded apartments. The result is that, because of all these conditions, people get infected with tuberculosis. They still get treatment too late and/or inadequately. And thus, with all the progress and the affluent society, we get new cases of tuberculosis; and the old ones are not cured completely, though frequently they become cases in an inactive stage.

Older people, especially among the poor, do have tuberculosis. It is important for several reasons. First, the mortality rate among older people due to tuberculosis is higher than that of young people who have the same type of tuberculosis. As one investigator (Myers in Minneapolis) has shown, older people do not respond to the above-mentioned antibiotics as well as younger patients. Apart from that fact, their resistance is lower and their nutritional status on the whole inadequate. Secondly, people and even doctors do not realize that the cough of the old man or woman is due not to old age but just to an active tuberculosis. Thus, the old people get the treatment which they need, and the isolation, much later than they should. And thirdly, tuberculosis among the old people is a problem of public health because, if not detected, they spread the tuberculosis in their environment. Many coughing grandpas or grandmas are responsible for the tuberculosis of their grandchildren, whom they infect when they kiss the children, embrace them, and coddle them with all their love.

For all these reasons, tuberculosis among old people is not a disease which can be neglected. Generally speaking, any old person with a chronic cough is a suspect of having tuberculosis, unless otherwise proven. The mobile X-rays of the chest cars which travel from district to district in order to detect a latent TB are a great boon; but I have the suspicion that the old people take little advantage of this free opportunity. And even if they are caught and TB is found, the card of the health department which informs them that they should see their physician because an ailment found on the mobile X-rays does not necessarily mean that they are running to see the doctor or unit or clinic. It would be more effective if the health authorities would deal with TB as they do with venereal diseases. The people with gonorrhea or syphilis are compelled to be treated either by their private physician or at a health clinic. Such a compulsion does not exist in cases of TB, and the people with discovered TB remain a menace to public health and continue to spread the infection, unless they undergo treatment voluntarily.

We do not have to discuss cancer of the lungs. It is not specific for old age. There is an increase of lung cancer in older people, but there is generally an increase of cases of lung cancer in all age groups; therefore, cancer of the lungs cannot be attributed to the aging process.

It is different with pneumonia. Pneumonia too occurs in all age groups. It can be found in children and infants as well. But pneumonia in children and young people responds easily to antibiotics. Their resistance is great and, correspondingly, the mortality from pneumonia and even morbidity—the rate of sickness—is comparatively small. In the aged, pneumonia is a leading cause of death. The resistance is low, the antibiotics do not work as well as in young people, the heart is easily overstrained by the impact of the infection, and the result is death, sometimes within days and even hours.

Curiously enough, death from influenza in elderly people decreases, though we actually do not have an active antibiotic for influenza as we have it for almost all types of pneumonia.

As far as I can judge, the reason is the more frequent vaccination against influenza of older than younger people, who tend to neglect such a vaccination with the optimistic view that they will not get influenza—and if they do, they will get rid of it in no time.

The older people are rather pessimistic and afraid of sickness and death. Therefore, they tend to go to the doctor for the one or two vaccinations which are required in a year. Immune reaction is in this case not likely, because it would occur in all age groups, and would not explain the decrease of influenza cases and death from it in old age.

The leading respiratory diseases in old age are chronic bronchitis and emphysema. The causes of chronic bronchitis and of emphysema are: (1) smoking for many years, (2) infections, (3) air pollution, (4) occupation, (5) occasionally allergy, (6) heredity, (7) changes in the blood vessels, especially in the arteries, (8) aging.

It is necessary to point out that all the above-mentioned eight possibilities can occur as a cause of a non-specific respiratory disease in younger people as well as in older (apart, of course, from aging, though the other causes can result in a premature aging). However, as explained before, an infection, for instance, in younger people does not have such a deleterious effect as in older persons. If we take the causes one by one, we can easily understand why respiratory diseases play such a great role in old age. Smoking, for instance, can cause cancer in younger or older people. But, if one is a smoker, it means that with age there is simply a greater number of years in which a person smoked, and so the damage is more profound. A lot was written about the relation between smoking and cancer, but people do not realize the close connection between smoking and chronic bronchitis plus emphysema. As the Advisory Committee to the Surgeon General of the United States Public Health Service reported: smoking is the most important of the causes of chronic bronchitis and increases the risk of dying from chronic bronchitis and also from emphysema; cough and sputum-production, or the two combined, are consistently more frequent among cigarette smokers than among non-smokers. Smoking is associated with a reduction in ventilatory function; among smokers there is a greater prevalence of shortness of breath.

That infection plays a great role in respiratory disease, is easily understood. We inhale air 24 hours daily, and there is in this way plenty of opportunity for germs to reach the bronchial tubes and lungs. The germs can reach the lungs also by the way of the arteries which supply the respiratory organs.

We read nowadays a lot about air and water pollution. Considering that at least 70% of the population in the United States live in large cities, where the air pollution increases with the increase of industry and of the number of automobiles, it is clear that there is a growing danger of sickness due to air pollution. It was noticed that the number of deaths of patients with chronic diseases of heart and lungs increased considerably with the increase of air pollution.

Regarding occupation, it was long known that certain occupations—especially miners, diamond polishers, and similar occupation-holders—have, as the compensation boards now recognize, occupational diseases of silicosis and other pneumoconioses which are caused by inhalation of dust particles of coal, diamonds, copper, and other non-ferrous metals; and this results in fibrosis (hardening and loss of elasticity) of the lungs and development of air-flow obstruction. The same permanent respiratory impairment occurs in occupations when workers are exposed to certain vegetable dusts, molds, fungi, grain dust, or to irritating gases in chemical and other factories.

Allergy plays a certain but not a great role in the development of a chronic bronchitis. There is, of course, a close relationship between allergy and bronchial asthma. And, while an asthma can disappear without leaving any traces, nevertheless the frequent condition of an asthmatic status when a person has an asthma more or less permanently is the cause of a chronic asthmatic bronchitis.

Heredity plays a certain indirect role in the development of respiratory diseases. There are people who incline to frequent bouts of bronchitis and/or pneumonia, and some who do not.

There is a family history of prevalence of non-tuberculous lung and bronchial disease, frequently more among the male members of a family than among the females of the same family. Possibly it is due to the fact that women started smoking only recently, while men smoked for centuries. There is also a hereditary factor in the constitutional type. We distinguish between the asthenic and pyknic type of persons. The asthenic is usually thin and tall, and his or her chest is narrow. The pyknic type is broad-shouldered and heavy-set, with a wide chest. Contrary to expectation, the thin and narrow-chested asthenic people do *not* incline to bronchitises and pneumonias. They do incline to tuberculosis, though infection with tuberculosis germs can happen to anybody, at any age or any type. But somehow, the TB infection occurs more frequently in the asthenics. On the other hand, the broad-chested, heavy-set people incline to bronchitis and pneumonia. Some of them have many times a pneumonia and/or bronchitis in their lifetime. The typical example is the late English Prime Minister Sir Winston Churchill. If we consider that constitution is hereditary, then we can understand the influence of heredity on the origin of respiratory disease.

The final two causes of chronic respiratory diseases are interrelated. The changes in the arteries occur in old age, primarily due to hardening, to sclerosis, to wear and tear; on the other hand, aging causes a decrease in the elasticity of the the lung tissue, a rigidity of the chest wall, and a diminution in the regulation of ventilation and of the cough reflex by which the expectoration takes place. If the sputum is not removed, it clogs the bronchial tree and fills the alveoli (the little bubbles, the vesicles which are the end-extension of the bronchial tree, just as leaves are the end-extension of the branches of a tree).

It is necessary to give some explanation of what an emphysema means. Bronchitis as a disease is so prevalent that the term is popular; and everybody knows what bronchitis means, though the importance of that disease is much less understood than it should be. Emphysema is not familiar to the general public, maybe because in most cases it is an end-product or a by-product of a chronic bronchitis, and it is not considered as a disease by itself.

What is emphysema? It is a localized or generally spread condition, acute or chronic, which is characterized by loss of elasticity and overdistension of the lung alveoli. The alveoli—the dead ends of the respiratory tree or system—become disturbed and can even burst. In its most common form it is chronic and causes a widespread partial bronchial obstruction (of the larger or smaller bronchial branches). The chief underlying cause is a chronic bronchitis, or bronchial asthma, or both. Usually there is also present a chronic infection and loss of elasticity of the tissues surrounding the bronchial tubes. The loss of elasticity is important. The walls of the alveoli are stretched and thin. The rupture of the walls between the small alveoli causes the formation of bigger air-sacs of all kind of sizes. There is a reduction of the number of tiny arteries, and the larger arteries of the lungs are exposed to more wear and tear, resulting in sclerosis. These changes in the lung arteries then cause widening of that part of the heart which supplies the lung arteries with blood and oxygen. The airways are dilated in inspiration and normally contract in exhalation. However, in the condition of emphysema there is a spreading obstruction of the larger, and especially of the smaller and very small, bronchial tubes. This over-inflation of the lungs (like an overblowing of a balloon) leads to stretched and narrowed tiny arteries of the alveoli of the lungs and to loss of elastic tissue in the walls. In this way the lungs slowly increase in size. The chest cage tends to a position of almost permanent inhalation, with the result that the diaphragm becomes low or flat. The volume of each breath decreases, and the air which remains in the lungs is not exhaled and increases in amount. At the same time, because of the abnormal condition, the supply of oxygen to the blood is decreased because of blood-vessel deficiency and poor mixing of the inhaled air and the air which remained in the large air sacs. The normal supply of oxygen decreases to 80-70% (instead of being 95%), while the usually-exhaled carbon dioxide remains and increases in contents. All this is a slow but progressive process, and causes shortness of breath due to mechanical airflow obstruction and lack of oxygen. The patient is hungry for air, and strains all his resources to get oxygen. This causes overexertion of his heart, especially of the right side of the heart, which is responsible for the respiratory circulation. Then comes a congestion in the peripheral blood vessels and the patient becomes bluish, especially in the lips and the face. He suffers from what is called "cor pulmonale," which means a heart condition which is due not to a defect of the heart itself but due to an overstrain of the heart by the defect of the respiration.

The so-called senile emphysema does not differ much from the emphysema as just described. In old age there is osteoarthritis of the spine, with less mobility of it and of the ribs which are attached to the spine in the back; and in addition to the general effects of the emphysema there is a gradual lifting of the ribs and of the breastbone, and the fixation of the ribcage in a position of inhalation.

It should be understood that, in general, respiratory diseases are very common among elderly people; and all investigators agree on the importance of chronic non-specific changes in the bronchial tubes and lungs in advanced age. Very often it is difficult to distinguish between various types of respiratory diseases, and one disease flows over into another. Sometimes it is even difficult to say whether we deal with a disease, or with an expected change in the respiratory organs due to the wear and tear of age. Just the same, on a statistical basis all over the world it is found that there is a high incidence of chronic non-specific lung diseases in patients over 65 years old. Males are more affected than females; as said before, it may be due to smoking.

Because of the overall changes in the respiratory tree, bronchitis often changes in a bronchopneumonia, which is a significant cause of death in the aged.

In the prevention and treatment of non-specific chronic lung diseases of the elderly patients, the total personality of the patient has to be taken into account. There is no type of prevention or treatment which is good for every elderly person. It depends on the diet, food habits, on the constitution of the body, on the general attitude towards health and sickness, and on the will for recuperation. The treatment will be the same as in younger persons—antibiotics, cough medicines, oxygen, vitamins, good food, and good nursing care. Just the same, the results—good or fatal—will depend on the personality of the patient and his or her general health.

Whatever it may be, one should always remember that bronchitis—acute or chronic, a so-called cold, emphysema, or pneumonia should be treated with the utmost care in elderly patients. Their respiratory system is very sensitive and frail. Negligence can lead in no time to a castastrophe. Therefore, it cannot be emphasized often enough and strongly enough that respiratory diseases are leading causes of debility in old age, and should be treated with due respect.

CHAPTER XIV

DISEASES OF DIGESTION IN OLD AGE

It is interesting to see the usage of language among laymen when it is a question of organs and diseases. Some medical expressions become a common property of everyone; some are just not used. The word *abdomen* is Latin in origin, but so are many words in daily usage. Nevertheless, the word "abdomen" is not used. Commonly, it is called the belly, though nobody talks about diseases of the belly. Peculiarly enough, even the organs in the lower part of the belly are not called by their proper name. One should speak about diseases of the intestines; but this is so named only by the highbrow, by intellectuals. Again, commonly, the intestines are called "guts." But nobody says, "I have a disease of the guts"—just as hardly anybody says, "I have a disease of the intestines." People do talk about bellyache, but rather jokingly or figuratively, or use it as a vulgar expression. The organs of the abdomen which serve the digestion have one common name—stomach. "Stomach" in the layman's language is everything—almost from the throat down to the rectum—which serves digestion. That includes the esophagus, which brings the food to the stomach, the stomach proper, the duodenum, the small and the large intestines. Sometimes, in the description, the layman distinguishes between upper and lower stomach. But, on the whole, any bellyache is a stomach ache. There are some small exceptions: these are the appendix and the hemorrhoids, commonly called piles. Of course, the liver, the spleen and the kidneys, the pancreas gland, are not included in the word "stomach"; the diseases of these organs are known as separate entities, and rightly so. And they shall be treated as such in this book, in separate chapters.

Now, from the medical point of view, we have to discuss the digestive system in its separate parts, because each of them presents different diseases and different problems; and the more so when we consider the organs of digestion from the point of view of old age.

To start with the esophagus, which means the tube which leads from the mouth to the stomach and brings the food to it, there are hardly any diseases of the esophagus which are specific for old age. Cancer of the esophagus occurs, of course, in old age, but it occurs also in younger people. Varicose veins in the esophagus are due almost exclusively to alcoholism and are connected with liver cirrhosis. But alcoholism occurs just as much in young people; and how soon the varicose veins in the esophagus appear depends not on age but on consumption of alcohol. True, one does not get them soon after having become an alcoholic. Frequently, it takes years for those varicose veins to develop. But I know enough cases when the daily steady consumption of large quantities of alcohol in any form started very early as teenager. Thus, with early alcoholism the varicose veins of the esophagus can appear and lead to a catastrophic bleeding at young or middle age. If they appear in old age, then it is a question of the beginning and of the development of liver cirrhosis, and old age is only incidental.

A frequent disease which is nowadays more often than before diagnosed is a hiatus or esophagus hernia. What a hernia is, I do not have to explain. It is just a medical term which is accepted by the population, though it is just as Latin as the not-accepted "abdomen." In plain English, a hernia is just an enlarged hole through which a part of the intestines comes through and bulges through the skin of the abdomen. In a case of a hiatus or esophagus hernia we have the same occurrence. The esophagus runs through the chest until it ends in the stomach, which lies in the cavity of the abdomen. In order to do so, it has to go through an opening in the chest—namely, in the lowest wall of the chest which separates the chest from the abdomen and which is called the diaphragm. If the hole gets too wide in a certain position, a part of the stomach slides into the chest cavity through the hole in the diaphragm. The hole is called the hiatus; therefore we have three names for the same condition: hiatus hernia, esophagus hernia, or diaphragmatic hernia. I call it a condition because it is actually not a disease, rather a defect. And people can live with it sometimes all their life without knowing that they have such a defect. If I describe it among the diseases of old age, it is not because it occurs in old age only. It can happen in any age; and some of the hiatus hernias are even congenital—that is, inborn, as a child can have at birth any other defect. And the reason why these esophagus hernias are now more easily detected is a better X-ray technique and a better understanding of the complaints of a patient who suffers from a hiatus hernia. Certain of the hernias are more common in old-age, just the so-called sliding ones. They are seen on X-rays and they disappear, depending on the position in which you make the X-rays. The old age plays the role of causing loss of elasticity of the soft tissues and less tightening of the muscles which surround the hiatus hole. Therefore, more stomach tissue can enter the chest—similarly to the hernias in the groin which also occur in any age, but are more common in elderly people whose muscles there are not so elastic and give in.

The result of an esophagus (hiatus, diaphragmatic) hernia is, in general, mild and of little consequence. Just like the other hernias, it leads ocasionally to an operation which consists in tightening of the opening in the diaphramatic wall. But if a patient is sensible and obeys a few simple rules, the hernia in the esophagus will cause very little trouble.

It is not the purpose of this book to give detailed treatment of diseases; it is enough to say that a hiatus hernia can hardly be prevented, that it cannot disappear by itself, that it cannot be cured by any medical treatment, only surgically. But a patient can help a lot to avoid trouble from that hernia. Apart from other advice, the main course of prevention is to avoid heavy and big meals. The reason is purely mechanical. There is plenty of room for plenty of food in the stomach. However, if only a part of the stomach squeezes through the hole and is in an awkward place where it has no business to be in the first place—namely, in the chest—and if that part is filled and overfilled, then one has to become uncomfortable. The food cannot well squeeze through the hole down to the rest of the stomach, or only with difficulty. Then, in order to get rid of the discomfort, one has to throw up the food. And that is what happens when that part of the stomach is overfilled by unreasonable patients. And another reminder: the hernia slides, just like a baseball player, and it depends on the position where that part of the stomach is situated—in the abdomen or in the chest. And here comes a simple rule: don't lie down after the meal. Sit or walk for an hour, or stand, thus giving the stomach an opportunity to bring its upper part down into the abdominal cavity, instead of being in a horizontal position and preventing the sliding of the esophagus hernia into the chest cavity. These are simple rules if one has a hiatus hernia; but, like any rules, they are frequently not obeyed, with unpleasant consequences. One thing is sure: nobody dies from having a hiatus hernia; and it does not shorten life or make one disabled, unless he or she behaves too foolishly.

The stomach presents different problems in old age. There are actually no stomach diseases which can be attributed to old age except one—namely, atrophy and shrinking of the lining of the stomach, with inactivity of the glands of the stomach. Such an atrophic stomach can occasionally be found in younger people too; but, generally speaking, it is more likely to be found among elderly people. If not for any other reason, it is sufficient to remember that in old age all glands are working less or not at all (like, for instance, the ovaries in a woman after menopause), and the stomach glands are no exception. And, if they are not working, hardly any stomach juice is produced; and with other causes combined it leads to an atrophy (shrinkage) of the lining.

The stomach condition which occurs especially in old age is practically harmless. The lack of acid and juice production can be easily substituted by adequate medication. It does not have any serious post-effects and does not require any special treatment; and, definitely, it does not affect the life and well-being of the patient.

People will hear a lot about cancer of the stomach. Of course, it occurs frequently in elderly people, as all cancers occur more often with age. But, as long as we don't know the cause of cancer, we cannot consider it as a disease of old age—the more so because cancer very often is found among children, not only in adults.

The duodenum, so called because its length corresponds to the width of twelve fingers, is as a name not popular among laymen. It is often known as the second part of the stomach; and though there are very many differences between stomach and duodenum, this expression is not out of the way, because in many respects the digestion of food is done in both. When the food enters the stomach, the digestion starts, and what is not digested in the stomach continues to be in the duodenum. What chemistry for that process of digestion is not available in the stomach is found in the duodenum, in order to split the food in its digestible components.

Now, if the duodenum as such is not well known, one disease of it is very popular—namely, the duodenal ulcer. Of course, we have stomach ulcers and duodenal ulcers, and the public calls all ulcers stomach ulcers; but important from all points of view is the duodenal ulcer. Here again, one has to stress that a stomach or duodenal ulcer is not an old-age disease. However, though it is considered as a disease of younger people (and in fact the latest research has discovered that ulcers are not rare among teenagers, even 12-13 years old), one has in this case to emphasize that ulcers, stomach and duodenal, are not rare in elderly patients. For some reason, if an elderly person has stomach trouble and vomits or passes blood in the bowel movement, laymen incline to declare that the patient surely has a cancer. It is true that a cancer can cause bleeding, loss of weight, of appetite, vomiting and stomach pain, but an ulcer does the same as long as it is not recognized and treated. And in many cases the activity of the stomach and of the duodenum, which is needed for the development of an ulcer, can be blooming in old age just as well as in younger people. The main cause—if not reason—of an ulcer is the production of hydrochloric acid by the stomach.

There are glands in the stomach which produce this acid, and they work overtime. We spoke a short while ago about atrophy and shrinking of these glands. But, as I said, it happens but rarely; while ulcers of the stomach and of the duodenum are so frequent that they can be considered as a curse and effect of the modern civilization. Of course, it is not true that you have to be an executive and have plenty of money in order to get an ulcer. It is true that, even if the overproduction of acid causes in some cases an ulcer, this is not the reason why people get ulcers. You have to have a so-called ulcer personality in order to get an ulcer, because the main reason for the development of an ulcer is the nervous condition of the patient —his or her tension, his or her penned-in emotions which are not given vent abroad. Usually, ulcer patients are not screaming or shouting when they are emotionally upset. They are what we call introverts—contrary to extroverts, who easily explode, show their nervousness, make life unbearable to their environment; but they themselves do not suffer from their emotions. The whole development of an ulcer depends on the irritability and overactivity of the so-called autonomic nervous system. It is called autonomic because it has a kind of autonomy in its function.

It governs and directs our internal organs, such as the stomach and intestines; it has influence on the function of the glands, on blood pressure, and so on. How decisive the role of that nervous system is, is easily proven by the fact that an ulcer heals if the part of that system called the vagus nerve is cut away from the stomach. In such an operation, called vagotomy, you leave the ulcer in, and it heals by itself just because it does not get the irritating influence of the vagus nerve. That does not mean that the nervous condition of the patient changes; he or she remains the same—tense, apprehensive, emotional. But after such an operation the nervousness is no more transmitted to the site of the ulcer.

The reasons for nervousness which lead to ulcers are manifold. In any case, if one has an ulcer personality, which may be inborn, he or she does not have to be rich or even to have a responsible position in order to get an ulcer. In my experience, just the poor, insecure, elderly people (and not only elderly) get ulcers, because they become tense and apprehensive due to their financial difficulties to make ends meet. There is even something inherent in their poverty which leads to ulcers. Because they are poor and depend on the good will of their employers and any other people with whom they have to deal in order to make a living, they have to stay quiet, at least externally, even if they are upset and possibly wronged. In other words, they have to take it, though they don't like it, and internally they are boiling mad. The same I observed among patients living on welfare assistance who depend on the good will of their case-workers and investigators, who can by a bad report regarding their behavior cause a cut in their allowance when every penny counts. You can find ulcers also in old-age homes and nursing homes, when the inmates greatly depend on the good will of the nurse, even in regard to getting a bed pan or being allowed to be brought by wheelchair to the recreation room. In short, the story of the ulcer as prerogative of an executive or financial tycoon is a gross exaggeration. A tycoon can have an ulcer, but a welfare recipient can have it too.

It was necessary to devote that much space to the ulcer disease because it is common in old age and often overlooked, because not expected and therefore neglected. And, while ulcer is curable and sooner or later heals, it has many pitfalls and dangers. An elderly person can get a perforation of an ulcer just as often as a younger one and have a massive hemorrhage, which in older, debilitated people is even more dangerous than in younger ones. And the treatment and prevention of ulcers, with their complications, does not differ in old age from that of younger patients. The healing of an ulcer is a long-drawn business in any age group, but it may take even longer in elderly people. That is one of the reasons why older people are often advised to undergo an operation for an ulcer, because the danger in case of complications is much greater.

CHAPTER XV

CONSTIPATION AND DIARRHEA

Somebody coined a saying: human life can be divided in three periods. When a person is young, he or she thinks only about sex; when the person becomes middle-aged, the center of the interest is food, good eating, plenty and frequently; and in old age, the third period of life, the center of interest becomes evacuation, the bowel movement. Of course, such a philosophical saying has to be taken with a pinch of salt. But basically it is correct, even if a young person eats and eliminates, and a middle-aged person can show plenty of interest in sex. Just the same, as a doctor I was always amazed how, with advancing age, the problem of having a regular and abundant bowel movement becomes more and more important in the mind of an elderly person. I would go as far as to say that the pre-occupation with b.m. is one of the first signs of the approaching old age. That does not mean that an elderly person does not care for eating—some are gluttons and never stop eating; but at the same time they would also worry if they would not have a regular b.m. As far as I can judge, the TV and radio commercials which stress the importance of "regularity" in advertising their products appeal primarily to elderly people. A young person does not care and is rarely afflicted with such a problem. In middle age there is some interest and some watching for regularity, but it is not of overwhelming importance as in old age.

Before dealing with the problem of constipation, I would like to explain the problem of diarrhea—which, though less spread among the over-65 population, might be much more serious than constipation. Diarrhea is actually a symptom of irritation and/or inflammation of the large bowels. They are the instrument of elimination of the waste after digestion of the food in the stomach and duodenum and its passage through the small bowels, where a further splitting of the food and partial absorption into the body takes place. If the elimination is too much precipitated, and if the b.m. is not properly formed and becomes loose or watery, we have the picture of diarrhea. Diarrhea is often called by laymen "dysentery." In calling it dysentery they occasionally confuse the doctor, because they mix up a symptom and complaint with a disease. Dysentery is a specific disease caused by germs and parasites and is characterized by diarrhea, by bowel movement 3, 4, 5, or 10 times daily. In so far, dysentery and diarrhea are identical; but by far, not every diarrhea is due to dysentery. Practically, considering the whole population of North America, the cases of dysentery caused by germs and parasites are statistically negligible.

However, plain diarrhea is more common and is not caused by germs or parasites. The one reason for diarrhea in old age is the previously-mentioned shrinking of the lining of the stomach and of its glands. Thus the food is not properly digested and goes down undigested and coarse. It runs, so to say, through the whole intestinal tract, and that produces diarrhea. One has to know a little about the physiology of the G.I. (gastro-intestinal) tract in order to understand the problem of diarrhea and constipation. The food after digestion moves through the bowels by peristalsis, which means movement similar to that of a worm or caterpillar; namely, contraction of one part of the bowels, which pushes the waste or food a little lower down towards the rectum. Then comes relaxation of that part and contraction of the next one, and so on. In other words, the waste and food are squeezed through the bowels towards the exit. If one has diarrhea, whatever the cause, this peristalsis or movement, as described, becomes violent, and so fast that there is no time to make the waste solid and formed. The first cause of diarrhea—lack of proper digestion due to shrinking of the lining of the stomach—is of lesser importance. It does cause diarrhea in some cases, but not always. If one examines the stool, one can easily find undigested particles of food and, not infrequently, whole pieces of meat or berries, if swallowed whole, not touched by digestion and looking exactly like they were before the food intake. But, just the same, diarrhea due to the stomach defect occurs only on and off, and not violently.

The most common cause of diarrhea, if not from an infection, is colitis. Colitis means an irritation and/or inflammation of the colon. The colon is the whole extent of the large bowels, starting with the appendix and ending with the rectum. Colitis is not a disease of old age; it happens even more often in young people. But you can find it on and off among older people, just the same. It is a psychosomatic disease in the beginning— that is, a disease which starts in the mind and develops in the body (from the words "psyche," or "soul" and "soma" or "body"). In other words, a person who is nervous transfers the emotion to a part of the body, causing it to function abnormally. Such a disease is also an ulcer of the stomach or of the duodenum, as described in the previous chapter. The same type of people who develop ulcers also develop colitis. However, it is necessary to stress the word *"type,"* because it rarely occurs that the same person has ulcers and colitis. For some psychological reasons which one would have to go far to explain, one patient, so to say, selects the stomach for the nervous disorder, and another chooses the colon.

Now, there are stages in the development of colitis. It starts with some greater frequency of bowel movements; the stool is still formed. Then the stool becomes more loose, later more watery. Mucus, similar to that in a case of a cold in the nose, appears in the stool; it is then the stage of mucus colitis. Later, blood appears together with the mucus—some blood streaks or drops, not a real hemorrhage. The consistency of the stool becomes more and more watery; the frequency can rise to 10-12 and more times a day. And, if no treatment of the colitis is energetically pursued, the colitis becomes in the final stage an ulcerative colitis with sores in the lining of the colon and a diseased appearance of the lining seen on X-rays (and with an instrument called a sigmoidoscope by which you can observe directly, through illumination, the lining of the rectum and of the lowest part of the rest of the large bowels, called "sigmoid").

For some reasons the colitis, though it can spread through the whole colon, is mainly confined to the lower part of the intestines, which are located on the left side of the abdomen and terminate in the rectum.

As I mentioned before, colitis occurs in all age groups, though not in children, unless they suffer from an infection by germs or from infestation by parasites. It is not frequent in old age, but it occurs. Colitis is a chronic disease which can last for many, many years, and it can start in middle age and continue in old age.

However, diarrhea through colitis and any other disease is a minor problem of old age, compared with constipation. It is not only that elderly people pay more attention to the regularity of their bowel movements than younger ones, but there is really a problem because so many patients in the old-age group do suffer from constipation.

Now, let us find out what is regularity and what is constipation. There are many people, especially among elderly patients, who are of the opinion that if they do not have daily at least one bowel movement, and an abundant one, something is wrong and they are constipated. This idea is also strongly suggested by advertisements of laxatives. Actually, it is not the case. It is very nice to have a daily well-formed and plentiful b.m.; it shows a normal function of the bowels—a good habit, especially if the b.m. comes like a clock, always on certain hours or before or after meals. We are slaves of our habits, and we can compel our body to adjust itself to those self-imposed habits. Whatever the habit is, if it leads to daily regular b.m., it is wonderful. But, it is not a must and a rule that this way should be the norm for everyone.

There are many people who have a b.m. only once in two or three days, and they too are normal. This is their habit to which they adhere without any discomfort; and they are perfectly well from their own and from the medical point of view. I even had a patient whom I observed for about 15 years who had a bowel movement only once weekly, and he is still well; and the X-rays and other tests did not show any irregularity or disease. Let us say that his bowels worked in a slow-motion way. Though this was an exceptional case, nevertheless it shows that there is no rule to what is normal: once a day, twice a day, once in two or three days, and so on—all this is normal.

A person suffers from constipation only if his or her habit changes. If a person normally has a b.m. every day and suddenly this does not occur, and he or she gets a b.m. either only after several days, or through one of the many laxative devices, then constipation exists—especially if, without a laxative, no bowel movement occurs on the third or second day by itself. A habit can change for many reasons (change of food, climate, travel, different hours of work or rest, and so on). If the result is a normal b.m. only after two days, instead of daily or twice daily, then it means that the body started to adjust itself to the new circumstances, and this is not constipation.

With all the explanation of why a so-called constipation is actually only a change of habit, one has to concede that elderly people suffer more often from constipation than the younger generation. Why? When one gets older, he or she usually has less physical activities and at the same time one eats more, and frequently a different food than hitherto. On retirement, people eat more and at different times. In big cities the average worker has a hasty breakfast; lunch he eats in a cafeteria or lunchonette, or occasionally he brings a sandwich from home. The main meal is in the evening. Now, the peristalsis—the bowel movement, which I explained previously—is promoted by intake of food. And though many people have a b.m. immediately after arising, just the same, the normal way is to expect a b.m. some time after a meal. Some have time for b.m. after breakfast, some don't; and during the journey to work, the urge for a b.m. dies down and people get constipated in this way—unless they have plenty of time after breakfast, or they acquire the habit of going to the bathroom after dinner, or they belong to the lucky ones who have the b.m. just on arising. When one retires, the whole schedule changes: breakfast does not consist of a hasty cup of coffee, but it is a leisurely affair with cereals, eggs, toast, etc. On the basis of this, one would expect that now the real movement of the bowels would be better than ever. But it does not happen this way. Human beings are slaves of habits. They have, as the Russian scientist Pavlov found out 50 years ago, a conditioned reflex. That is, their reflexes—and the b.m. is also a reflex—are subject to a condition which can be created artificially. As Pavlov's dogs ate only when a bell rang, so the bowels move only if the conditions of life and work remain the same. Therefore, if these change the leisure does not help; neither does the greater amount of food consumed, which should promote peristalsis. The result is constipation. Just like pilots of commercial planes and their hostesses have to re-adjust themselves to changes of time due to the speed of the jets, and to learn to sleep and to eat in different times than the environment in which they find themselves after only a few hours' flight, so a retired person has to re-adjust him or herself to the new conditions of life, and to acquire new conditioned reflexes. Some do, some don't. If they do, after a while the b.m. becomes normal; if they don't they become constipated.

Activity helps also in promotion of a b.m., and the lack of activity leads to constipation.

Many people have a b.m. only when they are active physically, even if they only walk. But with retirement usually comes laziness. Many activities are abandoned, and new ones are not necessarily started. And the new eating habits—more food and at different times—change completely the accustomed ways of life.

All this causes constipation. There is also a slowing down of the activities of the body itself with advancing age. In other words, the movement of the bowels becomes slower. So the elderly citizen is frequently a constipated one.

What to do about it, and how to prevent it? On the whole, I would like to emphasize that constipation is not a great calamity, and almost always harmless. It sometimes becomes a nuisance, and occasionally even dangerous. The danger is only in such an obstinate and prolonged constipation that the stool hardens and causes an intestinal obstruction which has to be removed by hook or crook. In most cases it can be dealt with in a comparatively easy medical way; but in some cases it leads to an operation. The nuisance value appears when in old age the bowels moves well until the stool reaches the rectum, and then it stops and accumulates. This is called rectal impaction —just a complete stoppage, like a dam. In such a case, even an enema does not help much; and a doctor or a skilled nurse has to enter the rectum with a gloved hand and physically and forcibly break up the hard pieces of stool and remove as much as possible, with the hope that the rest will give in and will be eliminated by a high enema and similar remedies.

One has to distinguish between two types of constipation. One is due to slowing down of the movement of the large bowels as described. The other is called spastic constipation and is due to opposite reasons: the bowels are spastic—that is, crampy— and the tightness of the cramp transforms the normal appearance of the large bowels from a long, wide tube, similar to a large bologna sausage, into the appearance of an accordion— small compartments divided one from another by a narrow artificial ring which is only functional. It comes and goes, resulting in larger and smaller compartments, and accordingly also widening or narrowing of the width of the bowels. This condition also causes constipation, which is easily recognized. The origin is nerves—cramps due to general nervousness; therefore, we speak about a spastic colon. Apart from the typical appearance on X-rays, it is recognized by the kind of stool which is eliminated by a person who suffers from that condition. Each pressure removes the stool from one or two or more compartments, and the appearance of the stool corresponds to the molding of the stool in that colon compartment. Usually they are small, hard pieces like pebbles or nuts, or long, narrow pieces like pencils—depending on whether the contraction, the cramp or the spastic condition, caused an inflated small compartment in the bowels, or tightened the bowel so that its width—the lumen, as it is called—becomes long, but as narrow as a pencil. Which one it is, is of no importance. In both cases the result is the same—spastic constipation; because either no stool comes out, or, if it comes, it comes only in small quantities in the shape described.

It is clear that any drastic measures which would speed up the activity of the bowels would make a spastic constipation only worse, and laxatives are prohibited. Relief is easily obtained by soothing the excited, over-irritated bowels, as by hot bath, heating pad, and medication which is counteracting nervousness and the spastic condition of the bowels.

Generally speaking, treatment of spastic constipation is easier by far than the ordinary, so to say, common garden variety of constipation.

Ordinary constipation consists of slowing down of peristalsis. In other words, the large bowels move much slower and occasionally not at all. The result is that the stool, which normally becomes already solid in the large bowels, becomes more and more solid, sometimes hard like a rock. And the harder it is, the more difficult it is to move it, with the resulting increased constipation.

Apart from the rectal impaction of which we talked before, the problem of constipation consists of two parts: one, to move the accumulated stool and to eliminate it from the body; two, to restore the normal function of the bowels. The first task is comparatively easily achieved. Any strong laxative will do it, such as castor oil, or licorice powder, or a high enema with plenty of soap and water—in order to reach from below the upper parts of the colon, and in order to loosen up the hard mass of stool. The same is done by the laxatives from above. If one or the other laxative works, the colon is cleaned up and everything is fine. The question is only: for how long? After all, food is being eaten. Stool accumulates again, and the problem of elimination in case of constipation arises again.

And here we come to the second part: what can we do to get rid of constipation? One has to know that constipation is widespread—that millions of people suffer from it, and especially in old age. So, even if it is mostly not serious, it is still an important problem. There are thousands of remedies and advices on what to do in case of constipation. One says, drink hot lemonade first thing in the morning; drink hot water in the morning; walk a mile before breakfast, and so on and so on. All these advices are how to fight constipation *without* laxatives. Now, these devices are harmless and can be used by constipated persons. What they do, from the medical point of view, is to induce peristalsis to bring the bowels to a condition of moving. If one succeeds in doing it, he has to be congratulated with the advice to do it regularly, daily—whatever it was that helped him or her; because the regularity of the advice, if successful, creates a new habit, a conditioned reflex by which the bowels will move.

Unfortunately, all these devices frequently do not work, and one has to look for stronger remedies in order to get rid of the constipation. Some people are obstinate. They don't want to use laxatives, and try all kinds of food to promote the bowel movement, such as raw vegetables, a lot of raw fruit, dark bread—in other words, food containing a lot of roughage. The idea is not bad, if one can tolerate all this raw stuff and roughage. Roughage is not digested; is not absorbed by the body, and therefore it appears in the large bowels poorly digested or not digested at all, and *can* cause bowel movement. I say *can*, because if the large bowels are, so to say, lazy, there will be only more accumulation of stool but not necessarily movement of it. And that is the crux of the problem. In the long run, after trying everything else, even the most reluctant constipated person will start taking laxatives.

The question is, is there a solution to the problem of constipation? Basically, yes—and practically, no. If one has plenty of time and just makes a habit of going to the toilet on a certain hour every single day, whether he or she has an urge or not, then sooner or later it becomes a habit—a conditioned reflex transmitted to the colon by the brain—and the bowel movement will come; maybe in smaller quantities than expected, maybe not every day. But with the help of the above-mentioned devices *and* the regularity of the toilet session, *plus patience* to wait, if necessary, for 15 or more minutes, one can break the constipation and return to a normal regular bowel movement without the help of laxatives.

But practically it looks as if the majority has neither the time nor the patience which is required, and they turn to the help of laxatives.

Now comes the question, how effective are laxatives and how harmless or harmful?

Regarding the effectiveness of the laxatives, there is no one answer. What is effective in one case is not in another case. All laxatives, without exception, are addictive, just like morphine or codeine or even heroin. As soon as you are used to taking laxatives, you won't have a b.m. without taking a laxative. Some of the laxatives are so strong that a better name for them is a purgative. To these belong, for instance, castor oil. But, if a constipated person starts taking castor oil regularly day after day, he or she will have the result of a diminishing return; that is, it will stop, for that person, being a purgative and will become a mild laxative or will not work at all. On the other hand, if you take a mild laxative like milk of magnesia, you'll find that, while one has a very good b.m. from one teaspoonful, another person will take two or three tablespoonfuls with hardly any result. So the action of a laxative is very individual—different in every patient. And there is definitely an addiction in the meaning that a person who is constipated and used to laxatives will have no b.m. if he does not take a laxative.

By the same token, even if one has to take a laxative day after day, it is again individual whether the dose has to be increased or not. I know patients who cannot have a b.m. without laxatives, but stick to one for years and do not have to increase the dose. And then, in other cases, after a while the laxative stops working: the dose has to be increased, or the laxative changed for another one. In short, there are no cases exactly the same. As the proverb says, "One man's meat is another man's poison." Therefore, there is no use to recommend one laxative and to condemn another. Each of them, and we have hundreds, is good for one person and does not work in another case. Generally speaking, if a patient observes that a laxative works, he should stick to it. If, on the other hand, it does not work or stops working, it should be changed for another, instead of trying to achieve results by increasing the dose.

And finally: is it better to wait for a b.m. even days, or is it better not to wait and to take a laxative? In the beginning of the discussion of constipation I mentioned under which conditions one can and should wait for a natural bowel movement. But if one is definitely constipated and no amount of waiting and trying causes a normal b.m., then I would say it is better to take a laxative, even if it means addiction to it. There is hardly any danger in taking a laxative if it does not cause purgation and diarrhea, but a more or less normal b.m. It is just the same if one suffers from headache and there is no specific reason for it, such as a tumor or any other serious disease. Then it is better to take something for the headache, like aspirin or anything else which takes it away, than to walk around with headache and to be disabled by it.

As I said, in old age constipation is a discomfort which preys upon the mind of an elderly person and makes one unhappy. It is a small price to pay to be more comfortable if it can be achieved with a laxative pill or powder.

CHAPTER XVI

GAS AND GAS PAIN

One of the favorite words used by most women in the office of a doctor or at the clinic of a hospital is "gas." Some have also "gas pain"; and any pain within the abdominal cavity, and frequently also in the chest, is considered as a gas pain.

Before talking about "gas" in general, let us consider the "gas pain." To start with, there is no such thing as a gas pain. What people consider as gas pain can be anything: an appendicitis, a gall-bladder attack, a kidney stone, a pre-menstrual pain, and, last but not least, a heart attack. There exists a harmless explanation of the so-called gas pain—namely, an acute cramp of the large bowels which shifts from place to place. It is in the upper or lower abdomen; it can start on the left and shift to the right, and vice versa. This expression "gas pain" is often dangerous because, when a patient believes he or she has "gas pain," then the calling of a doctor is being postponed until the pain becomes excruciating and develops into an acute heart attack; or an acute, possibly perforated, appendicitis; or an acute attack of the gall-bladder—or kidney stones. It is interesting that people believe that gas, which they know develops in the abdomen, can also cause "gas pain" in the chest. How, it never became clear to me; apparently people either have poor ideas about the separation of the chest from the abdomen by the diaphragm and believe that there is no real division between the organs of the chest and of the stomach, or they think that the gas pressure goes up into the chest and causes chest pain, which they declare as being due to gas. It is true that in a certain small number of cases the pain caused by a heart attack starts in the epigastrium, which is the stomach pit, so that it could be mistaken for the so-called "gas pain."

However, I have often found that even pain in an acute heart attack, which was located in the chest across the breastbone, was still considered as "gas pain." Conversely, a patient is very happy if you tell him or her (it is mostly her) that the complaint of pain is really due to gas. There is a condition, as described previously, of a spastic colon, which means that the colon contracts like an accordion; and this contraction or spasm causes pain, usually alleviated by antispasmodic medication, such as belladonna or atropine, or by narcotics and/or sedatives. In all cases I would strongly advise you to see a doctor in a case of "gas pain," because the underlying cause *may* be one of the above-mentioned diseases.

To return to the problem of "gas" as such, one has to explain, first of all, that the production of gas is a normal thing. Food is being digested in the stomach and duodenum. It is further split in the small bowels, and then the indigestible remnants, the waste, the roughage, go down into the colon and become what we call stool or b.m. The expression "bowel movement" is only a delicate expression for "stool" or "feces," because actually the b.m. would mean the *movement* and not the *product* of the bowels. But that is how people talk. Now, the process of the digestion causes the production of gas by fermentation, just like you get gas bubbles in the formation of wine from grapes or berries or apples. The usual gas is sulphur hydroxide (H_2S) which gives the unpleasant smell of the stool; there are also some other gaseous substances in the waste. In any case, this production of gas would not bother people and they would not talk about it, if not for the fact that some people produce too much gas or they don't eliminate it fast enough, with the gas remaining in the bowels; or they notice the overproduction by elimination of the gas in the process of having a bowel movement, which is often more than expected; or in many cases people are constipated, but just the same they get out a lot of gas while at the toilet. Occasionally, the elimination of the gas precedes and promotes the bowel movement, thus helping to get rid of the constipation.

If there is a condition of overproduction of gas and insufficient elimination of it from the bowels, then people have a "gas" condition. The abdomen (the stomach, in popular language) is blown up or bloated, so that a woman looks like she is 6 or 7 months pregnant. It is especially evident when the patient is slim, because there is a striking discrepancy between the abdomen and the rest of the body. This gas condition, however, is a nervous condition, due to holding the colon and the muscles of the abdomen in a contracted position. Very often it occurs after tension, aggravation, emotional upset, etc. Some people are almost always in tension, especially the introverts who do not cry or scream but have their nervousness inside. Such people are bound to have a lot of gas which sometimes gives them trouble, as described; but often it causes just an overexpansion of the belly without any particular complaints. Then it becomes a cosmetic problem.

But it has to be emphasized that, though in most cases there is a retention of gas which blows up the belly, the bloating and/or the big belly can occur without gas retention, only by the condition of the abdominal muscles. Everybody knows that women who have delivered several children have a large abdomen. In such cases the overextension of the abdominal muscles during pregnancy does not completely disappear after the delivery; like an overexpanded rubber band, it just does not go back to normal condition. It is especially the case when the woman is older and still gets pregnant. A part of the elasticity of the muscles is gone, and the muscle after overextension during pregnancy is just slack and the whole abdomen is bigger, out of proportion to the other muscles.

Just the same can happen not organically but functionally to any woman who comes to a doctor with a complaint that her abdomen gets big as in seven months of pregnancy. It is not always connected with a "gas" condition, because such a woman tells the doctor that the bloating does not disappear even if she passes gas. Usually, this swelling of the abdomen appears soon after an aggravation, excitement, fright, or after eating a large meal. The swelling can come suddenly and collapse suddenly, like an accordion. Dr. Alvarez, the editor of *Modern Medicine,* describes in the August 1966 issue such a bloating without gas in nervous women. He also found out in the medical literature that two investigators described such an "accordion belly" already in 1891, and in 1900 and gave it that name. This bloating without gas is due to contraction of the muscles in the back of the abdomen, and can be made to disappear if the woman is placed on her back with her thighs flexed on her abdomen. Some are able to bloat in either the right or left lower part of the abdomen, or only in the upper part. The great majority of the "bloaters" are women. In Dr. Alvarez's 92 cases there were 85 women and 7 men. All the women were nervous, due to an unhappy family life, either in marriage, or because they were not married, or were divorced. Some were nervously and mentally unstable; many were constant complainers; others had nervous breakdowns. The 7 male "bloaters" were also all suffering from nervous disorders. In short, the same people who suffer from "gas" and "gas pain" are the type of people who can have a bloated belly even when they have no overproduction of gas. It is important to mention that, just as a so-called "gas pain" can conceal a heart attack or any other serious sickness, there exists, on the other hand, the danger that a nervous person is bloated with gas overproduction—or without, as in the "Alvarez" cases—can be unnecessarily operated for imaginary causes of the big belly, such as appendix or gallbladder or ovaries, with the idea that the removal of these organs would make the bloating disappear. In other words, underlying these operations is the thought that the above-mentioned organs contain a focus, a source of the gas-pain complaint. Of course, the operation does not help; because such people need a psychiatric or psychological treatment or plain reassurance (after a thorough checkup) by the physician that nothing is wrong and that the gas condition was harmless.

The trouble is only that such nervous patients are usually also hypochondriacs, and that they would not believe their doctor, even after a most thorough examination. The result will be that they will start going from doctor to doctor, and from surgeon to surgeon, in order to prove to themselves that their complaints are due to a serious underlying disease which was just not recognized by the previous doctor.

To sum up: gas and gas pain are not a disease but a symptom, either of a serious sickness or, if none is found, of a chronic nervous disorder which has to be treated as such.

CHAPTER XVII

DIABETES IN OLD AGE

Diabetes mellitus, to give it its full medical name, is not particularly a disease of old age. It can and does start often in teenagers, especially, if they inherit it from diabetic parents; it is frequent in grown-up and middle-aged persons, and it is very frequently occurring in old age. If it is necessary to talk about diabetes in old age, it is for several reasons. To start with is the fact that in very many cases diabetes appears only in old age. Somebody is well up to the age of 60 or 65, and then suddenly, when his or her urine is routinely examined, the doctor or the laboratory finds that the urine contains sugar, which definitely was not the case in preceding years. With the sugar in the urine usually is also found an increased amount of sugar in the blood. So, this is one reason why we have to discuss diabetes in old age: it comes more often in the old-age group than in any other, and it *starts* more often in that section of the population.

The next reason is that the course of diabetes in elderly persons is very different from that in younger people. It is milder and less dangerous compared with diabetes in the younger generation, easier to manage and easier to control. The normal blood sugar, which vacillates as normal between 80 and 120 or, according to the latest corrections, between 70 and 110 (it depends on the type of test which a laboratory uses)— is high in a case of diabetes. It can be almost normal or as low as 130 or 140, or it can go sky-high up to 300 and 400. The higher the figure, the more dangerous diabetes becomes; it can lead to a diabetic coma which means unconsciousness and possibly death. So, the whole trick consists in keeping the blood sugar as low as possible, and if possible, to get normal figures. But, if not possible, we should try to keep it in the figures of 130-140-150. The urine sugar is less important because on an empty stomach it is often negative; that is, no sugar can be detected in the urine, and the blood sugar can still be higher than normal. Actually, the sugar appears in the urine only when the blood sugar reaches 160 or more, and is missing at a blood sugar of 130-140-150.

The whole diabetes business depends on the problem of the so-called Langerhans' islands. The pancreas gland, which lies in the middle of the abdomen near the stomach and duodenum, has groups of cells, called islands by the name of the discoverer, Langerhans. These cells produce a juice called insulin. Its function is to digest pure sugar called glucose or dextrose, which is the end-product of the splitting and digestion of starch and plain sugar—called in chemistry "saccharose." This glucose circulates in our blood, and its amount in the blood is what we look for when the blood test for diabetes is taken. Now, in a case of diabetes these insulin-producing cells are damaged; they still produce insulin, but their production is deficient. The less they produce, the worse is the diabetes; the blood sugar, which is controlled by the insulin, rises. The sugar of the food cannot be digested and is spilled through the kidneys in the urine. The lack of production of insulin causes also as a by-product a rise of acid in the blood, which we call ketosis; and that is most dangerous because it has an influence on the blood circulation everywhere, and especially in the brain. That is why we get a diabetic coma in such a case by disturbance of the proper function of the brain.

We spoke of diabetes in old age as being milder—but only under certain conditions. Diabetes in younger people is more dangerous because we cannot control it easily. Very often we have to use insulin as an injection in order to give the body what it cannot produce itself. Insulin was discovered about 40 years ago, and it is now given by injection as a substitute for the missing natural insulin produced by the body. Before the era of insulin people died easily from diabetes because it could not be controlled, often not even with a strict diet, especially when the island cells did not produce insulin at all. Insulin is life-saving. Theoretically speaking, if one could get as much insulin as he or she needs, there would be no need for a diet. But the more a patient eats of starches and sugar-containing foods, the more insulin he requires for its digestion. And, if some parts of his or her pancreas gland still work, they become easily exhausted by too much demand. As in a factory, there is a limit to the amount of production which can be achieved. So, a certain limitation of starches and sugar is needed. We have the impression that the insulin deficiency in old age is not as great as in young people, that the deficiency is due more to the wear and tear of the function of the pancreas gland. Of course, not everybody becomes a diabetic in old age. You have to have an inherent weakness of this gland, just like some women have an inherent deficiency of the ovaries which function poorly. However, the fact that this deficiency appears in old age only speaks in favor of such a diabetic. Accordingly, if an older diabetic does not abuse the deficiency of insulin in his or her body, and restricts the diet in respect to starches and sugar, one can expect that in most cases such a diet will suffice to control the diabetes. Diabetes cannot be cured, but it can be controlled by manageable proportions. Diabetes has to be controlled by diet and managed by either diet alone or with the help of insulin and the anti-diabetes tablets which were discovered in the last few years.

The diet as consumed by a diabetic person does not have to avoid starches or sugar-containing food. On the contrary, if a diabetic person would try to live without starches and sugar, he or she would endanger life, because starches and/or sugar are imperative for our well-being. We can be without starches for a little while, but we cannot be always without them. Such a diet is not only one-sided for anybody, but in a diabetic person it would increase the acid in the blood and cause ketosis as described, which is a danger signal. In other words, what is needed for a diet controlling diabetes is a reasonable restriction of starches and sugar, which would give the island cells an opportunity to produce as much insulin as they can without overstraining their capacity of production.

However, diabetics love food which they should not touch, and in older age the more so. Old people have little that gives them pleasure. They do not dance, or rarely; they have no sex, or rarely; they do no play an active role in sports, maybe with the exception of golf. Lack of activity in many fields leaves them the pleasure of eating. And, if they are diabetics, they minimize the danger of eating forbidden food and cheat whenever they can. There is an old Latin saying, *"Omnis diabeticus mendax"* which means, "Every diabetic is a liar." Of course, the meaning is that he or she lies in regard to the forbidden food eaten. Therefore, because of this craving for sugar and starches, it is difficult to manage a diabetic person and to control his or her diabetes. With the advent of insulin and the anti-diabetes tablets, this task is greatly eased. At least with the help of insulin and/or the tablets, the sting of immediate danger to life is taken out of the treatment of diabetes.

It can be said that in our times nobody has to die from diabetes. In the one or other way diabetes can be controlled and the life of a diabetic can be easily managed. Only complete disregard of the simplest rules for diabetes can cause danger and death from diabetes. Such fools exist, but, thanks to God, they are rare. The others are either sensible and doing well on diet and tablets, or they are less sensible, cheat and eat what they shouldn't, but at least they have the resort of insulin which makes up by the unpleasantness of daily injections for the cheating and for the lack of sensible understanding of the character of diabetes. It is, as in alcoholism or drug addiction, a certain weakness of character and lack of will power.

On the whole, diabetes as such is no more a dangerous disease in old age. There remains a fear of it in elderly people who cling to the daily routine of the urine test for sugar, which usually is performed religiously, often more than necessary. One can see the unhappiness on the face of the old man or woman if the urine shows sugar, and the contentment if the urine does not show sugar. While not denying the value of the self-testing of urine for sugar, it is my impression that this is overdone. It would have a meaning if the diabetics would consider this testing as a rule of what to do. Sugar present in the urine—therefore I should cut the starches to a minimum. No sugar in the urine—I can be more lenient with the diet. But in daily life it does not work in this way. If there is sugar in the urine, the patient takes one tablet more or 10 units of insulin more—or frequently the diabetic hopes that tomorrow the urine will give better results and continues eating as hitherto. If tomorrow the result is the same, he or she might think of taking more tablets or more insulin. But, if on the other hand the urine shows no sugar, there is even more reason to cheat, to eat more starches, fruit, juice, etc. than prescribed by the doctor. For these practical reasons, it would be better if the patient would test the urine less and visit the doctor for a blood test and general examination more often. Now, with Medicare paying the bill, there is hope that the diabetic will visit the doctor regularly, and thus the old-age diabetes will be better controlled.

Diabetes is not only a problem of having too much sugar in the blood and spilling it in the urine. It causes a repercussion all over the body; it raises the cholesterol in the blood; it causes an early development of cataracts in the eyes; it causes a premature development of arteriosclerosis—that is, hardening of the arteries—with resulting high blood pressure, coronary arteries disease and sclerosis of the brain arteries. It has a deleterious effect on the peripheral arteries, especially of the legs, with difficulty of walking—and even in some cases causing complete stoppage of the circulation and gangrene of the feet, leading thus occasionally to amputation. All these dangers inherent in the diagnosis of diabetes make it mandatory to control the diabetes, even if only as a preventive measure to avoid the serious consequences. These are not necessarily bound to the severity of the diabetes as such. For instance, one of the side effects of diabetes is a neuritis—an inflammation of the nerve—of the peripheral nerves, such as of an arm or of a leg. This neuritis is frequently found just in people who have a mild diabetes.

The same often applies to the peripheral arteries disease. I remember a man of about 50 who had a family history of diabetes but considered himself immune to the inheritance of diabetes. (It is known that diabetes is inherited from a diabetic parent, though not all children get it if only one parent has it.) I do not know how often his blood sugar was examined before I saw him. I only know that he came to me because he could not walk. He tried all kinds of remedies, including arch supports and space shoes. But when I saw him and found him suffering from a mild diabetes, he already had an extensive sclerosis of the main artery of one leg, and he had to undergo surgery in order to enable him to walk.

In short, diabetes is a dangerous disease—no more by itself, because it can be controlled by diet, tablets and insulin; but because of the effects of diabetes on the function of the whole body, and especially on the arteries and the blood circulation.

CHAPTER XVIII

DISEASES OF THE MUSCLES, JOINTS AND BONES

Rheumatism was and still is an all-embracing word. Any sickness, any complaint connected with muscles, bones, ligaments and joints was called rheumatism, and is still called so in the parlance of the average layman. In medicine, there is nowadays a classification and segregation of the diseases of these parts of the body, mainly due to better diagnostic methods and due to better understanding of the pathological changes which take place there.

(a) *Rheumatism.* We call rheumatism actually only the disease of the muscles, ligaments and tendons. The diseases of the joints we call arthritis, of which we have several types, each distinguished by its peculiar progress in the joint. Rheumatism and arthritis are not confined to old age; younger people can have them too. But rheumatic aches in bones and muscles are prevalent in old age.

What is *rheumatism?* We still don't know exactly what is going on in the rheumatic muscle. We only know that such a muscle aches on touch and pressure and on certain movements, and that the pain preferably comes *before* the change of the weather, like from hot to cold and vice versa, and even more so when the dry weather changes to a humid one—rain, snow and so on.

There are many theories why it is so, but no definite evidence. According to a theory which was published by me about 35 years ago, the rheumatic muscle contains more water which it absorbs from without and partly from within. This is especially the case before saturation of the atmosphere with moisture. Therefore, the remedies against rheumatism are working towards the goal to get rid of the superfluous water in the muscle, such as heat, baking, massage, exercise, etc. The action of aspirin is pain relief; how it works, why it does relieve pain, nobody knows. Possibly, if one accepts my theory, the perspiration which accompanies the action of aspirin and other salicylates takes away the superfluous water from the afflicted muscle.

In any case, it is statistically known that elderly people suffer more from muscle rheumatism than younger ones. The explanation lies probably in the fact that in older age there is less muscular activity which would work on the muscle in the same way as massage or exercise does for the relief of rheumatism. It is known that rheumatism does not affect people who have as an occupation hard physical work, unless they have to work primarily in conditions of exposure to changes of weather, such as farmers, bricklayers, builders, masons, contractors, cement layers, roadbuilders and so on. In all other elderly people, clerks, bookkeepers, physicians, lawyers, salesmen, etc., the muscles through lack of exercise become flabby. There is an invasion of fat into the muscle fibers, and they are exposed to diseases, infections and any other damage. It is interesting to note that in case of fever due to infection the first symptoms are the aches and pains in the muscles which are the premonition of the acute impending disease.

Rheumatism of the muscles and of the ligaments and tendons which connect them with the bones can be very painful. However, it is not a killing disease. It disables frequently for a short time, but with all the medical weapons which are nowadays at our disposal, the disability goes away soon, and the body is restored to normal—which means that muscular rheumatism does not leave any scars or other permanent changes.

(b) *Arthritis*, which belongs to the same family of rheumatic diseases, is a completely different story. It belongs to the family of rheumatic diseases because, similar to rheumatism, it is also prone to react to changes in the weather. Besides, the muscles, the ligaments, the bones and the joints form together a complete structure; they are our framework within which we have to live. And their action is interwoven; the sickness of one of them reflects on the activity of the others. However, even arthritis is not one entity, but there are several types which differ not only by development and progress, but also by age group.

(1) *Rheumatoid arthritis* occurs only in young people; it is extremely rare in older people, unless it started in young age and continued through middle age and is still existing in old age. In all my practice I remember only two cases of rheumatoid arthritis which started at the age of fifty; and these cases were exceptional, with some special reasons why this type of arthritis could occur in them. In any case, we don't have to elaborate on rheumatoid arthritis because it does not belong to old-age diseases.

(2) *Osteoarthritis,* contrary to rheumatoid arthritis, hardly ever occurs in young people, and is a most prominent and frequent disease of old age. The reason why it happens to elderly persons is simple: it is a wear-and-tear disease, due to use and abuse of the joints. And there is another distinction between the two arthritises. In rheumatoid arthritis are primarily involved the small joints, such as those of the hands. The involvement of the larger joints such as knees, comes much later. In osteoarthritis it goes the opposite way: the large joints, such as knees, hips, sacroiliac, spine are the first to be hit by the osteoarthritis. The small joints come later. The word "arthritis" means, actually, inflammation of the joints. This is especially true for rheumatoid arthritis, which is caused primarily by an inflammation. In osteoarthritis, the inflammation is a secondary, late sign: in the beginning there are symptoms and signs of the wear and tear. Therefore, the osteoarthritis is often called osteoarthrosis in order to emphasize that this disease is *not* due to an inflammation. The osteoarthritis or osteoarthrosis of the spine has a special name: it is called spondyloarthritis or spondyloarthrosis. It is the same, only pointing to the fact that this disease is concentrated in the joints of the spine—that is, in the joints between one vertebra and the next one.

If one examines X-rays of a case of osteoarthritis, one finds that the edges of the bones which combine to form a joint are not smooth but rough, and that at the same time there is a kind of an outgrowth of the bones. It is what we call "hypertrophic," a term which just means too much growing, contrary to "atrophic," which means diminution of growth. The reason is similar to the hypertrophic heart muscle which becomes bigger by overstrain—what we can call an enlarged heart. The same happens to a chronically overstrained joint. And it is remarkable that the beginning of an osteoarthritis depends on the abuse of the joint. Because we have so many joints—without them we could not move and work and use our limbs or turn our head—it hardly ever happens that all joints are equally involved in this degeneration of the joints. It depends which joint is more used and abused. For instance, one has osteoarthritis of the knees if the knees are very much used in the daily work, or if the legs have to support a heavy body, as it is the case in very obese people. Even in osteoarthritis of the spine, we distinguish and see great differences in the severity of it in the joints of the lower spine, the so-called lumbar spine; or of the thoracic (chest part) spine, or the cervical (neck) spine joints. Again, it depends on the use and abuse of this or that part of the body, and mainly through occupation—carrying or lifting or bending or twisting.

There is hardly any elderly person who does not suffer from osteoarthritis of some joints, and many suffer from osteoarthritis of almost all of them—though it never occurs that all joints are equally involved. It is a long drawn-out illness or condition. It is incurable, but frequently it gives some people hardly any trouble. In some cases the osteoarthritis is found only incidentally, when the person needs X-rays of the joints for any other reasons, such as an accident—or when, for instance, the spine becomes visible on X-rays made for kidney or stomach trouble.

On the other hand, in some cases the osteoarthritis becomes troublesome and causes a lot of pain and disability. This is the case in osteoarthritis of the knees, or in that of the lower back, when it disables sometimes for many days. The treatment does not differ much from that of muscle rheumatism. The same baking, heat, massage, liniment, bed-rest and later exercises. In lower-back arthritis or that of the neck joints, one can add an orthopedic corset or collar. Recently we got additional medical remedies such as cortisone, Indomethane and some other preparations, besides the old salicylates such as aspirin and so on.

We have to be frank: osteoarthritis is incurable and even progressive in the meaning that, with the flight of time, the diseased joint gets more degenerated, and more joints get involved. Sometimes the osteoarthritis does not progress—and we don't know the reason. On the other hand, all the mentioned remedies are palliatives, which means that they work against the complaints, the pain, the disability, without curing the underlying disease. There is also no surgery, unless it is a question of straightening some of the damage done by the osteoarthritis. It is logical even from the point of view of a layman that it would be impossible to operate on all joints, if, as usual, many are involved. And even if it is done, how to prevent new outcrops of degeneration in new, up-to-then-not-involved joints? The fight against osteoarthritis is a fight against aging, against wear and tear. In our present stand of medicine, we don't have a remedy for it which could be proclaimed as a cure.

But, we have also to count the blessings. Contrary to the rheumatoid arthritis of young age which cripples, osteoarthritis does not cripple the elderly who get it. It makes walking frequently difficult, especially if the lower back and/or the knees are involved. It may disable for a while, it may cause a lot of pain, discomfort and trouble. But it does not cripple or make for invalidism, and is neither a killing nor a life-shortening disease; and for that we have to be grateful.

(3) *Gout.* Gout is an ancient disease, known for centuries, which used to be considered as a disease of the rich and affluent who ate plenty of meat, drank plenty of wine, and finally got gout from such a life. In a way, gout was considered something to be proud of—a status sign that one is doing well and can afford all this rich food and the wines. This assumption of the cause of gout was taken for granted for such a long time that even in our time people think that you can get gout only if you eat good food and drink plenty of wine.

What is gout? Actually it is only a form of arthritis, a gouty inflammation of the small joints; in the first place it appears in the big toe, occasionally it can start on the hand. The inflammation is connected with the accumulation of uric acid crystals in the joint. Now, it is true that uric acid can be found in many foods, and especially in meat. From the food it wanders into the blood, where it circulates in small amounts and is being eliminated through the kidneys. This is why we can find uric acid crystals in the urine. All this metabolism of the uric acid from the food up to the elimination with the urine is a normal thing and does not cause gout. We all do it. The danger point is the question of *how much* uric acid is circulating in the blood, and whether we eliminate all the uric acid crystals. If we have too much uric acid in the blood, we are candidates for accumulation of uric acid crystals in our body. The normal values of uric acid in the blood is up to 7 mg. in 100 cc. of blood (100 cc. is about $3\frac{1}{2}$ ozs.). Anything below the figure of 7 is o.k., above it means trouble.

We can have trouble with the uric acid in two ways. If it stays in the body and the crystals accumulate in the kidneys without elimination in the urine, then they can cause a formation of kidney stones which can consist of uric acid crystals. Or, the same crystals go via the blood circulation into the joints of the feet or hands and clog them by formation of lumps which are visible in the joints, or they are in the joint without much external evidence. What causes the trouble is the following factor: one has too much uric acid in the blood and in the joints, eats spicy food heavily and drinks some wine or some other alcoholic beverage, and he or she gets an acute attack of gout, with a swollen, red, painful big toe or thumb. (It can be also the ankle or the knee, or two joints are involved at the same time.) The doctor is called and the easy diagnosis is pronounced—gout. An acute attack of gout can be precipitated by pressure from ill-fitting shoes, by surgery for any reason, by an infection. Sometimes, if a patient has heart failure and swelling of the ankles or legs, the doctor may give a diuretic injection which is supposed to remove the superfluous water and salt from the body. However, as a side result often it starts an acute attack of gout.

The uric acid stays usually in the soft tissue around the joint and is therefore deposited as a salt, called urates. These urates in the soft and bony tissue form bumps called tophi which are typical for gout. If one has a chronic gout for a long time, all the parts of many joints may be covered by these urate tophi. It is peculiar that these tophi which contain the salt of uric acid which is responsible for the gout and are situated in the soft tissue are very rarely the site of the acute attack.

As mentioned, the old idea of gout being a disease of rich people is abandoned. We know that a person can have a high uric acid content in the blood without knowing it until he gets an acute attack of gout. There are families where gout occurs more frequently, just as diabetes is inherited. The gout in some members of such a family may be dormant and not make any symptoms. In other members of the same family the gout may be pronounced. Gout can occur in younger people but is frequent in middle and older age—maybe, as in diabetes, due to less exercise and more food containing uric acid. We see also that there are periods when we see a lot of gouty patients, and in other periods gout is rare. For instance, in the U.S.A. gout has become very common in the last 10 years, and was rarely seen earlier. It can be said that this is because we live in an affluent society, and people can and do spend more money on food, thus increasing the amount of uric acid in the blood. But gout does not always go with affluence.

The most severe case of gout I ever saw was in a welfare patient of about 68 years who lived in a private nursing home where the food definitely was not rich in uric acid, meat was given in small quantities, and so on. This man had the so-called tophi (accumulation of urates in the soft tissues surrounding the joints) of a huge size around almost every joint in the body; if one had opened all the joints and removed the uric acid salt from all the involved joints, one could have collected maybe a pound of that salt. The case history of that patient did not reveal any overeating of meat and similar food containing uric acid. And again, with all the accumulation of uric acid in his body he did not have one single attack of acute gout in the several years when I treated him. Possibly due to the bland diet, isolation from infections by confinement to the nursing home, walking in soft slippers, not having any alcohol, and thus avoiding the usual external reasons which bring about an acute attack.

Gout has to be considered as a disease which represents a deficiency of the absorption and elimination of uric acid in the body, possibly also overproduction of it. In this way it resembles diabetes, where there is a deficiency of absorption and elimination of sugar. It is also a hereditary disease. Some people eat food rich in uric acid as much as they want, and don't get gout; some eat much less than usual and do get gout. There is also a greater tendency to get gout among men than among women. The ratio is about 20 men to one woman.

We have plenty of remedies to cut short an acute gout attack, starting with the old well-known Colchicin; and then we have new ones, such as cortisone, Indomethane, and so on. We have even medication to diminish the amount of uric acid in the blood, thus diminishing the chance of getting an acute gout attack.

Bland diet, avoidance of sharp spicy food, comfortable shoes, all this helps to prevent acute attacks. Regarding alcohol, it does not have to be avoided, but abuse is definitely not helpful. I have found that gouty patients tolerate poorly any wine, and especially sweet, heavy wine like port wine. (This was known long ago. In other times the typical rich John Bull type of Englishmen drank a lot of port wine and usually suffered from gout attacks.) They do tolerate in *moderate* quantities pure alcohol, such as whiskey, rye or bourbon, without precipitating an acute attack of gout.

Gout is a disease of middle and old age. In the acute form it can be very painful and disabling. However, only in very advanced cases can it cause a deficiency of kidney function. Generally speaking, gout is neither killing nor shortening the life-span of a person suffering from it.

(4) *Osteoporosis.* This is not a disease of the joints, but a condition with a typical change in the structure of the bones. It occurs almost only in women and is mainly due to deficiency of the function of the ovaries. Because in and after the menopause there is a decline of the activity of the ovaries. Osteoporosis is to be considered as a disease of old age. Of course, it can occur in younger women if their ovaries were surgically removed for whatever reason. It also starts sometimes shortly after the menopause—that is, in the early fifties. But its onset is very slow, and the symptoms of osteoporosis may not come to the fore before the age of 60 or more.

Osteoporosis is easily seen on X-rays of the bones, especially of the large bones. The bone structure is not so dense as it should be, due to loss of calcium, which is the most important mineral of the bone. This loss of the calcium softens the bone. It can lead to a compression of the vertebra bones of the spine and cause senile kyphoscoliosis, which means a senile hunchback. You see such women in the street. They did not have a hunchback in younger years; it came about with the development of the osteoporosis after the change of life—menopause. Frequently, it can be recognized when a woman comes for the first time to a doctor's office or clinic and her measurements are taken. She does not yet have a hunchback, but she is surprised when she is told her height, and declares that she must have shrunk because she is positive that she was one or more inches taller. And she is right: she did shrink due to osteoporosis and compression of the vertebra bones of the spine.

The usual complaint of older women in such a condition is backache. If the doctor attributes this pain to arthritis or advanced age, and the X-rays are not taken, the diagnosis of osteoporosis and its remedy are missed. Namely, because it is a specific female disease and is connected with loss of the function of the ovaries, therefore an improvement can be expected if and when a substitute treatment is given. The patient will be given ovarial hormones, usually with very good results.

Here I have to make two remarks. First, a person can ask why, if the disease is due to loss of the calcium mineral, should one not treat the patient with calcium. Of course, calcium as we have it in dairy products and/or calcium tablets is harmless and often beneficial. However, in the case of osteoporosis it is a question of *absorption*. Without addition of female hormones, the calcium will leave the body and will not enter the bones where it is needed. The hormones can be given by mouth in tablets or by injection, which works usually for quite a while.

Here comes the second remark. Female hormones given to an elderly woman can and do sometimes overshoot the mark. They can not only help the bone disease, but can also cause a bleeding from the vagina. In such a case, a panic occurs. The publicity about cancer is so widespread that a vaginal bleeding is considered as a sign of a cancer. The more, because ovarial hormones are often blamed as a cause of cancer, and because it is true in certain selected cases, many women refuse to be helped because of the cancer scare. It can be definitely told that in the doses as prescribed by the doctor and under his supervision, there is no danger of a cancer from such treatment of osteoporosis. And further, in order to avoid such unnecessary bleeding, the female hormone is given with a very small amount of male hormone in order to neutralize any overaction of the female hormone. Therefore, hormonal treatment of osteoporosis is safe if given under a doctor's supervision. Osteoporosis causes backache and therefore discomfort. Because the bones lose the calcium, they become porous (that is the meaning of the name "osteoporosis" —porosity of the bones) and therefore brittle, and can break easily. And any fracture in old age is a serious disease because of poor knitting of the bones and of possible complications.

In short, osteoporosis is not so harmless apart from the backache which it frequently causes, and should be treated by the doctor without hesitation.

(5) *Low Back Pain*. This kind of pain is very common in elderly people, much more common than in younger ones; and the reason is that lower backache is frequently due to degeneration—wear and tear—of the joints and bones; and that, of course, occurs rather in advanced age.

What is lower backache? One has the pain in the lower part of the spine, in the so-called lumbar spine, then even lower in the sacral and sacroiliac region, in the tailbone; and the pain can and often does radiate into the sciatica nerve, which runs along the leg (usually either right or left, never at the same time in both legs). This pain can result from many causes: it can be due to an injury of the soft tissue, such as muscles and ligaments and tendons which are attached to the bones and joints, and that occurs for external reasons, such as lifting of heavy things (if one is not used to that), or sudden bending or twisting of the body. I have seen it happen to people who had a sedentary occupation, and then either took up golfing or carpentering, or bought a summer home and started gardening, with all the physical work which is connected with it. In other words, they get a muscular or ligament sprain or strain from unaccustomed work. We usually call it lumbago, or sciatica if it goes to the leg.

One can get lower backache also from an infection if some germs enter the lower back structure. Or, the lower back pain may be due to a spreading of a cancer which is in a different area of the body. For instance, a lung cancer can spread to the spine, and a cancer of the prostate in a male can spread to the lower back and cause a most severe pain.

However, apart from a violent overexertion and/or an infection, both of which can occur at any age, lower back pain is prevalent in old age. The reason is that a younger person has more elasticity of the soft tissues of muscles and ligaments, and a normal structure of bones and joints. In older age, the elasticity is greatly diminished and the joints and bones degenerate, as shown in previous chapters. Therefore, the lower backache in elderly males and females is a very frequent complaint with which they go to the doctor.

It is very important to find out the cause of that lower backache. As shown, in females there might be a special reason for the backache. In males it might be connected with the prostate gland, which the females do not have. Both sexes can suffer from an infection, from which old age is not immune. And both definitely are bound to have a larger or lesser degree of a degenerative osteoarthritis, with its changes of the joints and their adjoining bones; and this is the most frequent cause of low back pain in elderly people. However, one should not have the notion that his or her backache must necessarily be due to arthritis, and accept it and do nothing about it apart from taking a few aspirin tablets.

There is no reason for resignation and acceptance of low back pain as an inevitable complaint of old age. It is true that it is common and not always easy to cure or to improve. But our diagnostic facilities are nowadays very good, and we have many ways of treatment which can terminate or greatly diminish low back pain.

CHAPTER XIX

DISEASES OF THE PROSTATE

The prostate is a gland which only males have, just as ovaries exist only in females. It is a gland which produces a juice which mixes with the seed of man, and therefore it plays a certain, though minor, role in sexual intercourse and in the reproduction of the human species. It lies between the rectum and the urethra, which is the canal which leads from the urinary bladder outside and conveys either the urine on urination, or the seed (semen) on ejaculation of it at the end of sexual intercourse.

The prostate can get an infection, and then it is inflamed. This inflammation is called prostatitis. It sometimes comes due to a venereal infection with gonococci, and becomes a part of a gonorrhea. Or the infection can affect the prostate from innocent causes, such as an infection and inflammation of the bladder, which we call cystitis. The prostate can get infected and inflamed also via the blood circulation, if the blood vessels carry germs, which can come from any place in the body.

However, this prostatitis or inflammation of the prostate gland is rare in old age and common in young people. It sometimes comes after too much sexual activity, when the gland gets enlarged with blood and overexerted together with the other male organs. Even gonorrhea which one can get at any age is rare in older men because they are more mature, more cautious, and take the necessary precautions in order to avoid an infection.

More frequent in old age is cancer of the prostate, and such a cancer is rare in younger men. Why it is so, we don't know. There is the possibility that cancer on the whole is more frequent in elderly people and that, just as women get in older age a cancer of the womb, just so men get a cancer of the prostate gland. There is an additional reason: in older age the prostate undergoes changes, and these changes might be a breeding soil for the development of a cancer. We have many theories about the origin of cancer. None are proven; and as long as it is so, we just don't know why one organ is more frequently the site of a cancer and another less frequent. We only know that, in the case of the prostate gland, contrary to other organs, a cancer occurs almost always in older age, and hardly ever in young people.

Now, this cancer of the prostate gland—which, as I pointed out, is a part of the male sexual organs—differs from the usual cancers in that it can be treated not only by surgery but also by hormones—namely, female hormones, which can be given by mouth as tablets or by injections. If they do not cure the cancer of the prostate they at least stop its further growth and destruction of the body, *provided* that the diagnosis is made *early enough* before the cancer has started spreading either in the vicinity of the gland or via the blood into remote organs. Of course, surgery—removal of the prostate and its adjacent tissues—is the primary treatment. But then female hormones are given in order to stop further spreading of the cancer in case the operation did not catch all the malignant tissues, the remnant of which might be as small as a pinhead and still cause spreading of cancer, destruction and death.

In addition, there are inoperable cancers of the prostate. Plainly spoken, these are cancers which were not recognized early enough—usually by negligence of the patient, who took the symptoms lightly and never thought of cancer. Then the physician and/or the surgeon find out that it is too late for operation. In the usual cancer, the patient is more or less doomed. His life can be, maybe, prolonged by radiation either with X-rays, or radium or cobalt; but, generally speaking, there is hardly any hope for survival.

Not so with cancer of the prostate gland. With intensive and incessant treatment with female hormones, plus small additional surgery, the progress of the cancer can be stopped, and there occurs even a regression of the malignant tissues. The life of such a victim of cancer can be prolonged and the patient can continue a useful and active life for many years to come.

With the problem of operation of the prostate is connected the old-age disease of a benign enlargement of the prostate. It is estimated that at least 80% of all men get sooner or later an enlargement of the prostate, and the majority have to undergo surgery. Some statistics claim that even 80% is not enough, and that the enlargement of the prostate occurs in 90% of men. It is medically called hypertrophy of the prostate and has nothing to do with malignancy and cancer. It is actually a hardening of the tissues and general enlargement, which can go in two directions. As said before, the prostate lies between rectum and urethra—the canal leading from the bladder to the outside via the penis. The lucky ones get the enlargement in the direction of the rectum; they may have trouble with the bowel movement because the feces have to go through the bump formed by the enlarged prostate; but as long as this enlargement does not push into the direction of the urethra canal, they are all right.

However, in the great majority of cases the prostate pushes towards the urethra canal. The result, and almost the first symptom that something is wrong, is the so-called hesitation. A man stands up for urination because his bladder is full and he has an urge, but it takes several seconds, and in more serious cases a minute or minutes before the first drop of urine comes out. If the bladder is not too full, the whole attempt to urinate becomes futile, nothing comes out. The reason is pressure of the prostate tissue on the back part of the urethra canal. The bigger the prostate, the greater is the pressure, resulting in a partial obstruction of the canal. Finally, it comes to a complete mechanical obstruction and no urine can be passed. In that case, the doctor has to push a tube—a catheter—through the obstructed canal up to the bladder and relieve the accumulated urine. If such an obstruction recurs, there is no other way to help the patient but surgery.

Another frequent symptom which brings the patient to the surgeon is night urination. Some people have the habit of getting up at night to urinate. The majority don't do it. But whether they go at night or not, if the frequency of night urination increases, then something is wrong. It is also important to recognize that such an occurrence is not due to a cystitis—that is, to an inflammation of the bladder—because in that case there is frequency all day long, not only at night, which is characteristic for prostate enlargement. In mild cases, the night frequency occurs 2 or 3 times. But in severe cases a person has to get up and go to the bathroom 4 or 5 times during one night, which becomes a nuisance, even without the above-mentioned obstruction; and finally it leads also to an operation.

In case of a prostate enlargement, the bladder is not emptied completely during urination. First a small part and gradually a larger and larger part of the urine remains in the bladder after urination; that is what is called residual urine, and the more urine remains as residual, the more serious is the condition. The urine stagnates and deteriorates; it also causes back pressure, and some of the urine is pressed back into the ureter and to the kidney, thus causing an irritation and inflammation of the kidneys.

In short: an enlargement of the prostate, though it has nothing to do with a cancer or malignancy, is a very unpleasant condition which in the majority of cases leads to surgery.

Here it is necessary to emphasize that, at the present stage of medical science, there is no other course of treatment of an enlargement of the prostate but an operation consisting in removal of the gland. All remedies, including hormonal treatment and/or massage, are not worth a penny and should be considered as quack medicine.

When to be operated depends on the degree of obstruction. If one has the nuisance of too much frequency of night urination, or he has to be catheterized—that is, his urine has to be removed by a doctor through a tube—then the operation becomes inevitable and even urgent. In milder cases one can wait, because the development of the enlargement is a very slow process. The enlargement can be detected in a check-up at the age of 50, while the same person may have to have the operation 10 or 15 years later. The average age of men operated for an enlargement of the prostate is between 65 and 70; though occasionally a man of 50 needs already an operation, and on the other hand it may become imperative only at the age of 80.

What kind of operation is being done, and what are the complications?

There are 3 types of surgery for the removal of the prostate obstruction, and the complications, if any, can occur in any of them—though the type of operation selected by the surgeon depends on the general condition of the patient. The 3 types of operation are: the transurethral, the suprapubic and the perineal. In layman's language, this means: transurethral—going into the bladder with a tube similar to the catheter of which we talked before, armed wtih a fine, sharp knife, and cutting of the bulging *part* of the prostate gland which causes the urinary obstruction. It is the simplest operation. The wound is internal, inside the bladder, and causes the least trouble for the patient, though like any wound it causes bleeding and might cause an infection. But these are dangers inherent in any operation; you can have them when you cut a finger. The advantage of a comparatively minor operation is countermanded by the fact that you do not remove the whole gland, but only the bulging part. That means that, if there is a tendency of growing, the prostate will continue to grow, and sooner or later we shall have the same problem of obstruction. However, as said before, the growing of the prostate is a very slow process, and it might take 10 years before another operation becomes due. If you have a debilitated old patient of the age of 70 or more, you take a chance and do a transurethral prostate operation.

The other two methods both lead to the same end: complete removal of the prostate gland. Not so long ago, only the overgrowth was removed and the prostate was left. This type of operation was abandoned because the prostate started growing again, and not rarely the patient, after some years, again had urinary trouble and obstruction. The two types of removal of the prostate are actually only surgical methods. One surgeon prefers one type, like suprapubic, which means going into the bladder and prostate from above through the abdomen. In the perineal method the surgeon operates from the back, going to the prostate in the region between the rectum and the penis, where it is situated. There are advantages and disadvantages in each of the methods, and it is not the layman's business to dictate to the surgeon which method he should use.

There are, however, some points which a patient should know and be prepared for. One is that, before the bigger operation, the urological surgeon performs a minor operation—namely, he cuts the seminal cords which lead from the testicles to the penis and through which the semen or seed is conveyed for ejaculation at the end of sexual intercourse. This is done in order to prevent an infection of the testicles as a post-effect of the prostate operation. The result of this minor operation, which is done by cutting the cord through the scrotum (the pouch in which the testicles and the cord are lying) is that the semen which is produced is ejaculated, not outside as in usual intercourse, but inside the bladder. It becomes what is called a dry run; the semen is not deposited in the vagina of the woman, and therefore such a man becomes sterile. Considering that a prostate operation is usually performed on elderly people, it seems to be a minor matter—the artificial sterilization due to the cutting of the cord. This does *not* make a man impotent, and he retains the feeling of ejaculation as before. Just the same, a patient is entitled to know that this precautionary surgical measure will make him sterile. We still have plenty of men of over 65 who would not mind producing an offspring in old age, and some marry a young woman who can have children. Such people should be warned that such an operation is going to be done. It is not a *must;* a patient can declare that he is willing to take the risk of a testicle infection, and does not desire to have the cutting of the cord done. The prostate operation can be just as successful.

In a later chapter we shall discuss the sexual problems of old age in detail. In respect to the prostate disease, we have to make some additional remarks in this respect. The problem is: does the removal of the prostate make a patient impotent after the operation? The answer is, basically, no. If an elderly man was potent before the operation, he can expect to remain potent after the operation. There are some cases when the potency is diminished or gone after the operation, regardless of the type of operation performed. In other cases, potency is even improved. In the majority of cases it is a psychological problem, and the sexual activity before and after the operation depends on the female partner, on her willingness and her sympathetic attitude towards that problem. This is one of the reasons why a married patient after an operation for prostate trouble regains his potency sooner and better than a bachelor or a widower. In an operation, certain nerves are cut; in a prostate operation some nerves leading to the male sexual organs are also cut. This *can* lead to impotence due to organic reasons, just because those nerves which play a role in potency are not working. It can be expected that the function of those nerves will be restored in due time. The safer surgical method in regard to potency is considered the suprapubic one, which does the least damage to those nerves. However, the question of potency of elderly men is not that simple; it will be dealt with in a separate chapter. Here it was only necessary to explain to a layman who has to undergo a prostate operation what the pitfalls are, in order not to be surprised at the outcome after the operation.

The complications after a prostate operation are not different from those in any other operation. Generally speaking, in the standard of surgery now prevailing, one does not have to fear a prostate operation; he can count at being safely at home within 2 weeks. One complication can occur—urinary incontinence. In most cases, if it comes, it is only temporary and due to the lack of tonus (vigor) of the muscles which close the bladder after urination. In some people, incontinence appears as a sign of old age with or without operation—just a weakness of the bladder muscles. In some people this weakness appears only after the prostate operation. If the muscle functioned well before the operation, the continence will be restored soon. Only in very few debilitated persons, the urinary incontinence may become a permanent feature. On the whole, one should not be afraid to have the operation performed because of such possibility.

The advantage of getting rid of the urinary obstruction is so great that all possible complications which might never occur should be discounted.

CHAPTER XX

WOMEN'S CHANGE OF LIFE AND WOMEN'S OLD-AGE DISEASES

The change of life, or menopause, as it is called in medicine, is an important period in the life of a woman. Literally, it means that the menstruation stops and no formation of eggs in the ovaries takes place anymore; and, accordingly, a woman cannot get pregnant. When a woman starts her menopause is a highly individual thing. It depends on the function of the ovaries. Some women have very active ovaries; in others the menstruation is weak and short. Therefore, the first type of women will have a late change of life, and the second ones will have it very early. In this way, one woman can menstruate yet at the age of 50, while the other stops at 40 or even earlier. On the average, the change of life *used* to occur at the age of 45-46. For not-yet-clearly-defined reasons, most likely due to the general improvement of nutrition, vitamin intake, easing of a woman's work by the many appliances which give a woman more leisure and make the work less strenuous and less exhausting, women stop menstruating and come into the period of change of life later than 10-15 years ago; it is now common to hear in the USA and other more affluent societies that a woman still menstruates at the age of 50. Therefore, though rare in practice, theoretically it is possible for a woman who menstruates at the age of 50 to get pregnant. And, as a matter of fact, I knew a case in my practice when a woman of 50 delivered a healthy baby. Pregnancy in women of 45 and more is nowadays quite common.

If we take these changes into consideration, we shall understand that, on the one hand, a woman of 45 or 50 is, contrary to her mother, still young at that age and not old, but only middle-aged; and, on the other hand, the problem of change of life with its after-effects becomes a problem of old age.

Well-known is the complaint of flushes after the cessation of menstruation. Women used to have them between 45 and 50; it takes about 5 years for getting a new hormonal balance in the body, which has to get used to the fact that the ovaries have stopped working and producing female hormones. The female body gets a different type of metabolism, and the lack of those hormones causes a complete change in the function of most glands and even of the heart and blood circulation, and also of the nervous system. Therefore, the name—change of life—is a very correct one; from the medical point of view, it is really a change from the former life.

Just the same, the actual change of life does not belong to old age, if we accept the definition that old age begins at 65, the time of retirement and Medicare. Even if the flushes continue occasionally into the sixties, it is not common, and there is some special reason if the flushes are still bothering a woman at the age of 65 or more. However, we have also a so-called postmenopausal syndrome—that is, signs and symptoms seen in a woman after she finished with the menopause and believes that she would now be free from female troubles. Unfortunately, it is not the case. It is true that she might not have flushes any more; she does not have to worry about menstruation or pregnancy. But then new complaints appear which are connected with her sex.

As mentioned in previous chapters, some diseases occur in women mostly after change of life. Such is diabetes or a coronary disease. As explained, diabetes occurs in elderly women more frequently, primarily due to change of *way* of life—that is, more leisure and more food. The hormonal change hardly plays any role in the development of diabetes in older women, because we see the same occurring in older men. However, there is hardly any doubt that the female hormones protect a woman to a great extent against heart attacks and coronary disease. While the women are in childbearing age, the proportion between men and women suffering from coronary disease is 10 to 1. After the menopause the proportion is 1 to 1. We also mentioned the influence of female hormones on osteoporosis—the disease of the bones, with their brittle condition and diminution of calcium content. Of course, some men also have osteoporosis, but the cases are rare and due to some special reasons.

The main female problem after the menopause is the aging of the woman's sexual organs. To those belong not only the so-called "private parts," but the whole feminine appearance: the condition of the breasts, the distribution of the fat layers, the appearance of the skin and the condition of the hair. All this together makes a woman externally a woman.

Let us start with the sexual organs proper. There is no doubt that cancer of the womb, and especially of the cervix—which is the mouth or the part of the womb protruding in the vagina, and can be even felt with a finger—is quite frequent in elderly women. Therefore, such a woman should have a regular check-up, at least once yearly. To this gyneocological examination belongs a "Pap" smear, which means a slide smear from the cervix of the womb—called "Pap" because it was first introduced by Dr. George Papanicolaou. It shows under the microscope two things: first, whether there are malignant cells on the smear which would confirm the suspicion of a cervix cancer; in such a case, because of early detection, most cases of women with a cancer of the womb can be saved by an operation and removal of the womb. Secondly, by the same slide smear it is possible to evaluate the production of female hormone and to decide whether any treatment for hormonal deficiency is needed. A "Pap" smear is nowadays considered as a routine examination by a gynecologist and by most general practitioners for all elderly women, or any women who show some female disorders.

The benign tumor of the womb, the so-called fibroid or myoma, is a tumor of the muscles of the womb. It is not a cancer and does not change into cancer; it grows slowly. It is very common among women, almost as common as enlargement of the prostate in men. However, it is not harmless, because it frequently becomes very large and presses upon the surrounding organs. If it is near the lining of the womb—it causes bleeding.

Either menstruation (if a woman still menstruates) becomes very heavy, profuse and continues longer than a normal menstruation should, or bleeding occurs out of time: and occasionally it becomes a real hemorrhage. Also, it presses upon the bladder and causes a frequency of urination, not because of an inflammation of the bladder but due to mechanical pressure. For all these reasons an operation, called a hysterectomy, is frequently performed.

Who should or should not have such an operation? If the fibroid tumor is small, if it does not cause bleeding or any other complaints, it should and can be left alone. As said, it is not malignant and cannot harm otherwise. If it is very large and causes bleeding and/or pressure symptoms, it has to be removed. In most cases, such an operation is done at the age of change of life or later. Therefore, the loss of the womb at an age when childbearing is out of question is not important. Apart from not having children, the woman remains a woman for all practical purposes; and I would like to emphasize that, from the point of view of sex, there is no change whatsoever. In older age, the surgeon often performs an operation which is called total hysterectomy, which means that not only the womb but also the ovaries are removed. Usually, even if they are normal, it is done as a precaution, in order to avoid a possible second operation for ovarial tumors which also occasionally develop; because the ovaries not infrequently grow tumors which, in many cases, are malignant. Therefore, in elderly women a total hysterectomy, when a fibroid has to be removed, is advisable.

There is no way to treat a fibroid tumor by medical means. It happens just in older women that a fibroid stops growing and does not cause complaints. As said, in such a case no operation, even if the existence of a fibroid is known, is necessary.

Next we come to the vagina, which undergoes changes in old age.

Because of lack of female hormones, there occurs a drying, irritating condition of the vagina, and especially of the outer part of it, called the vulva. The result is itching and, because of the dryness, difficulty in sexual intercourse; it is what is called senile vaginitis. Female hormones can be given in such a condition, and not necessarily as tablets or injections. An ointment containing female hormones is available. It has a double effect: as an ointment it lubricates the vagina and eases the intercourse; the female hormones of that ointment give just as much hormone as needed for the vaginal condition, without causing the side reactions which are possible in the use of tablets or injections.

The itch can also be due to diabetes; as a matter of fact, in elderly women sometimes the first sign of diabetes is the itch in the "private parts," which is very embarrassing. With diabetes, and occasionally without it, we see fungus on the lining of the vagina, which causes irritation and itch. All these diseases are comparatively easy to cure by local treatment with ointments, chemical paints, douches and suppositories. But these ailments have to be treated, even if they are harmless, because the irritation, the itch and the scratching cause wounds which can easily be infected, and then, of course, need treatment like any other infection.

The senile vagina gets another trouble, too—namely, what is called rectocele and cystocele. It is a lowering of the suspension of the vagina by elastic fibers. The elasticity in old age is lost to a great extent, and either the upper part of the lining of the vagina is lowered and folded, and then it is called cystocele because it is connected with the bladder; or the back part is lowered and folded towards the rectum, and therefore it is called rectocele. In severe cases the whole vagina is pushed down and forwards so that its lining is protruding to the outside; it can even come out completely, so that instead of an opening the vagina presents a bulge, just like a glove which is turned upside down.

There are two ways to deal with such a condition of old age: either an operation, by which the surgeon fixes the vagina tight with stitches so that it cannot protrude or fold; or a doctor inserts a rubber ring which holds the vagina in natural position. Of course, the second way is possible only in mild and new cases; if this condition has gone too far, it cannot be repaired by a ring. It is similar to a hernia in the groin. In some cases a truss holds the hernia back; in more advanced cases the protruding part of the hernia cannot be pushed back by a truss, and such a patient has to undergo an operation.

Here I would like to say a few words about treatment with female hormones. There are many women who are afraid of being treated with female hormones because the hormones are supposed to cause a cancer. The answer is that, if there is a history of cancer in the family of a female patient or any inkling that the patient might have a cancer somewhere in her body, treatment with female hormones is out of the question. The hormones by themselves do not produce a cancer, but if there are malignant cells in the body, the addition of female hormones can promote the development of cancer. Pre-cancerlike conditions may be stimulated by the hormones to convert into malignancy.

On the other hand, if the hormones are given under supervision of a doctor, they can greatly help in some conditions. Small doses of the estrogen female hormone can help to cut down the frequency of hot flushes or even abolish them completely. There is no reason why a woman who suffers much from menopause (it is only a small minority) should continue suffering, if she can be helped by hormonal treatment. Osteoporosis is not cured by hormones; you need calicum, vitamins, etc. in addition. But again, female hormones in small doses help. And as mentioned before, the senile vagina can be restored to normal by a hormonal ointment. Then, why not give the hormones? It is just the same as refusing penicillin for an infection because some people are allergic to it. You just have to discriminate and to see which cases should be treated with female hormones and which not.

Here we come to the other feminine characteristics and in which way they change by old age.

One female characteristic is the distribution of fat in the body. It causes the formation of the well-known, described, and praised feminine curves. If a woman does not have the curves, she becomes angular and her body resembles that of a man. The curves are formed by the breasts, by the abdomen, by the hips and by the thighs. With aging, these curves and the distribution of the underlying fat change. The breasts are sagging, and the reason is that the fat content of the breasts diminishes without diminution of the glandular part—that is of the milk ducts. There is also a loss of the elasticity which supports the keeping of the breasts in position. The change of life and the consequent aging adds to the fat structure of the female body. Women generally tend to gain weight when the ovaries stop working. The weight gain in a woman is primarily in the lower abdomen, in the buttocks and hips, and in the thighs. But, while in a young woman this distribution of fat is just hinted at and gives her a gracious feminine look, in the elderly one it is exaggerated and you see a protruding "stomach," big hips, large buttocks and thighs, which are all of them out of proportion to the rest of the body. Even if a woman is not exactly fat, these characteristics of the post-menopausal age are visible to a discerning eye.

There is no remedy to these ravages of age to female beauty. It can be prevented from exaggeration by certain diets, by exercise, by massage, but it cannot be avoided. There are, of course, exceptions, and occasionally you see a beautiful old woman; but it remains an exception, and the beauty of an elderly woman is usually her charm, her pleasant character, which emanates through her eyes, her smile and behavior, which show the characteristics of her soul. In such a case the femininity and the maternity are interwoven, and such a woman can attract even a young man who seeks in a woman a mate and a substitute for a mother.

Again, there are cases when the curves are not exaggerated. The fat content in those places is not increased but, on the contrary, diminishes. The loss of fat makes an elderly woman angular, less feminine and older. Even without a reducing diet it happens by the malfunction of glands which can work in one direction or another.

This brings us to the two other secondary female characteristics, namely, skin and hair. They have been well-known and praised by poets since ancient times as a part of the beauty of the female body. But the skin has elastic fibers which keep the skin stretched over the muscle. The skin glands lubricate the skin (sometimes too much in teenagers, and brings them in despair when this over-lubrication causes a shiny and pimply skin) and gives it a smooth appearance, pleasant to touch by a male hand. It becomes an erogenous zone, that is, a source of male lust. The hair is also usually lustrous. It grows much more in a woman, but not on places where the hair becomes a male characteristic, such as a beard and/or a moustache.

The aging process changes all that. The glands dry up and the lubrication of the skin is diminished, if it does not disappear completely. The elasticity is gone. The hair is brittle and becomes gray, by losing its pigment, and also falls out. While a woman hardly ever gets bald, her hair is, however, thinning and falls out. It still grows, but wherever it falls out, it does not come back. It is interesting to note that the falling out and thinning of hair have become more pronounced in the last ten years, though we eat better, take more vitamins, etc. In one of my conversations with a leading dermatologist, he discussed this problem and phenomenon. His opinion was that the beauty parlor's hair teasing and dyeing is responsible, at least to a greater part; and the cosmetics used for improving of the skin are not good to its appearance, either. It may be that it applies to some cases. And if a woman loses her hair, "teasing" and dyeing it does not help, either; and some cosmetics do cause allergic reactions in some women. But, considering that women have used cosmetics and have done all kinds of things to their hair for thousands of years, we cannot blame just the fashions of today for the changes in the skin and hair of the women. Rather, as far as I can judge, the loss of hair is due to the nervous tension in which we live; and, in combination with personal worries and troubles, it causes in susceptible cases the loss of hair. The graying of the hair was always attributed to nervousness and troubles, as in the famous stories of people who got gray overnight due to a sudden shock. The stories were never scientifically confirmed, and in any case it does not apply to the graying of the hair in aging people. It is just plainly a loss of pigmentation, a natural bleaching due to insufficient production of pigment by the glands, which become deficient in old age.

So, we have to accept the changes of the appearance of skin and hair in elderly women as a sign of aging. Of course, men are not different in this respect. But, somehow, the baldness and the gray hair, the lack of elasticity of the skin, are accepted—not as a wonderful thing; but somehow it does not greatly diminish the value of a man as a man. In some cases, as with a politician, a big mane of white hair is considered a sign of distinction, and baldness as not a great handicap in life (even regarding success with women)—apart from actors and entertainers who have to use artificial hair-pieces to cover their bald heads.

It is different with women. First of all, they do not accept old age as such. They want to stay young, attractive and unchanged. At the bottom of their heart, they believe that they are as attractive as they were as younger women. On the other hand, in their home, when they look at the mirror they cannot deny the ravages of age, the changes of the body, of the breasts, of the skin, of the hair. They notice the blemishes of the skin, the sagging of the breasts, the thinning and/or the graying of the hair. They also notice the sprouting of a moustache, the growth of some hair on the chin—masculine characteristics, which appear not so rarely after cessation of menstruation and loss of production of female hormones. And they get panicky. They look for remedies, just as their ancestral grandmothers tried for thousands of years. They are the prey of quacks, of television and radio and newspapers, of advertisements which promise them a restoration of their youthful appearance, if they will only use this or that cosmetic—and several of them for each defect in their appearance. And so they use day creams and night creams, baths, dyes for the hair, teasing and changes of the coiffure, to make themselves attractive.

From the medical point of view there is no objection to all this beautifying of the female body, as long as all these procedures are not harmful. Here, we have to emphasize that female hormones have no place in beauty preparations. They will not change the loss of the elasticity of the the skin and remove blemishes, or restore the appearance of the breasts, or let the hair grow again. On the other hand, the addition of female hormones for that purpose can be harmful, because they are used without a control and can be taken in an overdose and without discrimination, in some cases contributing to cancer development.

The best way to preserve the female appearance in old age is cleanliness in a meticulous way, neat clothing, and work. Not overwork, but just a continuation of household chores, cooking, washing, mopping, sewing, washing of clothing and so on. Also maintaining interest in daily life, reading and writing, and helping family members and others. In other words, though one has to slow down and to take it easy in old age, that does not mean that life stops with old age and retirement, and that one has only to sit and wait for death. In respect of feminine appearance, activity is a very important contribution to good looks and maintenance of good health. It is not the addition of cosmetics which improves good looks, but the resolution not to give in to old age and to continue life and activities as before, though at a slower rate. In this way old age comes later, and a woman stays younger for a longer period of time.

A few more words about the modern ways to improve good looks, to preserve youth; in other words, to fake youthfulness. Wrinkles which come with aging do not go away. They can be removed surgically by plastic operations which smooth out the skin but give a rather mask-like appearance. There is no guarantee that the result of such an operation will last forever. The same applies to removal of pouches under the eyes. For a while, it helps; but the skin has lost its elasticity, and all the big expense and torturing oneself for plastic operations may be in vain. New wrinkles can appear, new pouches can form. And what about the neck, with its aging skin and wrinkles? How far can one go, even a rich woman, with the plastic operations?

Next come the breasts. Sometimes they are too small, not too well-developed. The plastic surgeon can put some artificial material under the skin of the breasts and let them appear bigger, more feminine. Some years ago, when we did not yet have the cult of the big breast, women underwent operations to diminish the size of the breasts. I still see sometimes the fine scars from such cosmetic operations. It is also not a coincidence that wigs are now in fashion. Fashion usually comes with some specific need; the loss of hair in women is new and more frequent than ever. The new fashion of wigs is very convenient. It covers up for the lack of hair, which was always an adored part of female appearance. It is interesting to observe that the teenagers' fashion moves also towards longer hair, not only in boys but also in girls—who wear it long and longer, though not so coiffured as it was done at the time when their mothers were teenagers and had long pigtails. To the same category belongs the teasing of the hair in a high hairdo which fakes a lot of hair with a minimum of hair on hand.

Whatever methods are used by women to improve their appearance, to conceal their real age to look young, is perfectly all right from the medical point of view as long as it does not harm and does not look ridiculous. One has also to remember that in our times there are still many elderly women who have to work in order to make a living. They have to appear younger, otherwise they would not be hired, and if their age is discovered, they would be fired. Their dyeing of the hair, their cosmetic endeavor to conceal their chronological age, is perfectly legitimate. But even a housewife who wants to appear younger if only in her own or her husband's eyes is right in applying feminine wiles to look younger. It has the value of a psychological tonic, it gives a moral satisfaction to a woman. From these points of view, in moderation, all this has our medical blessing.

CHAPTER XXI

OLD AGE AND OBESITY

Obesity as such is a difficult problem in all age groups. In old age it becomes a problem full of pitfalls, a controversial issue which has many aspects; and each of these constitutes a problem by itself.

The fact is that Americans in general are obese, and the same applies to most affluent societies all over the world. Obesity is also not specifically a problem of old age; there is a prevalence of obesity in both sexes and in every age. However, while in younger people overweight is primarily a psychological, sociological and cosmetic problem and only rarely has an influence on health, in old age it is first of all a health problem, and adds to the several troubles which surround the aging persons.

The first question in regard to obesity is: who is obese? Even this question cannot be answered simply; because the standards accepted for a normal weight at a given height and age vary much and change constantly. The reason why they change is the standard accepted by statisticians, mainly of life-insurance companies which try to find a common denominator for acceptance of risks: good risks, moderate risks and poor risks. Basically, it is considered that a lean person is a better risk and has a greater life expectancy that a fat person.

Generally speaking, this assumption may be correct, but it does not apply to all cases. Putting aside the consideration of life expectancy, one can come to a common denominator in regard to obesity in declaring that an obese person is a person whose weight is above the average in a given society and in a given country. In the U.S.A. in particular, this average is higher than among semi-starved populations of the so-called backward or underdeveloped countries. In plain English it means that, in poor countries, where the people have no money to buy food, they tend to be lean and obesity is a sign of affluence, or riches —of course with some exceptions, such as people with glandular trouble, or people who like to eat and, while they have no money for anything else, they contrive to find ways and means to satisfy their appetite, so to say, by hook or crook.

In the U.S.A. nobody starves, though we have plenty of poor people. The reason is that, even on welfare support, the money given is calculated to give a welfare client sufficient money to buy modest but sufficient food to maintain a balanced diet with an amount of calories in the food to keep the welfare recipient in good health. And people who work may spend a great part of their salary or wages on food, and they are evidently well-nourished.

Thus, we can accept the premise that the Americans are well-fed and in most cases overfed, especially compared with other nationalities who, with less calories intake, manage to keep good health standards.

We see people who eat well and remain lean. We see—occasionally only—people who eat very little and are obese. Those two categories are exceptions and belong medically to so-called pathological cases; there is something wrong with their body organs.

For the average person it can be said: if one eats well, one gains on weight. If one has no appetite, for whatever reason it may be, one is bound to lose weight. I know, and I hear it daily in my work as a doctor: "Maybe I am obese, maybe I gain weight, because my glands do not function well, my metabolism is out of order." Just the same, one hears that the obese person hardly eats anything, has only one or two meals daily. But if you go deeply into the matter and investigate, with plenty of time to spare, the eating habits of the person in question, you will find that the obese person really eats once or twice daily; but either compensates for the food deprivation by taking too many calories at one meal, or just nibbles on chocolate, candy, cookies, and cake between meals, or drinks plenty of liquid such as orange juice which contains a lot of sugar. The result is the same or worse than having 3 straight meals, because this nibbling or drinking is not considered as a meal, and therefore "does not count." In short, the situation is simple: you eat more than you need, and you gain weight; you eat less than you need, and you lose weight; you eat just as much as you need, and your weight remains stationary.

Assuming a person is obese or overweight according to all medical and statistical standards, in which way does it hurt health and life? There we go back to the question of obesity, according to age. If not excessive or overweight in younger persons, if they do not suffer from heart diseases or high blood pressure, it is primarily a cosmetic problem of appearance, and a psychological problem of ridicule, of insecurity, of unhappiness, of loss of attraction by the opposite sex, and so on. In old age, when the question of looks, of attraction, of appearance becomes secondary (though it does not disappear—older people also want to look nice and attractive), the obesity problem has to be discussed from the point of view of health, sickness and span of life.

On the whole, we have in the U.S.A. more older obese persons than younger ones. And there is a reason for it as we shall explain in a moment. Let us first find out how obesity originates. One eats more than he or she needs for the maintenance of health. The food is burned by the body and absorbed. If one eats too much of it, it is being deposited as a fat layer. Some foods are better burned and used for energy. To that category belongs protein, in the first place: protein means meat, fish, cheese, part of the milk, egg-white. Vegetables, if they do not contain starch or only very little, are also burned well or eliminated with the bowel movement. Fat is also not immediately deposited as a fat layer, unless it is consumed in large quantities. The main culprit in formation of fat layers and obesity is the third main ingredient of our food, namely starch. And starch means sugar, to which it is converted in the chemical factory of our body; so we have to count sugar and all food containing sugar, and all starches, such as flour, cereals, potatoes, macaroni, spaghetti, noodles, rice, and all food made from flour, which means bread, cake, cookies, crackers and so on, and so on. Mind you, we need starch and sugar for our health, but much, much less than an average person eats. On the average the American daily menu consists of a fruit juice, of cereals, of toast, of potatoes or rice or spaghetti, and of sandwiches—which means again bread, regardless of the inside contents of the sandwich. And what about doughnuts, cake, ice cream made with sugar, and last but not least fruit, such as oranges or grapefruit or grapes or bananas or apples or pears or peaches, of which every one contains plenty of sugar?

All this means a large amount of starch or sugar calories which, if in excessive quantities, are deposited in the body and contribute to obesity.

In old age, there is, generally speaking, more leisure and less activity. That means that an elderly person requires less calories than in younger age. However, because of abundance of time and little to do, there is a great temptation to eat more, and more frequently. The result is that an elderly person eats not less but more than he or she needs for maintenance of good health—and slowly but surely, even if he or she was lean in younger age, becomes obese, and has overweight.

The overweight causes a lot of trouble. The heavy weight of the body makes walking difficult, and so there is even less exercise than before; if the legs are not too bulky, the obese person is top-heavy; his weight has to be supported by the legs. The body is like a house built on slender pillars. The pillars—the legs—are standing on the knees, which give in in their structure, the joints become arthritic. The heart has to pump a lot of blood to sustain the blood circulation in the gross structure of the obese body; the overworked heart muscle becomes flabby, the heart enlarges, and its overwork causes shortness of breath. The blood circulation is also disturbed; in the legs develop varicose veins because of stagnation and slow motion of the blood in the veins of the legs. The arteries, because of too much fat circulating in the blood, become clogged, narrowed in their width, and with calcium mineral become hardened; and the arterial tubes cannot bring enough blood and oxygen to whatever organ needs them most. An operation, if urgently needed in the belly, becomes more difficult because the surgeon has first to cut through layers of fat before he reaches the diseased internal organ. Correspondingly, the healing is protracted and slow, and frequently complications occur. Because of all the disadvantages, a surgeon is very reluctant to operate on obese persons, and, whenever feasible, advises the patient to postpose the operation, and in the meantime to try to reduce.

If there is a tendency to diabetes, it hits sooner an obese than a thin person. Why, if the same inheritance factors exist, a lean person should escape and the fat one gets diabetes, we don't know, but it is a well-known fact. The fat person has a tendency to respiratory diseases (not to TB), and especially to pneumonia, probably for two reasons, first, there is a certain type who gets pneumonias and has a tendency to obesity. It is called the pyknic type. Usually such people have a big frame, are broadshouldered, and have a wide chest. Secondly, the obesity causes shortness of breath, not only by the performance of the heart but also because the breathing is shallow; the fat person does not inhale or exhale properly, with the result that the lungs are not sufficiently ventilated, the breathing capacity is diminished, and that in turn causes new respiratory troubles.

The final verdict in regard to this long history of the condition called obesity is not a good one. In principle, it shortens life and causes sickness and at least disability, especially in the meaning of not being able to do many things which a person should be able to do regardless of age. However, I said in principle, which means theoretically, it is so. Practically, obesity does not always have such a gloomy prediction and course. There are plenty of fat people whom their obesity does not disturb at all and who are not disabled and not sick either. It is a question of adjustment, of making the best of it and of trying to lead a normal life even with the handicap of obesity. How, we shall see in a moment.

What can be done about overweight, about obesity? And in our case, old-age obesity?

The treatment of old-age obesity differs from that in

younger people. First of all, if reducing is necessary, it cannot be done by starvation, pills and injection. It is wrong for young people but it is deleterious, and can lead to disaster in old age—to start with, sudden loss of weight has a bad effect on the skin, as described in previous chapters. It can lead to a dropped kidney (the kidney is upheld by a fat capsule; if this capsule disappears, the kidney goes down in the belly with resulting kinking of the ureter—the tube which leads from the kidney to the bladder—and urinary trouble); the other organs also are lowered and occupy a wrong, unnatural position, exercising pressure on the organs from which they should be separated, and which they now touch and disturb in their function. Secondly, a sudden loss of weight causes a disturbance of blood circulation, a sometimes not-desired lowering of the blood pressure. Thirdly, it causes a maladjustment of the metabolism, of the function of the glands.

If such a sudden loss of weight is additionally achieved with the help of reducing pills, which contain an extract of the thyroid gland and amphetamines, and usually also laxatives, a real revolution occurs in the body. The normal bowel movement is pushed into a frantic activity by the laxatives. The thyroid extract accelerates the function of that gland, causing fast heart-beating and a nervous irritation. The amphetamines, while for a while diminishing the appetite and craving for food, overexcite, overstimulate, and cause an elevated blood pressure and insomnia, or at least a disturbance of sleep. The injections are usually diuretics, that is, they push the kidneys to a stronger action with a longer elimination of the urine from the body, thus giving the illusion of loss of weight by a temporary loss of fluid from the body—and sometimes causing dehydration, which means excessive fluid loss and excessive dryness.

All this should not be done in old-age obesity. The organism of an elderly person is not able to adjust itself promptly to new conditions of metabolism, of the functioning of the circulation and of the nerves. The whole complex mechanism is slowed down. The elasticity is lost or greatly diminished, and whatever adjustment is necessary has to be done gradually in order not to upset a precarious balance. Therefore, radical changes in diet and in medication are out of the question. Great losses of weight are neither desirable nor advisable. The problem of obesity has to be approached from a different angle. First, one has to ask himself: has the elderly person always been obese, or did that happen only in recent years? Secondly, how much damage does the obesity do to the organs? How do they function in this old-age organism? Are there noticeable changes due to the obesity or to old age? And thirdly, what can we expect from a weight reduction?

If the answer to the first question is that the elderly person has always been obese—and under always we mean many, many years, since middle age or even as a youngster—then the situation regarding reduction of weight is almost hopeless. In even a most radical reducing regimen you can achieve weight loss which will promptly return to normal as soon as the regimen is slackened. In such cases, if the weight does not go steadily up, but the overweight is *always the same,* it is better to leave the obese person alone—not to try to impose on him or her any restrictions which would make the patient unhappy and would lead nowhere.

The second question, how much damage the obesity does to the organs, is the most important one. We have to distinguish between damage observed and found as due to old-age changes, and between changes which are definitely due to obesity or worsened by obesity. If the damage is due to old age, the problem of obesity is secondary and less important. If the fat layer, on the other hand, threatens the well-being, the health and the life of a person, something has to be done about that. With that is connected the answer to the third question, namely, what can be expected from a weight reduction?

There are four major diseases of old age in which obesity can cause a worsening of the condition. There are: an arteriosclerotic heart and high blood pressure, bronchiectasis and emphysema of the lungs, osteoarthritis, especially of the knees, and peripheral arteries disease of the legs. None of these old-age diseases is due to obesity; but all of them get worse, if and when an elderly person is or gets obese. The reason is mainly mechanical. A heavy body has to be supplied with blood and oxygen by the heart. The heart in such a body simply has more work to do, undergoes more exertion, and becomes weak and flabby, with resulting more shortness of breath; and this condition can result in heart failure. Loss of weight does not change the arteriosclerotic condition, but it lessens the burden, the load which the heart has to carry. The blood pressure can be high in lean persons too; but if a person inclines to high blood pressure, sometimes considerably, a gain of weight increases the blood pressure.

Bronchiectasis, which means widening and formation of pouches in the lowest part of the bronchial tubes, and emphysema, which means overexpansion of the lungs, are very common in old age. And again, overweight does not change them but makes walking and breathing more difficult; especially in emphysema, where the shortness of breath is a common feature —and it is easier to breathe when one has less weight. By the way, the shortness of breath in emphysema is different from the shortness of breath of a heart patient and has to be treated in a different way.

The people who suffer from osteoarthritis of the knees have difficulties in walking and going *down* stairs because of the joints of the knees. But, again, apart from the origin of that arthritis which is often attributed to obesity, an overload of weight on the knees makes walking more difficult. And the same applies to the hardening of the arteries in the legs, which is due to arteriosclerotic changes and causes pain in the legs on walking. Here the load of overweight is an additional mechanical difficulty.

I would like to stress that none of the mentioned diseases disappears after reducing, and even after a most drastic weight loss. They become only a little less severe; the symptoms are less pronounced; the patient feels better. He or she has less complaints, even if, objectively, the diagnosis remains the same.

The next question—What can we expect from a weight reduction?—is mainly answered by the relative help which is given to old-age diseases by the weight loss. However, to lose weight is not too difficult: but to *keep* the weight loss indefinitely, not to regain the former poundage, is extremely difficult. Here we go back to the problem: is the weight loss as such desirable? We saw already in what cases it is desirable, and we should expect that an elderly person will in such cases do his or her best to obtain an appreciable (from the medical point of view) loss of weight. In all other cases, when the weight of a person is not a medical problem, it is better to leave such a person alone; just to accept that he or she is obese, as long as the overweight is not excessive.

The main reason for such an attitude is the fact that the fight against obesity should have started long, long ago, namely, in childhood. An obese child will become an obese adolescent, and the obese adolescent will continue to be an obese adult until he or she will be an obese elderly person. It is not a question of metabolism (though very occasionally it is the case), and not even of heredity, but mainly of habits. Obese parents who love to eat will imbue the habit of eating well and plenty in their children. They will worry if the children happen to to be poor eaters, and they will try their best to induce their children to eat well. In the ethnic minorities of the U.S.A., the Jews and the Italians are the greatest culprits in this respect; but you can find this attitude towards food among all ethnic groups, races or origins.

In respect to obesity or leanness there are only two groups of people: those who love to eat and accordingly become obese, and those who consider eating as something which you have to endure, to do in order to stay well and healthy. This second group will keep their weight standard. They might not be thin but they never become obese.

Obesity was treated in all kinds of ways, starting with complete starvation, then with all kinds of diets to suit every taste —and the result was always the same. One can lose weight by any of the diets, but as soon as the person in question gives up the diet or only eats more than prescribed, the weight comes back with a vengeance. So maybe we should say, as Dr. Astwood wrote 1962 in his article "The Heritage of Corpulence," "At present obesity is incurable."

However, we don't have to be so pessimistic; it is possible to lose weight, and the obesity can be conquered—but provided, we don't ask too much and take into account human nature. For old age, the standard of weight loss has to be: one and, tops, two pounds per week. Of course, a patient who has a good sense of humor told me that at such continuous loss, one would still lose 52 or 104 lbs. in a year. Theoretically, she was right. But practically, the trouble with any loss of weight is that nobody can keep on a certain diet permanently. Whatever you eat becomes, if continuously eaten, monotonous and therefore boring; and one therefore tends to go on a binge, and to give up the best intentions in the world. In addition, there are too many temptations, especially if one loves to eat. Therefore, a continuous loss of weight week after week is an illusion and never occurs, unless there is an underlying serious disease.

The loss of one or two pounds per week in an elderly person who needs reducing is practically easy to achieve, either by general reduction of food intake by 10-15%, or by a more drastic reduction of intake of starches, which, as we have shown, have the tendency to deposit themselves in the body. And in elderly people, especially of the female sex, the favorite spots of deposit are the thighs, the belly, the hips and the buttocks—just the parts of the body where a fat layer is the least desirable. In any way of weight reduction, if and when the desired weight is achieved, one can occasionally commit some dietary sins; I allow my patients who are even on a strict diet, to have one meal per week whatever they want. It does not change the general pattern of weight loss, and on the other hand it gives the patient a psychological boost that once in a while he or she can indulge and does not have to think about calories, weight or have a guilt complex of not having followed doctor's orders.

In general, one has to confess that the fight against obesity is a losing battle—unless medical science comes up with some invention as to how good-tasting food, rich in calories and fattening, can be eaten with delight and pleasure and leave the body without harming it, and without being deposited but eliminated in a harmless way. Substitutes for good food, of which we have a myriad, just don't taste. In the meantime, until such an invention appears, it is a tough fight against obesity.

The battle against obesity is not completely hopeless. An observation was made that, regardless of diet, people who are physically active do not gain weight as easily as inactive persons. As said before, one reason for old age overweight is the tendency to less physical activity and more eating. Now, not every activity is good for the elderly and aged. One has to consider the inherent wear and tear of the body, with lack or lessening of elasticity and of the speed of reflex-action. Therefore, activities which may be beneficial have to be restricted in old age. As a matter of fact, except for special cases, one can generally recommend only a few physical activities, and these are: (1) walking, (2) swimming, (3) bicycling *(not motorcycling)*, (4) golfing. Golfing is actually only a modified walking and has to be considered from this angle, not as a sport but as a physical activity which is harmless and beneficial to the requirements of old age. Walking is the easiest and most important physical activity. It keeps, like all the other four above-mentioned exercises, the circulation going and the muscles active. One has to learn to walk, especially in the USA, whree there is a temptation to use the car for any reason whatsoever, even if the goal is within walking distance. Going uphill is not for everybody, because it is much more exertion, but going on an even level and at a steady, easy pace is a wonderful exercise which does not cost anything, gives one a fresh aspect and outlook on things and people, and keeps one in fresh air, with more oxygen (even with the air pollution) than at home.

I have here to mention that all the walking at the office by the man, and all the walking from the living quarters to the kitchen by the housewife, are *not* a substitute for really brisk, continuous walking. The miles done at home do not count, because the walk from room to room is short and interrupted by standing or sitting. I do not mind window-shopping or walking in the street, but I do mind shopping as such. Like walking at home, it does not count. One can start by walking ¼ or ½ a mile, and slowly increase the daily walk to 4 miles daily.

Bicycling is outmoded in the USA; it is still very much alive in Europe, and especially in Holland. The millions of bicycles in Europe are also giving way to the car, as in America, with the resulting increase of coronary diseases, peripheral arteries trouble and all the other signs of hardening of arteries.

Swimming for a good swimmer, if done daily and not to excess, is just as healthy for elderly people as for youngsters. But of all four physical activities which I recommend for elderly persons, walking has the priority. It can be done everywhere; you don't need any contraption for it. It hardly depends on the weather (apart from a pouring rain, it can be done in any weather), is cheap and healthy. A daily walk of 3–4 miles keeps you alive and healthy, longer, and reduces, as a by-product, the pot-belly. However, one has to point out that any of the above activities as such are *no substitute* for a moderate way of eating. Regarding calories, the walk as a reducing device is hardly worth mentioning; it is worth, calory-wise, only a few calories. But, combined with moderate reduction of food intake, it will counteract the regaining of weight, should one have the tendency to do so.

The obesity of elderly people is a problem. But with use of common sense, and with some help as indicated, it can be checked before it becomes deleterious to health in old age.

CHAPTER XXII

LACK OF APPETITE IN OLD AGE

While obesity is a serious problem in old age, loss of weight due to lack of appetite is a minor problem. The reason is that there are much fewer elderly persons who complain of lack of appetite and therefore of loss of weight than obese aged, and that the solution of this problem is comparatively easy.

We have first to eliminate lack of appetite in persons who used to eat well and then suddenly lost their appetite and started losing weight. In such a case, the first suspicion is a serious underlying disease, and in most cases it means—cancer. Therefore, one has to undergo tests for cancer, especially of the stomach and of the bowels, which cause the sudden or progressive loss of appetite. If a cancer is out of question, the second possibility is an underlying other serious disease, such as a disease of the blood, anemia and so on. If there is a clean bill of health, one has to look for other reasons, which are partly organic but mainly psychological or even mental.

An organic reason may be lack of teeth and no artificial teeth—bridges or dentures. A person without teeth cannot chew and is therefore limited in his or her choice of food. Soft food which can be eaten without chewing is frequently tasteless, or not appealing and not provoking a desire to eat, even if spices and salt are added. One has also to remember that many elderly people are not supposed to eat spices or salt. So that food in such a case is missed. Another organic reason is, sometimes, lack of gastric-acid juice in the stomach. Though ulcers with too much acid occur in old age, you see more often lack of acidity in the stomach in that age. It is not always a sign of disease; it is just that the glands which produce gastric (stomach) juice do not function well any more, just as other glands function poorly in old age. Lack of juice production in the stomach causes, sometimes, lack of appetite; the stomach just does not respond to the view of the food. In the famous experiment of Pavlov the scientist could see how the stomach juices of the dog responded to the view of the presented food, how they increased in quality and quantity. The same happens in a normal human being but it does not have to be the case in older people with lack of stomach juice. In this way, also, lack of appetite develops.

The other possibilities lie within the sociological aspect of the life of an elderly person. One can find that the lack of appetite frequently occurs in lonely people. A widow or widower, or an old spinster or an old bachelor, living all by him- or herself. It is hardly worthwhile to cook for one person; there is no incentive to cook elaborate food. Therefore, one buys canned food which is easy and quick to prepare. The food in this way prepared is monotonous, and it is just a question of eating it as an obligation to be fed in order not to starve without any pleasure, which is and should be connected with the process of eating. Such a person may be well-nourished and frequently is by eating bread, ready-made cereals, cookies or cake or canned meat—all foods ready-made, without having to go through a long process of cooking.

We see also that the lack of incentives can cause a lack of appetite in hospitals, nursing homes and other places where there is a mass-production of food for many people. Not only is the food not individually prepared to the taste of the eater, but being served every meal is not conducive to appetite-development. This applies especially to women, who are often proud of their skill of cooking. Take it away from them and they will lose their appetite. The same woman who eats very little if and when she eats all by herself, will eat well and with appetite if she has one or more guests for whom she has to prepare a meal. On the other hand, a lonely person who goes to a restaurant for an occasional meal will eat slowly and with good appetite, not leaving a crumb, because the meal is a feast, eaten in a different atmosphere surrounded by other people;

while at home it is boring and monotonous. One has also to remember that many of the old people have very restricted resources. They have to calculate how much money they can spend on food, and the bought food items frequently do not correspond to what they would like to buy to eat, because they cannot afford it. The result is that they buy and eat in order not to starve, but there is no question of being happy about the forthcoming meal. One does not look forward to it and accordingly has no appetite.

Some old people lose their appetite and start losing weight if they suffer from a senile depression; and this depression does not have to come in very advanced age. It frequently comes in women after menopause; but most often in the sixties. Such persons have no appetite whatsoever. And if the depression, as often is the case, lasts several months, if not years, they lose a lot of weight, causing a suspicion of an underlying malignancy which is not the case. But the lack of appetite due to depression belongs already to psychiatric problems of old age, and about that we shall talk later.

Generally speaking, lack of appetite in old age, apart from serious diseases which can occur in any age, is a symptom or at the best an ailment without serious consequences. Such people are often lean and have a good figure. They are rarely undernourished. But if they are, this is easy to correct, much easier than overweight and obesity.

CHAPTER XXIII

ANEMIA AND OTHER BLOOD DISEASES

There is no special type of blood diseases, including anemia, which can be the result of aging. Leukemia, most known of blood diseases, occurs more frequently in children than in adults and is definitely rare, though not impossible, in old age. We actually still do not know how leukemia starts. We call it blood cancer. We know that in that disease there is an overwhelming increase of the white cells in the blood; but why, we don't know—just as we don't know why one person gets a cancer and another not, and why one gets a cancer of the stomach, and another a cancer of the brain. Therefore, we don't have to discuss leukemia and similar blood diseases in a book which is dedicated to diseases which are especially connected with old age.

However, though again, anemia can occur in any age, there are several reasons why anemia is frequently seen in elderly people.

First of all, we have to distinguish between pernicious anemia and secondary anemia. We know nowadays that pernicious anemia—which was called pernicious because it was a fatal disease—is due to deficiency of the B12 vitamin in the body, and that by taking enough B12 a person with pernicious anemia can live as long and as well as any other person. A fact is that pernicious anemia is frequent among elderly people. It is only a hunch, a guess, but I would consider it as a well-educated guess, that the prevalence of pernicious anemia and the deficiency of the B12 vitamin is due to some food deficiency; though we cannot say for sure which food ingredient is missing in the diet of elderly people. Everybody—or, let us say, most of the people who are interested in such matters—knows that at the beginning of the treatment of pernicious anemia the patients were fed large amounts of liver, and primarily raw liver, until it was discovered that the healing ingredient in the liver was the vitamin B12; and that made obsolete the feeding of the liver or of liver extracts as it was done at the later stage of the treatment of pernicious anemia.

In order to go further with the argument regarding the importance of the diet in the origin of the pernicious anemia, let us talk first about the second and most prevalent type of anemia, namely, the secondary anemia. This anemia is called secondary for the simple reason that it occurs as secondary to another disease or health-condition; in other words, it is a post-effect and not a sickness by itself. And it can be assumed that, with the disappearance of the first condition, the second one—the anemia—will also disappear, as it is usually the case.

Now, there are obvious reasons for a secondary anemia, and some which are not so obvious. It is obvious that a person becomes anemic if he or she suffers a great loss of blood, as, for instance, after a profuse hemorrhage—let us say, from the vagina in a woman, or from a bleeding stomach ulcer or from any other severe bleeding, like a knife-stabbing or gunshot which penetrates a large artery or vein. Sometimes a tremendous hemorrhage, and even a fatal one, can occur when a large artery or vein bursts. For instance, a bursting of an aneurysm—that is, a blow-up of the main artery, the aorta—could be fatal in no time. But even a big varicose vein in the leg can burst and shoot the blood up to the ceiling.

These are obvious reasons for a secondary anemia; and, apart from a bleeding ulcer and occasional bleeding from varicose veins in the esophagus (that is, the pipe which leads from the mouth to the stomach), where hemorrhages are not uncommon, the other instances mentioned above are comparatively rare. Less known is the fact that small bleedings can also cause an anemia, especially if they are small but very frequent. To these belong nosebleeds, small bleedings from hemorrhoids, or profuse menstrual bleedings even if the menstruation is regular and does not take longer than 4-5 days. In the latter case, the explanation is simply the fact that the female body just does not have time to reproduce the lost blood before the next menstruation occurs. The above-mentioned small blood losses from hemorrhoids, nosebleeds, etc., cause an anemia because the bleedings and the blood losses are so insignificant that the body has no incentive to replenish the loss and does not give itself the effort to reproduce the lost hemoglobin (the blood coloring) and the red cells. But, though it may be each time only a few drops of blood, in the long run it counts and causes a secondary, usually mild anemia.

The treatment of such secondary anemias, whether due to a massive hemorrhage or to small blood losses, is simple. A blood transfusion will replace a great loss of blood; the cause, such as a bleeding ulcer or a burst vessel, will be eliminated. In a frequent small blood loss, the cause—hemorrhoids, bleeding spots in the nose—can be cauterized. A too-strong menstruation can medically or surgically be brought under control. The existing mild secondary anemia can be cured with doses of iron, liver, vitamins, etc., as long as the cause of the anemia is eliminated.

However, even if we discard all the above-mentioned causes of secondary anemia, we still find a lot of cases of such an anemia in older people. If we find them, we have to look for the cause. Otherwise we could not cure the anemia and we could miss an important cause, and thus hasten death and overlook an underlying disease.

The first reason for a secondary anemia in older people, if it is not due to the above-mentioned causes, is an undetectable cancer. Very often a cancer is hidden somewhere in the body. It might be minute in size. It might not spread to the surrounding tissues or organs, and still cause an anemia—which is not rarely the only clue in the detection of a cancer in its first stage, when there are no other obvious signs. If there is a definite anemia with diminution of the number of the red cells and of the percentage of hemoglobin, one has to undergo a very thorough checking with X-rays, etc., until such a possibility of a cancer as the cause of that anemia is discarded. One has to remember that malignancy rises with age. Cancer is more common in older people than in younger ones, and therefore any danger signal should be carefully watched.

But, supposing all the above-mentioned possibilities are reviewed and eliminated, and the elderly person still has anemia, where do we have to look for the cause? The answer is in the diet. In the previous chapter I mentioned already, that, even if obesity is more common among aged, there is still a percentage of elderly people who do not care for food and who consider eating as a sort of a curse, something which has to be endured but not enjoyed. That applies especially to lonely people, to the widows and widowers, to the old bachelors and spinsters who live by themselves in small apartments and rooms in residential hotels, and who also not infrequently have to live economically in order to make ends meet on Social Security or any other small pension, and therefore economize also on food. Here comes the coincidence of lack of appetite when one eats all by himself and the need for buying of cheap food. The cheapest food and at the same time the easiest to prepare, is starch. Bread, cereals, potatoes, rice, noodles, macaroni, and so on are cheap; they are either ready-made or easy to make for a meal. Protein, such as in meat, in fish, in cheeses, in eggs, is more expensive, and also requires more elaborate preparation. Therefore, it is often discarded from the diet or eaten in minute quantities. But blood production depends on the consumption of protein, and the deficiency of protein in the diet causes the anemia in old age which we call nutritional anemia. It comes either as a post-effect of a lack of appetite or of an unbalanced diet with deficiency of proteins. Therefore, even if a patient takes all kinds of iron, vitamins, etc., it improves the anemia temporarily; but if there is no radical change in the mode of life and of food consumption, after a short while, when the iron tablets are finished and the old, starchy food plus some vegetables becomes a staple ingredient of the diet to the detriment of protein, everything returns to the previous condition, and the patient again becomes anemic.

It is also a socio-economic problem which has psychological

undertones. Some of the elderly people used to eat well and food rich in proteins, in younger age. When they become old and lonely, with married children living maybe far away, and the financial resources greatly diminished, from time to time, for remembrance of things past, they go on a binge. They have a heavy and very expensive meal at a restaurant, plenty of steak and even wine, and very often a meal which they can hardly afford and which their stomach hardly tolerates. So they are afterwards at home, suffering from indigestion, full of remorse—and at the same time it becomes clear to them that, in order to make ends meet, they will have to be doubly economical. The result is, after such a binge (which has no value from the medical point of view), more unbalanced diet and, slowly but surely, development of old-age nutritional anemia. The answer to this problem is obvious—change of habits.

CHAPTER XXIV

ALLERGIES IN OLD AGE

There is a very common fallacy that allergies of any kind are common in young people and rare in old age. Generally speaking, an allergy can start in the first days, weeks or months of life; and some babies have so-called diaper rashes due to allergy to some detergents or materials. Later, new allergies can develop, such as allergy to flowers or any other plants, which can start at a very early age of some months or years. Some children are allergic to certain foods, milk, wheat, and what-have-you? The refusal of a child to eat certain foods is not always based upon bad behavior, on being spoiled. A child has some natural instincts which tell him to avoid certain foods which might damage the digestive or respiratory system, or the skin. An allergic child becomes most likely an allergic adolescent and later an allergic adult. And such an allergy can continue to old age, though not necessarily so; because some of the childhood allergies disappear in adult years. A child allergic to wheat or milk will drink and eat that food without any consequences as an adult. Even asthma, hay fever, and other similar allergies can disappear with maturity.

But, on the other hand, some allergies appear only later, in grown-ups and at old age. Asthma, for instance, does not always start in childhood; it can develop in adults. The same applies to other allergies, such as skin rashes due to use of cosmetics or detergents. And old age is no exception to the rule. Basically, behind every allergy lies a nervous component. It may be 80% allergy to dust or dog hair or cats or detergents; but 20% is due to nervousness, to stress, to tension, to emotional disturbances. After all, not everybody is allergic to certain foods or materials or animals. So it must be somehow connected with the personality of the allergic man or woman. By the same token, the same person does not always have an allergic reaction towards the stuff which causes that allergy. On an off, the person eats the food, inhales the dust, touches the animal, and nothing happens. If allergy were a total reaction, it would always produce the same result. But it does not, which proves the point that it is connected with the emotional condition of the person.

This is the general idea of the origin of allergies. As applied to old age, it makes not much difference. If basically an old person is allergic—suffers, let us say, from asthma or hay fever as a young or middle-aged person—there is no reason to expect that because of aging he will become less allergic. On the contrary, with age you can expect that there will be more post-effects of the allergy due to wear and tear in the course of the years. For instance, the asthmatic person will develop a chronic bronchitis or an emphysema, as described in the chapter about lung diseases. Or, if an allergy of the skin exists, the duration of such an allergic skin reaction can bring about a permanent change of the skin, a condition of eczema or of a chronic inflammation of the skin. But such post-effects can occur at any age if and when the allergic condition persists for a long period of time. Only in old age, due to disturbances of the blood circulation and changes of the organs, you can expect more pronounced changes and post-effects.

There are, however, plain allergies, such as food or drug allergies, which start in old age. It is not easy to explain why a person who was not allergic to these substances all of his or her life suddenly cannot tolerate them; but it is a fact, well-known and nowadays seen more frequently than before. A person eats shrimps or grapes for many years without any disturbance, and all of a sudden, at old age, gets hives or an itch after eating that food, or develops an inflammation of the skin after using a detergent which was used for many years. The answer may be in the fact that old age is by far not a tranquil period of life, without any aggravation or stress or tension or anxiety. It may be that, physically, on retirement there is no more hustle and bustle to come to work on time or to return, to catch a bus or to be caught in the rush hour. But, in a way, there is tension due to the fact that the income diminishes, and in most cases one has to learn to make ends meet more than ever because the income is usually fixed and the financial reserves low. All this results in tension. Aggravation can come through family frictions, or controversial opinions among friends, and so on. If we accept the premise that a great part of an allergic condition is due to emotional influences, then it would be understood that pent-up emotions and tensions give vent to an outbreak of an allergy. If you travel to New Hampshire or Florida at the period of hay fever, you will be surprised to find that the majority of the hay fever sufferers waiting there for the end of the pollen season are elderly people. And not only because they can afford it timely due to retirement and no pressure of job, etc., but also because they do develop the hay fever allergy to a greater degree than the young ones. They just cannot take it physically, and therefore escape to New Hampshire or Florida.

If and when an elderly person gets an allergy, the treatment will be the same as in younger ones; but the post-effects will depend on the general health condition of the patient. In most cases the allergy is rather a nuisance than an impediment to health and life.

CHAPTER XXV

ACCIDENTS, FRACTURES AND SURGERY IN AGED PATIENTS

Among older people there is a high incidence of accidents which not infrequently are fatal, either immediately or sometime after the occurrence of the accident. This was found in many surveys on a national, state or local scale; also in reviews of operations at hospitals on older patients who had accidents and required surgery; and also in statistics of accidents which happened in nursing homes or any other institutions for aged people.

There is a consensus of opinion among all investigators regarding the reason for the high proportion of accidents in aged patients and generally in older people; namely, the fact that the great majority of people over 65, up to 80%, suffer from one or more chronic conditions which are connected with aging, such as: heart disease, high blood pressure, arthritis, rheumatism, diabetes, poor blood circulation or slowing down of mental abilities, etc. These conditions do not have to be dramatic; they do not necessarily make the aged person an invalid. He or she with one or several of the above ailments very often lives by himself and caters for himself or herself, cooks, cleans the room, etc. But just the same, these health conditions make such a person more accident-prone. Many of the accidents which occur 3 times as often in aged as in younger people are due not to a slippery street or floor or rug, but due to the fact that the person in question has a slowing-down of reflexes, or does not see well where the wet spot is, or where the step is, by miscalculation of its height. It is interesting to find out that most accidents of that type occur either in the bedroom or bathroom and/or toilet. There are also certain hours when the accidents occur more often: such is the time from 6 to 10 a.m. when the aged person gets up, washes, dresses, prepares breakfast, and again in the evening between 6 and 10 p.m., when the person prepares for dinner and sleep. In the afternoon most of the aged rest, and that cuts down on the incidence of accidents.

Accidents can be of all kinds. Frequently, they occur in crossing the street and in pedestrians' collision with cars whereby the driver should not be always considered as responsible. The slowing down of reflexes, the hesitation whether to cross the street or not, the sudden fright of a car, and going back while the driver expects the pedestrian to continue the journey forwards, the frequent ignorance of the traffic rules—these cause a lot of car-collision accidents which are due to the behavior of the elderly passerby. Frequently it is a fall from the bus while stepping down by not seeing the step or miscalculation of the height of the bus step to the ground. The poor vision plays a great role in the accidents of aged people, but also the poor blood circulation in the legs which "buckle under" and cause a fall. The other reason is dizziness, which may be due to high blood pressure or poor cerebral circulation, or an attack of Menière's disease of the ears.

A lonely person, afflicted with one or more of such health conditions, will just the same cook for herself or iron, if it is a lonely elderly widow or spinster. She will sustain an accident by burns from the hot pot or from a hot iron. But the majority of the accidents of old-age people are falls. They fall in the street, in restaurants, in supermarkets, but most of all at home. Very often the fall ends with a fracture, due to the fact that osteoporosis and any other change of the bony structure causes a weakening of the resistance of the bone, and a fracture follows. Most common is a fracture of the hip (about 35%), then fractures of the wrist (about 16%), and then fractures of the upper-arm bone or humerus (14%). Fractures of the ribs are quite common, but they hardly ever require hospitalization and therefore escape statistics. Pelvis fractures among elderly people are not frequent, but they occur. Either they heal by themselves after a rest of 1-2 weeks; or, if they cause a simultaneous tear of the bladder, which on and off happens, such fractures are in the majority of cases fatal because they require an immediate operation in an area which is already contaminated by urine oozing out of the torn bladder, plus internal bleeding. Of course, fractures of ankles occur too; but percentagewise they are less common than the above-mentioned fractures.

If a fracture demands only a cast, it is a comparatively simple matter. Whether a fracture will "knit"—that is, whether the broken pieces of a bone will unite—is not necessarily a problem of age. You can be surprised how well a bone "knits" in a woman of 80, and how occasionally poorly in a woman of 45 or 50. We don't know the exact reason, but we generally expect a person in good health, without mineral, vitamin or hormone deficiencies, to unite the broken pieces of the bone well and to have a working extremity again in 6 to 8 weeks. However, one can expect more debility in an older person, and accordingly, more time will be required for healing of a fracture in such a case.

Of course, hip fractures, which are the most frequent fractures of aged people, belong to a special category. To begin with, they always require an operation and a long post-operative care. As preparation for that operation is also important, the knowledge of the general health condition of the patient is needed—especially of the heart, blood pressure and blood count. One has to know that, with a fracture, there is connected a tear of vessels and a loss of blood in the surrounding soft tissues of the hip and of the thigh; this can amount to more than two pints and has to be replaced by transfusion, if the operation should be successful. However, the operation, even if it is not an immediate emergency, should not be postponed for longer than 24 hours; because, with passage of time after the injury, the complications and the mortality rate increase. Most of the medical conditions which the patient has can be studied and treated during the period of convalescence, which is, unfortunately, very long anyway.

Not always is an internal metal fixation of the hip possible.

During the operation, and sometimes already by X-rays, there may be ample evidence that the bone fracture is complicated and the bone itself osteoporotic. Thus it will not hold any fixation. In such a case, the wise surgeon will not operate, or he will stop the operation if he finds unfavorable conditions, and will decide to treat the fracture by traction or by some other procedure, even if the results are not as good as by operation and fixation.

The main task during the operation is to do it not only well but fast, because the old organism cannot stand a prolonged operation and a prolonged anesthesia. The nature of the anesthesia is not so important as the method of its administration. The induction should be gentle and slow. The blood pressure should be watched doubly carefully, because older people incline to rapid lowering of the blood pressure to a very low, dangerous point. In general, spinal anesthesia by injection of the anesthetic material into the spinal column is by far not the best method of anesthesia for the elderly patient, because it often causes a dangerous lowering of the blood pressure. If general anesthesia cannot be given, local anesthesia and nerve block are advisable.

Of course, the after-care of a hip fracture is just as important. It depends on the doctor as much as on the patient whether he or she will walk or not. If the doctor encourages the patient to try to walk first with a walker, then with canes, then with one cane, and with the help of a nurse or relatives, and a physiotherapist surpervises the progress, then there is great expectation that the patient with a hip fracture will walk again in due time. Otherwise, the patient will be confined to a wheelchair for the rest of her or his life. It requires a certain courage to stand on one's feet after such a fracture, and there is a certain amount of psychological despondency and resignation to invalidism from which the doctor and the relatives have to pull out the patient. There should be the will of the patient to walk; if this exists, there is good hope that the patient will walk.

And that brings us to the general problem of surgery in aged patients. On the whole, surgery, if it can be avoided, should be avoided. Apart from the fact that elderly people cannot stand anesthesia well, as mentioned above, because of the many chronic ailments which accompany old age, one can expect complications after any operation. It is clear that careful evaluation of an elderly patient before an operation, and especially if it is an elective one, should be done. Nevertheless, even with the preparation of the heart and blood condition by digitalis and/or blood transfusions, the mortality rate in patients over 65 undergoing surgery is about three times as high as in patients under 65. Just the same, older people also get an acute appendicitis or an acute inflamation of the gall bladder, or an intestinal obstruction; and surgical intervention is still the almost only treatment for most types of cancer, which is more prevalent in older age groups than in younger. Even with the most careful preparation, in the presence of chronic disease, the mortality rate, according to many surveys—such as that of the University of California School of Medicine, or the Ohio State University College of Medicine, to give only two examples—in old patients is about 20 to 25%, while for the same operations the death rate in younger people is only about 6%. On the other hand, the important thing is not the chronological but the physiological age and the general health. In the same statistics it was found that without a concomitant chronic disease the death rate in patients over 65 fell from 21% to 14% and less, which is still high, and shows that in people over 65 you have to expect complications even without a high blood pressure or chronic bronchitis or emphysema or bronchiectasis or any other obvious disease because there is already a wear and tear of the organs, a deterioration of the blood circulation, and so on.

All this speaks in favor of having elective operations, such as gall bladder, prostate, hiatus hernia, hemorrhoids, chronic appendicitis, or fibroids, done at a younger age—not to postpone them for a time when a comparatively easy operation can become a major project. Wherever possible, such conditions should be treated medically and not surgically, if and when they occur in old age.

In case of emergency, you have no choice if an operation becomes imperative. There should, however, be a pre-surgery care, which is crucial in aged patients. Not only should the anesthesia be kept to a bare minimum, but also the after-care should be extremely good, and the patient has to be watched day and night. Ideally, it would be advisable to keep such a patient after an operation in an intensive care unit, or in a special unit for geriatric patients.

As a consolation, it is necessary to mention that, notwithstanding all the mortality statistics, it is amazing to find how often people of 80 years and more go through an operation with flying colors and leave the hospital sometimes sooner than younger persons. It is often found that people over 70 get a kind of a second wind or a second youth, and go through diseases without complications. And, again, one has to say that chronological age is frequently not the indication of how a patient will behave in sickness and operation. His general health and his will to live and to overcome all obstacles are the main factors in cure and recuperation.

CHAPTER XXVI

ALCOHOLISM IN OLD AGE

Alcoholism is not a problem of old age only; we have plenty of alcoholics also in younger people. In some social layers of society, alcoholism starts very early. They start to drink regularly and plenty as teenagers, and continue until, in the middle age of 30-40, they become addicted alcoholics who cannot live without alcohol—and that in increasing amounts. If I speak of social layers where alcoholism is prevalent, I mean the poorest and the richest. It is less common in the middle class. All this for sociological reasons. The poor and very poor drink as a means of escape from the surrounding misery, unhappiness, unsolvable problems, and the dim future ahead. The cup which cheers, if drunk in excess, gives oblivion for a while. The teen-ager who sees the drinking of the parent or parents imitates their way of life, and finds taste and sometimes also forgetfulness of the petty injuries and unjustices which surround the youngster. In the case of the very rich, the before-dinner cocktail or cocktails is a custom; and out of one or two drinks it becomes a series of drinks. The son and occasionally the daughter who observe the ritual want to participate, and as early as possible— with or without the permission of the parents. The result is early drinking at teenage parties, resulting in orgies, car accidents, and vandalism, as we saw not long ago as publicized happenings in the suburbs of New York, and which were not unique. Most likely this happens everywhere in the United States without too much publicity, and most probably also in Europe and any other so-called affluent societies and civilized countries.

To return to old age, we had to give the introduction in order to understand that in most cases old-age alcoholism is not a disease (and you have to call it a disease, like any other addiction) which starts at that age, but which has its origin in much younger age, even in teenage, and becomes more and more a habit as one gets older.

How widespread alcoholism is among people over 65 is difficult to calculate statistically, for the simple reason that many of the alcoholics stay at home and are not violent, even if they cause misery to themselves and to close relatives. They are known as alcoholics if they are admitted as such to psychiatric institutions or have to be taken in because of a liver condition and other concomitant disease. Statistics from the New York State Department of Mental Hygiene show that 7 percent of first admissions for alcoholic mental diseases to state hospitals are over 65 years old. And, of course, this is only a small percentage of old-age alcoholics who do not have mental conditions, but are alcoholics just the same.

We have to understand who is an alcoholic and who is not. It is not the amount of alcohol consumed which makes a person an alcoholic, but the dependency on alcohol. If a person must have alcohol, even if it is one or two cocktails per day, if he or she cannot function without the drink, such a person is to be considered as addicted to alcohol just the same as a heroin, morphine or codein addict. And in due time, as in all addicts, you can count on an increasing number of drinks an alcoholic must have, until he or she does not function at all, and the whole life-interest is concentrated only on getting a drink. One of my patients who used to be an alcoholic told me that in the AA meetings there is an old saying, "One drink is too many, and 1,000 drinks not enough." On the other hand, some people are used to a drink before dinner, a cocktail or two, and that does not make them alcoholics, even if it is more than one or two drinks, as long as they can stop when they are told so by their doctor; or if for any reason, they don't have or cannot get alcohol, they can function just as well.

The problem of alcoholism in any age is a social one, and especially in old age. It is interesting to find out that in some ethnic groups alcoholism is rare whether they customarily drink alcohol or not. Italians, for instance, habitually drink wine with their meals, but rarely to excess. I remember vividly how a patient of mine, born here of Italian parents, told me that he went to a small place in New Jersey where his parents lived on the occasion of Thanksgiving Day. When the mother asked him before dinner whether he would like something to drink, he said, yes, he would like a Scotch and soda. While during dinner wine was supposed to be served, she thought that he might want a soft drink. When she heard his answer, she started to cry. On his inquiry why she cried, she said that he was a drunkard if he wanted Scotch and not a soft drink, or at best a glass of wine. Drinking of wine in Italian families does not lead to alcoholism. And, by the way, his mother was right, because he died at the age of 55 from liver cirrhosis due to alcoholism, due to drinking of hard liquor—not of chianti or any other wine.

The same phenomenon you can observe in other ethnic groups, such as Chinese and Jews. The Jews are, in regard to alcoholism, unique. They have bars and liquor stores. In Eastern Europe they used to have in some countries almost a monopoly on liquor distribution. According to the Jewish religion, apart from the Passover night when there is an obligation to drink 4 glasses of wine, every religious ritual starting with circumcision, then in all other ceremonies, and in Sabbath blessings, wine drinking is a part of the ritual. Just the same, alcoholism among Jews up to a few years ago was virtually unknown. You could not find Jews with mental alcoholic disorders in any psychiatric institution, and alcoholic liver cirrhosis is still extremely rare among Jews. There is a whole literature which tries to explain this abstinence phenomenon. Some claim that it was due to the fact that Jews were always a persecuted minority who had to have all faculties intact in order to be able to defend themselves, which was impossible if under the influence of alcohol. This explanation is not unlikely, but it is not sufficient. However, if one coordinates all the facts which are common to all the ethnic groups who are known to be temperate in the use of alcohol, you will find that the common denominator is a closely-bound family community, with parental authority which was obeyed by the children, with respect for habits, customs and usage of food, drinks, etc. If the children were imbued with these qualities, they propagated them to their offspring until it became a customary ethnic trend which, if transgressed by any member of the tribe, was frowned upon and brought a kind of moral ostracism.

With the loosening of the family bonds, of religion, of tribal customs, you will find that alcoholism exists also among Italians, Jews, Chinese, etc.

One has to understand that alcohol as such, drunk in small quantities, is the cup that cheers, brings a better mood, and serves as a mild tranquilizer. It also has very few side reactions, if imbibed in small quantities. The trouble with alcohol is only that it is addictive, easily obtainable, and comparatively cheap. Therefore, it serves its purpose to a greater degree than it should; and in larger quantities it starts damaging the whole bodily system, especially the brain and the liver plus pancreas. And because the only obstacle to drinking excessively is either lack of money or will power, which is lacking in all addicts—and alcoholics are no exception—therefore we find such a great multitude of alcoholics.

Why does one elderly person take to alcohol and becomes an addict? The answer is not a medical or chemical but a sociological one. Alcoholism is escapism. The first and main reason is loneliness. If an elderly person has few friends or none, if the relatives do not care for him or her, if the elderly one has no hobbies which would occupy his spare time, if the aged does not belong to a club or organization, he or she will take to the bottle—especially if one is used to drinking moderately in previous years as a young or middle-aged person. First it is a consolation and a compensation for loneliness. Then one notices that one can sleep better, and soon it becomes a habit. The amount of imbibed alcohol increases until one falls into the bed and sleeps—or, rather, is unconscious—from too much alcohol. And, from drinking late at night, maybe while watching television, it turns to drinking before dinner, then before lunch; and finally drinking becomes the essence of the lonely life of an elderly person.

Of course, loneliness is the main but not only psychological reason for drinking. Let us be clear about one thing. There are very few people who become alcoholics from drinking wine, and hardly anybody in the United States. The Americans are not wine drinkers, like the Italians, the French, the Greeks, or the Spaniards. They drink hard liquor, whiskey, bourbon, rye, Scotch and gin. The taste of hard liquor is not such that a person drinks because he or she likes the taste of whiskey or gin. One can get used to the taste, but that does not mean that it is loved by the drunkard—contrary to the wine, the taste of which can appeal to the palate of a person and induce one to more drinking.

So the reason must be psychological. Apart from loneliness, there may be grief after the loss by death of a mate or of a child or even a close, dear friend. Occasionally, it may be due to a chronic, invalidizing and incapacitating disease. Sometimes, anger due to neglect by close relatives or because of mandatory retirement, while one feels to be still in the prime of life and mental abilities, and a general feeling of rejection induce overindulgence in alcohol by previously moderate drinkers.

Whatever psychological reason brings about alcoholism, the result is more or less the same—namely, addiction with consequent mental deterioration, delirium tremens, liver cirrhosis with accompanying bleeding esophageal varicose veins, water accumulation in the belly and, sooner or later, death. Mentally, there is a marked loss of memory, often violence; neglect in regard to habits, to clothing, lack of appetite, and disregard for conventional behavior or consideration for others. A New York Bowery alcoholic bum is the typical extreme example of a chronic alcoholic.

There is hardly any medical treatment of alcoholism. The chemical "Antabuse," widely propagated some years ago, did not bring the expected results but plenty of undesirable side reactions, and fell practically in disuse. The same applies to other medical remedies. It is, of course, possible to bring an alcoholic to an institution where he or she will be taken care of and "dried up" in a comparatively short time—that is, sent home sober. How long such an alcoholic will stay sober is a different question. It can take days or weeks before an alcoholic falls back into his alcoholical habits. The best results are still achieved by the non-medical organization of "A.A.," which means Alcoholics Anonymous. It is an excellent organization, staffed primarily by laymen—namely, former alcoholics who volunteer to help fellow alcoholics by staying with them day and night during their alcoholic stupor, not allowing them to drink, feeding them, taking the abusive words and deeds of their patients, and leading them to attend the A.A. meetings. The meetings are in a way "revivalist" meetings, but they work. And the A.A. helps countless alcoholics to become once more useful members of the society.

There is only one "but"—the A.A. is a voluntary organization, and an alcoholic has to want to be helped. He or she cannot be forced, and under pressure the action of the A.A. is useless and worthless. As in all cases of addiction, not all alcoholics want to be helped, even if their alcoholism ruins them and their families. Often they are too far gone to understand the need for help, and sometimes they are very happy to find in their alcoholism a solution to their problems. The real solution to alcoholism is the removal of the cause of it—to abolish the loneliness, the feeling of rejection, the feeling of uselessness, the anger, the grief. All this is a tall order and hardly possible; therefore, alcoholism is here to stay.

Prohibition, as it was experimented with in the U.S.A. on a grand scale, was and is, of course, a foolish solution. Whatever is prohibited has a special flavor of trying to beat the forbidden— a temptation to drink when one is not allowed. Hence the success of "bootlegging," as it applies to all things forbidden, such as pornographic literature, drugs, etc. As Alexander Woollcott used to say, "Everything I like is either forbidden or immoral or fattening"; and, of course, people do all the things, whether allowed by law or not. Prohibition is not a solution. Alcoholism is a social and psychological problem which is not limited to but—because of frustration and other erosions of life—more inherent in old age.

To cheer up a little the sad overall picture of the role of

alcohol in old age, one has to say that teetotalism is neither necessary nor even desirable for elderly people. In small quantities, alcohol helps and does very little damage. It is not a vasodilator of the heart, as it was thought to be and therefore recommended for people with angina pectoris and related heart troubles. The arteries do not widen, but a drink calms down the existing tension and anxiety if a person suffers from chest pain, and this is important in such a case. Because alcohol in small quantities, and especially wine, is a quite good tranquilizer, it helps one to fall asleep, and older people do suffer from insomnia. The appetite might also improve, as a good tonic improves it (which, by the way, usually contains a quite considerable amount of alcohol); because most elderly people suffer from deficiency of function of the digestive organs, and alcohol stimulates the production of acid in the stomach and its enzymes. It also contains more calories, and thus provides additional caloric energy and supplies more fluids which are needed in the frequent cases of dehydration in elderly people. Alcohol in small quantities, if not used in combination with other sedatives or tranquilizers or narcotics—when it can become hazardous by potentiation of the action—makes some elderly patients more alert, more enterprising, and more apt to undertake some social activities and social intercourse than without the stimulation of alcohol. Usually, though old people feel lonely, they have very little social interaction. One can see a ward full of old people who, instead of talking one to another, sit in his or her corner and do not pay any attention to the other. Each is completely indifferent to what happens to his wardmate—often even does not know whether he or she is still there or not. A small amount of wine, given at meals, was a stimulant to more sociability, to showing more interest, and to greater participation in group activities—as, for instance, reported by Drs. Zeake and Silverman in *Geriatrics* magazine. Of course it does not apply to all patients, and neither everywhere and always. It greatly depends on the basic character of the elderly patient. But let us say that alcohol in a mild form helps to thaw inhibitions, as it does also in younger people.

The meaning of alcoholism is best expressed in a story given as a fable in the Jewish Talmud. When Noah planted a vineyard after the Flood, Satan came to him and suggested partnership in this enterprise by praising himself as an expert. Noah consented. Satan then killed a lamb and sprinkled its blood on the soil when the vine was seeded. He did the same with the blood of a lion, then of an ape, and finally of a pig. And Satan's formula became the result of the drinking of alcohol. If one drinks a small glass, he becomes as gentle as a lamb; after two glasses he gets excited and stormy like a lion; after three glasses he is like an ape—loses his mind and imitates everybody; and if he drinks more and more, he becomes like a pig and wallows in mud and dirt.

This is, in a nutshell, the result of alcoholism on the human mind, and how it works in alcoholism. It applies to all ages, but it is more pronounced in old age where it becomes more hopeless, more devastating, and the most sad and humiliating. Alcoholism is a disease and has to be treated as such. It is to be hoped that medical science will find a solution to this manmade illness, too.

CHAPTER XXVII

SEX LIFE IN OLD AGE

In early 1965 there were 18 million people over 65 years of age in the United States. The number grows by approximately 1½ million annually. That means that in 1970 we had already 26 million people officially designated as Medicare people. Gently, they are called "senior citizens" or belonging to the "Golden Age."

Now, the sexual life of all these millions was, up to not long ago, an absolutely unknown territory, mainly for psychological reasons of the patients of that age and of the doctor. The older person was reluctant to talk with the doctor about his or her sexual life at that age; and, on the other hand, the doctor was embarrassed to ask questions about sex of people who might be the age of his father or mother.

However, these people are vitally interested, very confused, and want to have authoritative information about what is normal regarding sexuality in the old-age population, which grows from year to year and already constitutes 10% of the inhabitants of the United States. It can be stated that, with the improvement of general health and of the economic standard of the population in all civilized countries, such as in Europe, Canada, Australia, New Zealand, South Africa, Japan and some South American countries, the aging population increases, and their problems are everywhere the same.

The problem of sex in this sector of the population is so vast that one could write a book on this problem alone. Within the scope of this book on old age, it might be advisable to start this chapter with questions and answers as they commonly (but not too often or not often enough) are asked in conversation with a doctor. How little attention is paid to this vital problem of age in an aging population is best characterized by the fact that, in the 1700 pages of the two Kinsey reports on sexual activity, only *three* pages are devoted to the activity of the age group of above 50 years. Just the same, as one scans reports of gynecologists, urologists, psychiatrists and general practitioners which appear from time to time, one comes to some definite answers which can be given to questions asked, or which an elderly person would like to know. Here they are:

(a) *Sex in Men*

1. What is the sexual activity, on the average, of any age group?

Generally speaking, sexual activity declines with age. Young married couple have sexual intercourse four or five times weekly. Practically all males are sexually active at the age of 45. The frequency of intercourse drops with age. At 50 it becomes an average of about once or twice weekly. At 60, once weekly. While frequency diminishes with age, there is still sexual activity at the age of 70 in married men, and in 50% still at the age of 75 and older. In a study of 102 men, 1/4 of married men 71 to 80 years old had intercourse 13 or more times annually, showing that sexual activity is not uncommon even at that age. Of course, several did not have intercourse for many years before that age, either through lack of a partner (widowers or bachelors) or through impotence. The fact is indisputable that sexual activity in old age depends primarily on the availability of a (willing) partner, so that the chances for sexual activity in elderly persons are much greater in a married couple.

2. On what factors does the potency of a man depend, especially after 65 or even earlier?

Basically, impotence in men is primarily a psychological problem. There are definitely organic reasons for impotence, such as late diabetes, occasionally late syphilis, and neurological disorders; but they constitute a small percentage of the reasons for impotence in a man. The main reason, and that applies just as well to much younger men, is a psychological one. If, for instance, a man fails once in his power of virility, he can get scared and be afraid that from now on he will always be unable to perform a sexual act. It very much depends on his partner. If the woman is helpful, reassuring, and patient, she will easily restore the confidence of her man in his potency, and everything will be all right and will go smoothly. One has to understand that everyone has a certain pattern of sexuality which becomes a routine. If the routine is broken—say, by choosing or having another partner for sexual intercourse—then the same man can become impotent for purely psychological reasons. In older age, one should realize that, in the case of the change of partner—as in the re-marriage of a widower, usually to a younger woman than he—in the mind of the man arises the fear of whether he will be capable of intercourse with a strange and younger woman. If the new wife is not understanding and sympathetic in this situation, it can easily lead to a permanent psychological impotence and to an unhappy marriage—and this, even if the new wife is not interested in sex. But the feeling of failure and inadequacy will plague the mind of her husband and poison his attitude towards her. On the other hand, the knowledge of his disadvantage gives her the upper hand and can cause a domineering pattern in the mind of the wife, and cause further unhappiness.

3. Is there any guiding experience in regard to expectation of sexual life in older age?

There is a basic difference between the sexual life of married couples and single men and women. There is also a difference between the sexual life of lower and higher socio-economic groups of the population. There is also the fact that sexual activity in earlier life will bring about sexual activity also in older age.

To begin with the difference between married couples and single men and women, it is, first of all, a question of availability and of a routine inherent in the marital life. If a couple are used to regular sexual intercourse in younger age, they will continue, unless serious diseases interfere—maybe with some modification regarding the frequency—until very old age. If they are both alive and comparatively healthy, they will have intercourse even at the age of 80. It is different with single men and women, whether widowers or widows, bachelors or divorced. Such a person has to look for a partner. The sexual urge may be quite diminished; and therefore, even if a sexual interest exists, a single person in both sexes will rather give up, and slowly but surely, due to the lack of opportunity, the urge and the capability will die out. That does not mean that this will apply to all single men and women. The problem of sexuality in old age is highly individual. There are always men who will look for an opportunity to find a female partner, though only few of them will go to a prostitute, due to the fact that the urge diminishes with age. Even post-marital women after 50, though they do not have a legal partner, report that they have in about 37% sexual intercourse (compared with 83% of married women). However, after 60 only 12% of single women have intercourse, compared with 70% of married women of the same group of population. That does not mean that single women of the age of over 50 and above 60 have no sexual interest; only, the great majority has no opportunity and resorts to masturbation, which exists also in married women whose husband have lost interest in regular intercourse. But this kind of sexual activity is much more prevalent in the single-women group, as is logically to be expected.

There exists a fallacy in regard to the influence of sexual activity in early age on the potency of men in older age. Generally, people think that intensive sexual life in younger men causes impotence earlier, which is absolutely not the case. It is rather the opposite. It is like walking. People used to long walks in younger age will continue to walk at old age. The sexual organs do not get depleted in their activities unless there is definitely a great abuse. Otherwise, a man can start having intercourse at the age of 15 and still be able to perform at the age of 70, unless sickness and general debility interfere.

And here we come to the third group of these questions, namely, the influence of sociological and economic status on sexual activity. It is well known and documented that, in lower socio-economic groups, sexual activity starts much earlier than in higher socio-economic parts of the population. There are several reasons for it. One reason is overcrowding, leading to the possibility of observation of sexual intercourse in early age, and the desire to imitate what one sees in very early age. The other reason is the less-outraged view of an early pregnancy and illegitimate children, who are accepted without too much ado as something which happens and cannot be helped. The same applies to venereal diseases, which are also accepted as any other disease, without ostracism. There is also the reason of ignorance, or lack of education and lack of culture interests, with resulting concentration on sexual life as one of the few pleasures of life which one can afford—and the Devil can take the consequences. Also, financially, pregnancy and the upbringing of children are not such a problem. If the worst comes to the worst, there is always the welfare department which will take care of support in pregnancy and afterwards.

All this is a different problem in the higher socio-economic group. There is a taboo regarding early intercourse and, in general, sexual activity before marriage. Even now, with all the liberalism toward the sexual life of students, there is still a large percentage of girls who remain virgins until marriage, or have intercourse only with their fiancés in expectation of a very early wedding. Pregnancy before marriage in that group is a catastrophe. Either an abortionist is found for good money, which the lower group cannot afford, or the delivery takes place in a place remote from the usual environment and the child is given up for adoption, with all traces of the "shameful" episode obliterated.

Accordingly, these early customs and taboos lead to a different attitude towards sex also in old age. One starts with regular sexual activity late and finishes early. It is also dubious whether the women in that higher socio-economic group enjoy sexual activity to the same degree as in the lower group for the same negative reasons, as they are positive in the lower group; because sexual intercourse is frequently dominated by fear of pregnancy, of venereal disease, of discovery, and this fear kills the pleasure of women as frequently as the potency of the man.

Regarding the sexual life of men, there are yet the following questions.

4. At what age does a man lose the power of reproduction? That is, when is the end of his fertility, as opposed to potency?

Of course, without potency and the ability to introduce the semen into the vagina of a woman, there can be no fertility. However, due to artificial insemination, the answer is no more that simple; because, by masturbation, even an impotent man can ejaculate semen which can artificially be injected into the vagina and/or the cervix of the womb of a woman. Therefore, the two powers of potency and fertility have to be discussed separately. A man can have perfect potency and be sterile due to malfunction of the testicles, which produce only a semen without sperm cells or with a scanty, insufficient number of sperm cells; or a semen the sperm cells of which are not mature and cannot impregnate a woman. That can also happen after a disease which—for instance, mumps—can destroy fertility forever.

In normal conditions, fertility can be preserved for a very long period of time. Active production of live sperm cells may be present in extreme old age. If potency still exists and the female partner is of reproductive age, to become a father at 80 is a possibility. Biopsy of the testicles indicates a function consistent with fertility, and that is the case in about 75% of normal testicles in almost any age. This, however, has nothing to do with sexual desire and ability.

5. What influence has the removal of the prostate on the potency of a man?

Now, any of the three types of operations can cause impotence if the nerves which govern the penis and lie closely to the prostate are cut. However, the chances for such a misfortune are great in the perineal type, and therefore the chances for impotence after such an operation are much greater. It occurs even after a transurethral operation, which is the simplest of all three types; and it is not common, though it occurs, in the suprapubic type of the prostate operation. Therefore, in a sexually very active man, the suprapubic type of operation should be recommended, though no surgeon will guarantee that potency will not suffer. You have also to remember that, after all, a prostate operation is uncommon in younger people. Usually the patients who need the operation are between 60 and 70 years old, and not rarely even older—though, on the other hand, occasionally the enlargement of the prostate hits men of 50 to 60 years of age. Nevertheless, the question of potency is of lesser importance than in younger people, if there is the problem of either restoration of health or diminution of potency.

One has also to remember that, as mentioned above in previous questions and answers regarding sex in older people, potency is not only an organic but primarily a psychological problem. In some cases, the operation is a good excuse for discontinuation of sexual activity; either for the man who has a wife whom he does not desire sexually anymore, or for the wife who, under the cover of worry about the health of the husband, can escape a sexual life in which she is not interested any more.

However, if both partners are eager and willing, sexual intercourse is possible after any type of operation; though it is conceded that the chances after a perineal operation are much slimmer. Even an operation for cancer of the prostate, or even a removal of the testicles, as is frequently done in such a case—that is, castration—does not necessarily cause impotence, if there is no general debility.

One has to remember that the surgeons usually cut through the cord which brings the semen from the testicles into the canal which goes through the penis and causes ejaculation. This is a pre-operation procedure which takes only a few minutes; because the cord can be felt through the scrotum (testicles pouch), and a small incision bares the cord, which is then cut. It is a similar operation to that of cutting the ovarial tubes in a woman in order to cause sterility; only it is easy and simple in men, but the result is the same. This pre-operation surgical procedure makes a man sterile but not impotent. After the cutting of that cord, ejaculation still takes place but the semen, instead of being ejected into the vagina of the woman, flows backwards into the bladder and mixes with the urine, to be eliminated on urination.

To sum up the question of sex and prostate: a prostate operation does not usually lead to impotence. With willing partners and patience, the potency of a man can be restored to the stage it was at before the operation.

(b) *Sex in Women*

6. What influence has the change of life (menopause) on the sexual life of a woman?

From a general point of view, menopause as such has no influence on the sex life of a woman. If she had and liked sexual activity before the change of life, there is no reason why she should not continue. On the contrary, the loss of fear of pregnancy—the lack of need for contraceptives, which are often distasteful to women—should enhance the enjoyment of sexual activity. For many years, if not decades or even centuries, women thought that menopause means the end of sex. Now, with the more liberal approach to sex problems, with more literature on it, women talk occasionally to doctors about their sex life after menopause; and thus ignorance and superstition, including false ideas about sex in older age, can be dispelled, and in many cases women can be helped in that area too.

However, one has to remember that menopause usually occurs at the age of 45 to 50. A woman of that age is still young; she can be considered maybe middle-aged, but she is not old. Psychologically speaking, a woman who reaches the age of menopause occasionally has the idea that she loses her femininity. In cases of hysterectomy—which often has to be performed in even younger age because, let us say, of fibroid tumors—there can arise a psychological complex of inadequacy, of having lost a part of the body, of having become, in a way, a cripple. And if, as often occurs, flushes and increased nervousness appear as a post-effect of the menopause, then a menopause woman needs medical help, which is usually successful.

7. What is the average sexual activity in females?

According to Kinsey, the frequency of marital intercourse for females reaches its maximum a year or two after marriage; then it drops steadily to a minimum in the 51-60 age group. The average frequency is three times weekly for females married in their early teens, 2.2 per week at the age of 30, 1.5 per week by 40, once per week at 50, and once every 12 days by age 60.

It is all meant for married women. The sexual activity of single women, whether bachelor girls, divorced or widows, is less known. It is difficult to talk about their sexual activity, especially if in their environment extra-marital sexual life is frowned upon. It also depends on the availability of a partner. The older a single woman becomes, the more difficult it is for her to get a partner. She must be very attractive even in older age. She must be also more aggressive in order to get a partner, whether in marriage or just for sex. The competition is great. One has to remember that we have one million widowers against seven million widows in the United States. And there is a large number of older divorced women, and a proportion of single older women who never married.

8. Are there any organic reasons why an older woman could not have sexual intercourse?

Yes, there are. Sexual activity should not produce pain, but pleasure; otherwise it is meaningless. Now, old-age females whose ovaries do not function any more, who do not produce female hormones, suffer from a vaginal senile atrophy—that is, shrinkage of the lining of the vagina, drying up and therefore tightening it. The result is pain on introduction of the penis in sexual intercourse. The same can happen after operations for vaginal repair, as done when there is a drop of the vaginal wall—which also occurs due to senile changes and weakness of the ligaments which support the female sexual organs. In such cases, if there is a stricture after an operation, there is treatment with widening by instruments, if sexual activity is still desired. And intercourse, shortly started after such an operation, helps too to avoid strictures, tightening of the vagina, and should be encouraged by the doctor.

9. Is there any meaning to the sexual activity of older women?

On the whole, men are more sexually active than women, and that applies to young and older males and females. Apart from nymphomaniacs, women are not aggressive sexually; they give in to the aggression of the male, sometimes with pleasure, sometimes by convenience, habit or custom in the case of a married woman. If a woman had pleasure out of sexual intercourse in younger age, there is no reason why she should not enjoy it when she becomes older or old. Many older women are capable of greater sexual desire, response and enjoyment. However, just when the older woman who now has less problems at home, no fears of pregnancy, could enjoy sex, she finds herself restricted by debility, by illness, by the impotence of her husband or by lack of his desire for her as female; or by his death, which means lack of a partner. It happens not infrequently that a wife who was not keen on sexual intercourse in younger age and had no orgasm, and had sexual intercourse only in order to please the husband, in the course of the marital life develops an interest in sexual intercourse, experiences orgasm and pleasure, just at the time when the husband's interest and desire diminishes—especially if he has previously noticed her reluctance and objection to sex.

Deficiency of hormones in the older women can lead not only to senile vaginal changes, as described, but also to lack of sexual response. In some cases, when a woman is sexually not responsive, she may be helped by a course of male hormone injections, which increase the libido (sexual desire and pleasure). Usually, if she experiences sexual pleasure from intercourse after such a treatment and continues having sex, she will have orgasm and desire, also without further treatment. The male hormones cannot be given for a long time because they can cause male features in a woman such as growth of a moustache or sideburns, a deep masculine voice and so on.

However, a short course, sometimes even a single injection of a large dose, of male hormones can cause sexual stimulation in an older woman.

10. What about masturbation in older women?

Masturbation is a normal sexual outlet for anybody who has sexual desire and no means to satisfy it; that is, he or she has no sexual partner. Teenagers, and even subteenagers and children, masturbate. Up to 100% of males masturbate before they can have sexual intercourse, and usually start when they are getting erections—that is, at sexual maturity, which occurs at the age of 13-14. Girls get sexual maturity at the beginning of menstruation, that is, on the average, at the age of 12. However, masturbation is connected with the sexual phantasy of intercourse. In the man the erection and the ejaculation of semen gives the male sexual satisfaction, whether produced by intercourse or masturbation. Masturbation in girls, because not connected with satisfaction of erection and ejaculation, must be based primarily on a sexual fantasy of intercourse. Therefore, girls start masturbating, if at all, much later, as teenagers or in the early twenties—if they are still virgins or have lost their lovers and do not yet have another one.

Usually, regular intercourse makes an end to masturbation in males. In females, if the sexual activity does not produce orgasm and satisfaction, a woman will masturbate even after intercourse, if she still has a sexual desire. Basically, orgasm and sexual satisfaction in women is not entirely bound on intercourse, as in a man. It has to be connected with psychological satisfaction with her husband or lover. Any unpleasant thought, any anger, any aggravation invariably destroys the orgasm and sexual satisfaction in a female—contrary to the male, who has, so to say, male orgasm by ejaculation of semen regardless of anger, aggravation, or psychological dissatisfaction with the partner. That is the main reason for the existence of prostitution; in the intercourse with a prostitute there is no emotional involvement, only an automatic reflex of the male.

Now, to return to the masturbation of females in general and older women in particular. If a woman has sexual desire and has no outlet in intercourse with a male partner, she will masturbate. If she is a bachelor girl, a divorcee or a widow and used to masturbating in younger age, then it is to be expected that she will, as long as she has still a sexual interest, masturbate also in older age. And because of scarcity of partners, masturbation is much more frequent in older women than in older men. In a group of married women, aged 50, who had intercourse on the average of once a week, 30% were masturbating. Masturbation was still very prevalent at the age of 65 in married women. In single women masturbation incidents were nearly double those of the married group at comparable ages. They also experienced sex dreams more frequently than married women.

Is masturbation bad for health? No, not at all. This applies to all ages, as long as there is no abuse of it. The main damage, if any, is a psychological one. In a masturbating youngster, it gives him a life of fantasy which takes him away from the surrounding reality and makes him shy in the encounter with real girls—not the fantasy girls whom he conquers in the imagination while masturbating. The young girl has less damage; psychologically she also becomes introverted. Both suffer from a guilt complex in the feeling of committing a sin and doing something which should not be done—the more so because ignorant parents and moralistic books tell them how dangerous it is to masturbate.

Mature women who masturbate are the dissatisfied ones; they enjoy pleasure which they don't get in real life. The same applies to women in old age who by masturbation escape the misery of old, lonely age, full of disappointment and regrets about the mistakes made and the life wasted. At least in masturbation they have some vicarious pleasure which they do not experience in daily life.

So, as a doctor, one can only say: there is no damage to health or life in masturbation, and if the older women enjoy it and have no other outlet for their sexual interest and energy, let them enjoy it without feeling guilt or remorse. From the medical point of view there is no objection to it.

11. Are there sexual disturbances in older patients?

Yes, there are, and they are psychological and even mental. Frigidity in women is a badly-defined mixture which covers a lot of deeper psychological and other problems, some of them started at very early age, even early childhood. The old person's sexual pattern is the same as it was exhibited at the age of 16 or 17. Age alone does not diminish sexual desire. The rate at which man or woman slows up sexually in old age does not exceed the rate at which other activities have slowed down or stopped.

The most frequent symptoms of sexual disturbance in older patients are hypochondriac attitudes toward symptoms of disease, senile depression, persecution mania, and breakdown in marital relations. Disturbance is present when there is no sexual activity; when there is aggressive or destructive behavior towards partners or friends, or even mere acquaintances; whenever there is unfounded jealousy of other people and their imagined happiness. And, though it may sound peculiar, a loss of sexual satisfaction in old age—or the feeling that the satisfaction is missing —can lead to despair, which can be expressed by all kinds of psychosomatic or psychological symptoms. Underlying is the emotion that life is at an end. The clock cannot be turned back; and what was not achieved or fulfilled is lost forever.

To sum up: if an older woman can have sexual activity because she is lucky enough to have a husband, and one who still has sexual interest and ability, she should enjoy it; and if she experiences orgasm, there is nothing to be ashamed of and every reason for happiness. This is not because it is a sign of femininity, or of sexual attraction which she can still evoke, at least in her partner, though it is such a sign—but because sex is a part, and an important part, of life; and participation in every aspect of life is what we desire for every human being.

Part II

MENTAL HEALTH IN OLD AGE

CHAPTER XXVIII

MENTAL DISEASES IN OLD AGE

In old age we have to distinguish between mental diseases as they may occur more or less in all age groups, and mental deterioration which can be attributed to the wear and tear of age. Among mental diseases we have first of all to stress that one of them occurs only in young people, hardly ever after the age of 30, and that is schizophrenia—also called split personality or juvenile insanity. If we discard this disease, all other mental diseases can occur in old age too, namely: paranoia, also called persecution mania; manic-depressive insanity or mental imbalance, which consists of mania, of talkativeness, of restlessness, alternating with periods of depression, of sadness, of disinterest in any affairs or of the environment and not even interest in his or her own well-being.

(a) *Progressive Paralysis*

To these mental diseases we have to add progressive paralysis, which is a late effect of syphilis and which leads to insanity. This type of mental disease was quite common at the time when we had no proper treatment of early syphilis, and the brain became affected by that infection. With the advent of Ehrlich's salvarsan treatment and later of penicillin, the cases of progressive paralysis diminished in numbers. Also the treatment of that brain syphilis initiated by Wagner-Jauregg in Vienna, with malaria counterattacking the progressive paralysis, gave at least a hope for improvement and even for a cure.

There are, of course, mental diseases caused by other infectious or organic changes. There exists a mental deterioration due to diabetes, or due to a brain tumor, or due to typhus, or encephalitis (inflammation of the brain). But these diseases can occur in any age group, and are not confined to old age.

It is important for a doctor to distinguish between organic mental diseases which can occur in old age but are not necessarily due to old age, and brain changes which are due to old-age deterioration. The first ones belong to the field of psychiatry; and while the latter actually are also within the realm of psychiatry, nevertheless the burden of dealing with this problem lies on the shoulders of the family physician and of the family itself.

(b) *Senile Depression*

The most common and prevalent mental disorder of the aged is depression. Most people over 65, if they retire and do not lead a full, intensive life as before 65, are depressed. It is often connected with the problem of retirement; and of that we shall talk in a separate chapter. The depression can be due to organic brain changes, but it can also be due to a mental disturbance without an underlying brain disease. People are just depressed, and the range of depression can go from a very light to a very severe one. If they are depressed to a severe degree, they also deteriorate physically because they have no appetite, hardly eat anything and lose weight, sometimes up to 40 pounds.

The treatment of depression is very difficult. We have at least a dozen antidepressant medicines, but none of them can boast that it can cure depression; at the best there is some improvement, more alertness or more appetite. The main reason for such a depression of old age is a psychological one, a feeling of rejection, an awareness of age, of death approaching sooner or later. The rejection can be felt when a person feels perfectly well and is mandatorily retired from his job, which he fulfilled well a short while ago before he or she became 65 years old. The feeling of rejection extends to family and social life. The children look at the old father with the feeling that you cannot expect much in respect to advice and/or performance from an aged parent; maybe the advice given by the parent is due to senility. For a young man or woman a person of 65 or more is a tottering old; not an elderly, senior citizen who has accumulated wisdom and who should be listened to. The fact that the majority of the rulers of our world are old men is not appreciated by the young generation but, on the contrary, resented; and the drastic political conditions of our time are considered by the young generation as the best proof of the senility and lack of ideas of the older statesmen. That is one of the reasons why John Kennedy was so venerated by the young people all over the world; they saw in him a representative of *their* generation, from whom you could expect much. The accent on youth which you observe in our times only deepens the resentment and the dejection of older people. They see it everywhere, and after retirement they see it also at home, in their own family, where their ideas and advice are scorned. This adds to the depression of older citizens, men and women. The upbringing of children by the young generation differs from that of the older generation; and the old mother is being listened to by sheer politeness, without the slightest intention to do as the mother says and advises. The mother is not an idiot. She sees what is going on, and resents the situation and gets depressed.

Even in social life there is a slow but definite change. The retired man who was used to getting up early, to catch a train, to be expected home at a certain hour, suddenly stays at home; his colleagues and friends who may be only a year or two younger, continue their usual routine; and when they meet in the evening at parties or clubs or church or any social gathering, the slightly younger have to tell the usual daily encounters at the office or shop, while the retired man feels himself as an outsider. This too adds to the depression. For all these reasons one can consider depression as one of the most frequent and important mental disorders of old age.

(c) *Paranoia (Persecution Mania)*

Paranoia or persecution mania is also a not-infrequent mental disturbance in old age. It does not always take the extreme forms which require institutionalization of such a patient, though occasionally such paranoiacs become violent when they consider that they have enemies who have to be destroyed; and these "enemies" can be members of their own family, such as a wife or a husband or a child or a grandchild, and so on. In most cases, however, it takes the form of accusation of misdeeds performed by the so-called enemies who make their life difficult or miserable. One has to understand that traits of character which are inherent in a person, whether by heritage or by external influences, remain the same in old age; only, with aging these characteristics become more pronounced and, accordingly, more obvious. An economical person who always counted the pennies can become a miser in old age. A misanthrope who did not like social life can become a recluse. A person with a character of suspicion of people wanting to cheat him can become a paranoiac with a persecution mania. In short, character traits become exaggerated and develop into a psychological or mental sickness.

There is no treatment for such conditions. Contrary to the idea of many people that age mellows, it is not a general rule; it is highly individual. A nice person can in old age become even nicer; a bad person will with age become worse, and even evil. Old age is not necessarily a golden age for many people. It is in general a sad age when, apart from financial problems which are often more difficult than in younger age, there is a lot of bitterness and depression. This state of mind causes people to look for scapegoats, and thus develops a persecution idea: because it is in the nature of human beings to find the fault not in themselves but in others; in other words, to look for external and not for internal reasons.

On the whole, mental diseases are not very common among the aged. They are more prevalent among the young and middle-aged. The fact that we have so many old people in the mental hospitals is not due to mental diseases, but to mental deterioration. It is a fact that in 1912 only 13 percent of all new patients in mental institutions were over 65 years of age, while in 1960 they comprised 40% of all new patients. But there are reasons for this jump in percentage. First of all, the population of the United States gets older; as mentioned in previous chapters, we have now about 26 million people over 65. Secondly, many younger people can nowadays be cured or improved by the new drugs, by electro-shock and the other achievements of modern medicine, so that they can be treated as out-patients in mental institutions. And thirdly, as said before, many middle-aged people admitted half a century ago suffered from progressive paralysis due to syphilis, and the number of such patients is now minute. Just the same, the fact that 40% of patients in mental hospitals are over 65 constitutes a serious problem and has to be dealt with.

(d) *Physical Defects Causing Mental Disturbances*

Before turning to the problem of mental deterioration of elderly people and dealing with the so-called brain syndrome of those people—that is, the combination of symptoms which are related to the brain changes in elderly people—we have to emphasize that not all people who act senile are really senile. In many cases the change in the behavior of the elderly people is due to deafness which is frequently not recognized, or due to poor vision, or to physical weakness, or to loneliness, to lack of social intercourse with other people and lack of people to whom they could talk. We see as a result that people in such circumstances sometime talk to themselves, or start talking to strangers and even telling them their whole life story. Such behavior looks, of course, strange; and such people are considered mentally defective because they behave not quite as would be expected from people in a given routine environment. Half-deaf or deaf people often do not want to publicize their defect, and either speak too loud or too soft because they cannot estimate the volume of their speech. Half-blind people (we have a lot of so-called legally blind people who can read and walk without help and still are unable to perform like others) are very careful in their walking and avoiding obstacles which are none for normal people. Therefore their behavior might look peculiar to onlookers, and the strangeness can and frequently is attributed to a mental defect.

A correction of these defects, like proper glasses or provision of a seeing-eye dog, or a good hearing aid, or introduction to a social club where a lonely person can find company, entertainment and new interest, can change the whole pattern of behavior and restore the individual to a useful member of the community.

The most important mental disorder of the elderly is the series of symptoms which is connected with arteriosclerosis of the arteries of the brain. This causes a poor supply of blood and oxygen to those arteries, with a resulting malfunction of the brain centers which are fed by those arteries. Of these centers, the first victim is the memory center.

(e) *Memory Defects*

Memory starts at birth and ends only with the grave. It can be compared with archaeological findings. Each period of life puts a layer of memory in the brain sector where it accumulates and settles down. In the next period of life a new layer of memory settles down overlying the previous period, sometimes covering it so completely as to become invisible and forgotten. With each new impression, with new knowledge, the old ones are pushed aside as, superficially seen, not needed any more, and therefore obliterated from our conscious mind.

This process goes on all our life, one layer of memory piling up on the other, similarly to the formation of a new city or settlement on the site of an old city. When the archaeologists excavate a historical site, they go deeper and deeper, and sometimes they find one civilization buried underneath a later one up to the present time. Such a number of archaeological layers of old buried civilizations is described, for instance, in Michener's book, *The Source*.

Now, in our mind there is exactly the same accumulation of facts, of names, of figures during our lifetime. But we do not remember all the facts, all the impressions of a lifetime, unless one has a phenomenal memory which is a talent similar to a talent for painting or writing or for music or for languages. Usually, however, facts, happenings and impressions are lost, to be substituted by new ones. These old memories are lost to our conscious mind; but they did not disappear, they are only buried. Actually, nothing is ever lost. Our memory-center keeps all the happenings, all impressions, all facts as in a warehouse, to be taken out of it whenever necessary. Only sometimes it is a hard job to find it in the warehouse because of too much collection of facts and impressions. This is the reason why children have usually a very good memory; they do not have that much space taken up in that warehouse of memory, therefore it is easy to find what is needed.

As we grow older and gather more and more experience, the collection gets bigger and bigger and the layers pile up more and more. In order to find a way out of that maze, we make a selection. We chose what is important to remember and what is less important and and can be forgotten. This less important material is pushed away. In that selection we discriminate. We try to forget the unpleasant things and remember the happy moments of our life. The actress Ingrid Bergman was asked once by an interviewer what was the recipe for happiness, and she answered, "A good health and a bad memory." She was perfectly right. It is simple that good health is a first consideration, because illness mars any other happiness. But she was also right by saying that bad memory is a clue to happiness, because we try *not* to remember unhappy events of our life. One can see how we forget pain and discomfort which we had during illness and operations; how women forget the pain which they had at the delivery of a baby, and often soon afterwards get pregnant again and go through the ordeal of delivery all over again. The people who were in concentration camps with starvation and death-threat constantly before their eyes can continue living only by forgetting what they went through. The same applies to soldiers who went through horrors of war. They too can return to uneventful civilian life only when they succeed in forgetting.

In cases when this memory is too vivid, when the victims of horrors are living in their imagination through all these terrible happenings, they become mentally disturbed and require psychiatric help. But, apart from the sad memories of the victims of persecutions, of wars, even in daily life there are plenty of unpleasant impressions and happenings which we would like to forget and usually do. Let us say, we try our best to forget.

With the aging process, when the memory center—our "warehouse" of memory—is, because of hardening of the arteries, poorly supplied with blood and oxygen, our memory starts fading. We just do not remember things which should be remembered. The more involved the process of arteriosclerosis of that sector of the brain, the worse becomes the memory. An elderly person may not remember what happened yesterday, or the name of a close relative or friend, or, if the damage is severe, not even the words for objects of daily life. By the same token, an elderly person may suddenly remember very well happenings of 50 or more years ago, things which occurred in his or her childhood, and which the elderly person thought that these were forgotten long ago; and suddenly they come vividly into his or her mind. The explanation is that in a condition of arteriosclerosis the daily happenings are no more important. Such a person does not participate wholly in the daily life. These things are not as interesting as what happened when he or she was young and full of vigor and ambition. It is like taking a sponge and wiping out the recent writing on a blackboard; in other words, a return to childhood or adolescence, when everything was fresh and the impressions were so vivid that they stayed in the mind. Such occurrences prove again that memories are buried but never lost; they come back sometimes when needed and sometimes involuntarily. In the case of psychoanalysis for instance, it is the task of the analyst to pull out the old memories of childhood and early youth in order to come to the core of complexes from which a patient suffers, and which would be impossible if a memory would be wiped out forever.

In short—loss of memory is a selective process and discriminatory. If there is a completely overwhelming loss of memory, the person has severe brain damage and is near the stage of vegetation, with little hope of improvement.

There are probably dozens of remedies which were supposed to help to restore memory. The trainings of memory as advertised in the papers are, in cases of senile loss of memory, worthless because they do not touch the main reason for the memory defect in elderly persons—namely, the defect in the function of the brain. And no amount of exercise, of courses of memory-help, will improve the function of the brain. I doubt the value of such courses and memory-tricks, even in younger persons, because in younger persons who are physically healthy the lack of memory is purely psychological. People in younger age forget what they don't want to remember; it is sometimes painful to remember certain events in life, and because of the natural self-preservation instinct one forgets in order not to remember. Occasionally a person does not remember because he or she is not interested in the subject, and remembering some dates or names is just a superfluous, unnecessary and boring matter. On the other hand, a person will vividly remember trifling information about movie stars if one is interested in Hollywood life, just like there are people in England who know all about the royal family.

The memory in old age is erratic. The same person can one day remember things very well, and on the next day not at all. He has a complete blank, which can be very irritating to the relatives and to the elderly person himself. It is connected with arterial insufficiency, which varies according to the supply of blood and oxygen to the brain. It vacillates similarly to the coronary insufficiency in the heart. One does not always have chest pain which is connected with the insufficient supply of blood to the heart. One has good and bad days, and the same applies to the brain; one day the memory is not bad, acceptable; on other days it is almost a total blank. We do not have remedies which could cure a loss of memory; but any medication which improves the supply of blood to the brain will sooner or later have a beneficial effect on the memory—provided that the arteries which supply this section of the brain are sufficiently elastic as to widen on stimulation by medicine, and can bring a better supply of blood and oxygen. If that is the case, one can hope that the medication which dilates the arteries of the brain will also improve the memory.

It is also remarkable how inventive people are. If they know that their memory is defective, they will find ways to cover up the defect by some ruses to find out what they don't remember without showing that their memory is poor. In the long run they cannot deceive their relative or friends, but still one can cover up some huge blanks of spaces of memory which are missing, if other functions of the brain are intact. And that is the main problem; because, if one is smart enough, he or she just does not touch subjects when the memory comes to a test. One can write down some important items which one cannot remember. However, more important is how the rest of the brain functions; and here we come to the problem of senility.

(f) *Senility*

Ordinarily, accepted human behavior is regulated by the size of the brain and by the limited life-span of the cells contained in it. The brain cells, contrary to cells of other organs of the body, are irreplaceable; with age they deteriorate and die in increasing numbers, and thus impair the efficiency of the psychic and motor functions of the human being.

It is a natural, irrevocable process. But in some cases it is slow and starts at very late age; in others it comes early and even prematurely, just as in the cases of loss of memory which we discussed in the previous pages. It is connected with the general health of the person, and primarily with the degree of arteriosclerosis. It is also a question of luck. If the arteriosclerosis hits the arteries of the heart or of the legs, one has, of course, trouble. However, it happens the opposite way around, too—namely, the heart or the legs are in a comparatively good shape while the arteriosclerosis hits the brain arteries with poor supply of blood and oxygen, poor nourishment of the cells of the brain, with resulting deterioration and the so-called brain syndrome—that is, poor psychic function; in plain English, signs of senility.

There are many tests as to how to find out the degree of senility when there is only a functional disturbance, and when there is an underlying organic brain damage. The tests, done in all institutions for aged people, and in mental hospitals, are important because they give one a prognosis—a prediction whether there is hope for improvement or not. However, in most cases, if an elderly patient lives with members of the family, they will notice the mental deterioration and signs of senility without any tests. Just in order to give you an idea how the tests are done (it is only one of many), here are questions asked by the psychiatrist Dr. Alvin I. Goldfarb, who is also the chairman of the Committee on Aging of the American Psychiatric Association. The questionnaire used by him goes as follows: (1) Where are we (patient and doctor) now? (2) Where is this place located? (3) What is today's date? (4) What month is it? (5) What year is it? (6) How old are you? (7) What is your birthday? (8) What year were you born? (9) Who is the President of the U.S.? (10) Who was the President before him?

According to Dr. Goldfarb, if a person gets less than two of the questions wrong, he or she has a mild or no brain deterioration. If he gets from 3 to 7 of the questions wrong, he has a moderate brain damage. If he gets more than nine wrong, you can be sure that the patient has a severe brain deterioration and that the outlook is not particularly good.

The questions can be modified, and the answers are not exactly the same for every level of education and intelligence. The question of a birthday's exact date is, if it is not celebrated, of little importance and significance to some individuals. I know from experience that some of my Medicare patients had a lot of difficulties to make sure that they really achieved 65 years. Not only did they have no birthday certificates (and that applied especially to colored people born in the Southern states and to survivors of Nazi concentration camps), but they had occasionally only vague ideas about the date of their birth; while otherwise they were in perfect mental health. In my family we were 8 children, and the birthdays were not celebrated. We hardly knew when we were born; only, when we went to school we had to bring a note telling when our birthday was. The same can apply to question No. 6, when one is asked how old he is. Women give so often so many different answers to that question that they get confused themselves and do not always know how old they are exactly. And, regarding what date it is, if one lives a very monotonous life, in which one day hardly differs from another, it is not always easy to give a prompt answer to that question. Everybody experiences it during vacation time, when Thursday does not differ from Wednesday or Friday, unless there is a special event. I know that my patients, when they want to write a check for my fee, ask me what date it is or look at the calendar on my desk. And you will be surprised how many people are so engrossed in their petty daily life and are so little interested in politics that, especially in old age, they hardly know the sequence of Presidents. They might know the present President and forget who was the immediate predecessor. In short—the questions quoted above are relevant, but in some cases they do not apply to all levels of education, interest and intelligence. One can accept the diagnosis that, if somebody does not know the answer to any of the questions, something is wrong with his mental perception; and especially if one knows that the person who is interviewed previously used to know very well all the answers.

Basically, senility should be judged by comparison with performance in previous years. The greater the discrepancy in the performance, the greater is the deterioration, physical and mental. One can get old and still preserve physical ability and activities. There can be a physical senility—a man's inability to cater for himself, to look after himself, to do shopping, to clean, to wash, even to walk. This physical senility can simulate mental senility. If, for instance, a person is too frail to clean and to wash, and has no help and nobody to look after him, such a person can start accumulating dirt in the apartment by being unable to perform single household chores like washing dishes, pots and pans, or mopping the floor. It can also lead to lack of cleanliness of the body by postponing bathing, washing or showering. Clothing may be left dirty, stained, and not mended if torn. The same would apply to underwear. The result of all these happenings is filth. Now, if a stranger or a relative visits such a person, he or she would consider such a person mentally deranged for allowing the accumulation of such filthy conditions. Very often the basis is lack of money to pay help, plus pride of still having privacy and not having to go to a nursing home. Bad sight adds to the inability to see the dust, the dirt and filth.

With the physical frailty comes also a state of indifference, especially if such an elderly person lives all by himself, does not expect any visitors, and possibly has no relatives, or the relatives live far away. With this comes, not necessarily mental deterioration, but hostility and anger towards people who do not care whether they are alive or dead. And as a matter of fact, frequently even close neighbors do not care, do not visit, and do not know even whether these frail, elderly neighbors are still alive or not. I saw in my practice some cases of old, lonely people who died, and whose death was discovered only after some days due to the odor of the decaying body, because of which the police were called. They had to break in the door and find the body of a person several days dead from natural causes.

Just the same, we have plenty of cases of mental senility of all degrees. Some are slightly mentally defective: they still know what's going on, but they slow down in their daily routine life. One of the typical signs of senility is repetitiousness. A person apparently does not trust his or her memory and repeats the simplest thing said or to be done several times, or forgets that he or she told the story a few minutes ago and starts telling it all over again. One can forget to eat, or eats the same meal twice, having forgotten that she or he ate already. I know of a case when a senile person went to work at 5 o'clock in the morning under the impression that it was 10 a.m., and was surprised on arrival at the office that nobody was there and that the shops were still closed. These are comparatively minor mental aberrations. The real senility starts when a person gets completely confused, does not know where he is, has to be fed, washed, and dressed, hardly understands what one tells him or her, and behaves like a baby—including urinary and bowel movement incontinence, or without it. In any case, the complete mental senility converts a person from a human being into a vegetable, who lives only to eat, to drink, to sleep and to eliminate, and has no human interest in life. Frequently such a senile person does not recognize his or her closest relatives—a son, a daughter, a husband or wife.

What can be done in such cases? Here we have the extreme cases of institutionalization. And that brings us to the whole problem of human relations between old age and the rest of the community.

CHAPTER XXIX

SUICIDE IN OLD AGE

It is not widely known that the suicide rate among old people is exceedingly high, compared with the total population and with the younger people. We have in the United States more than 10,500 suicides recorded every year. The percentage of people over 55 who commit suicide is double of that of the total population. The highest rate of suicides for white males occurs at the age of 75 and over; for white females, the highest rate is in the menopausal years, at the age of 45-54.

There is also one very significant difference between a suicide of a young person and an elderly one. In both cases the cause of the suicide is an emotional crisis. But the emotional crisis in a young person, "the brainstorm" is transient; while it does not pass in an older person unless some radical changes are made. What is the cause of suicide in a young man or woman? A big quarrel which looks for an unbalanced person bigger than it actually is; a marital disagreement; a non-requited love; abandonment by a lover, male or female, and the end of a romance; a guilt complex because of something done which one regrets; fear of consequences, such as illegitimate pregnancy; fear of inability to cope with financial difficulties. All these reasons for committing suicide are transient and can be remedied. If the attempt of suicide is not successful and the person is saved, and the cause for the emotional conflict is removed, one can be sure that no other attempt will be made.

This is quite different in an older person. The best proof is the fact that, while for the whole population the attempt to repeat the suicide within the year, to finish the job, is only 2%, it is 6% for the repeat and successful suicide for the old-age persons.

There is, of course, a psychological reason for the high rate of suicides in older people compared with young ones. The main reason is depression and general despair of life. One reason is chronic bad health, whether due to arthritis or heart or lung diseases—in any case, a chronic disease which impedes enjoyment of life and normal functioning. That happens especially in lonely people who have to do things for themselves. Occasionally, suicide is attempted by hypochondriacs who imagine that they suffer from an incurable disease like cancer; and in order to avoid the pain and suffering which they connect with cancer, they rather commit suicide in order to avoid a final tragic, slow-in-coming death. Another reason for old-age suicide is financial stress. One has to fight daily in order to maintain himself at a time when the income is either greatly diminished or disappeared completely, due to inability to earn money. Even the fact of welfare subsidy does not deter suicidal persons from making an end to their lives. On the one hand, not everybody can manage well on the calculated minimum given to a welfare recipient in order to sustain his or her life; on the other hand, people on welfare feel degraded. They lost their dignity as human beings by having an investigation of their financial resources, of their family, of their insurance, if any; and they are ashamed of the fact that they have to apply for welfare, that their friends and acquaintances will know about that. And there are also the regular visits of the case-worker, who may have the best intentions but adds to the psychological indignity. A depressed suicidal person prefers death to this constant degradation of his dignity. Of course, not every welfare recipient is a candidate for suicide; it applies to people who become welfare clients at old age while all their life they could work and enjoy life, which had a meaning. Basically, welfare or no welfare, life has to have a meaning in old age. Otherwise it is not worthwhile to live it.

It is necessary to stress that only a small percentage of old-age suicides are suffering from a mental disease; only about 25% of the attempted suicides are psychotic—that is, mentally deranged—unless one considers that anybody attempting suicide is mentally unbalanced, which is definitely not the case. I remember vividly a case in my practice of an old woman of about 70 who committed suicide in full mental powers. She suffered from rheumatoid arthritis which came to her at late age (unusual for rheumatoid arthritis) and started crippling her and making her more and more disabled. She was a refugee who had just gotten compensation as restitution for her suffering in German concentration camps. She committed suicide with barbiturates which she saved for several months, receiving a small amount for insomnia. She left a note and a will in which she donated the money to some charities and distant relatives. She explained in her note that, while she could get domestic help or a nurse for her disability, she knew very well that her disease was incurable; and being alone, without a husband or near relative, she had no joy in life and no hope for a future. Therefore she would rather die peacefully as long as she could do it without suffering and without having always to depend on help from strangers.

One can, of course, argue that she suffered, apart from rheumatoid arthritis, also from depression due to her loneliness and former persecution by the Nazis. However, this is not the point. Important in this case, as in the 75% not-mental patients, is the fact that people commit suicide out of despair that they have no future and no point in going on living. In the 25% of mental cases who do commit suicide, it is usually fear which brings them to the end. In many cases, especially in institutions such as nursing and old-age homes where suicide is not infrequent, senility is often connected with a persecution mania. If one regularly visits such homes, one hears complaints not only about food but also about other inhabitants and nurses, even about doctors. Occasionally, one hears complaints about being poisoned or deliberately beaten by nurses or nurse-aids, or not being given food in order to starve them. Being helpless, unable to defend themselves, and having the persecution mania, such an old-age patient prefers to commit suicide in order to avoid being killed by others.

Generally speaking, old people commit suicide because they are lonely, poor, sick, insecure and afraid of dying all by themselves, nobody paying attention to them. Life has lost its meaning; they do not belong anywhere. If they commit suicide, they force the environment to pay attention to them; they become a paragraph in the papers, a subject of talk for a very short time at the institution where they resided. They are buried with the participation of a religious person; and finally, by lying in a cemetery, they are a member of a group of the dead —of a community in which they longed to be participants while alive. By their death, they restore the status which they had before they became old and lonely.

The whole problem of suicide in old age is not a medical, but a social and economical one. It has to be dealt with in the large scope of life as a whole in old age.

CHAPTER XXX

DEATH AND DYING IN OLD AGE

The attitude of elderly people towards death—how they feel about dying and death—has shown very conflicting results in the investigation of this problem by various psychiatrists and doctors interested in geriatrics, that is, in the science of old age. The reason is that this attitude towards the problem of dying and death is highly emotional and individual. It is almost impossible to define this attitude in the terms of elderly people as a group of the population; rather, we have to subdivide them into groups of personalities who show some common denominator which would characterize their attitude. And even then we still have to deal with smaller groups as subdivisions in order to gain a more or less correct impression, with the proviso that, as everywhere, there are exceptions to the rule.

We have to state, first of all, that there is a profound difference between the attitude of young people towards death and that of old people. A young person cannot imagine himself dying, especially if the youngster is healthy. They look upon old people who are condemned, so to say, by nature to death with a pity or sorrow. They just cannot imagine themselves dead, and if they hear that a young person has died, they would think consciously or subconsciously, "That cannot happen to me." They can imagine death by violence, but they do abhor the idea of slow dying by disease, deterioration and old age. This is one of the main reasons why young people volunteer as soldiers in a war. First, they are sure that they will have a great adventure and fun and will return safely home as heroes; secondly, if they think that they might die, that will be a quick death by violence, which is preferred to dying by degrees in old age. But, basically, they have a personal feeling of immortality. Though they know that sooner or later everybody is bound to die, they think that in their particular case it will be later, not sooner. They just don't entertain the idea of dying. They are too busy to enjoy life—period.

Completely different is the attitude of old people. They realize very well that, whether they are well or sick, they are approaching the period which ends in death. And, if there is a common denominator for all elderly people in regard to death, the name of the denominator is *fear*. They are all afraid of dying. Life with all its vicissitudes, all its unhappiness, is precious; one can have it only once, and if one dies, it is the end for good. But if fear is the common attitude towards death, there are, however, degrees of fear. For instance, deeply religious people of all denominations, whether Christians, Jews, Moslems or Buddhists, who believe in life after death, are less afraid of dying. I say *less*, because even with the inculcated beliefs in an afterlife there remains a certain doubt—or even, if no doubt, there is still an attachment to the life one has and enjoys while being alive. However, a deeply religious person accepts death not only as inevitable, but with the hope of eternity which will come after the death.

Apart from religion, there is a natural imagined wish for eternity which takes various forms in life. Children and grandchildren are the material proof that something will remain from one after death. In the life of the children will be a continuation of one's existence. He or she will not disappear completely. The face, the character will continue in another form. In this way such an attitude resembles the idea of incarnation in the Buddhist religion. Only, in the Buddhist religion one *personally* continues to live, though in a different form as another human being or an animal. But still he or she did not die, did not disappear completely. In children one also continues to live, and that is the law of nature. That is why the sexual instinct, the urge to procreate, is the most powerful instinct, from bacteria to human beings.

There are also other forms to promote continuation after death. There are the simple devices of stones with all kinds of inscriptions on the cemeteries. There are the wills in which money is donated for charities, educational institutions, etc., in order to perpetuate the memory and the name of the donor. There are the wills which force the children to do what the deceased wanted, at the peril of losing the inheritance. There is also the simple device of giving the name of the deceased to a grandchild in order to perpetuate the memory. All these devices are just a proof of the fact that people are afraid of death and cannot reconcile themselves to the fact that sooner or later they will cease to exist.

There are groups of personalities of aged who believe each in a different way, even if there is an underlying fear and the desire to live after death. As mentioned in previous chapters, many aged people are depressed because of financial difficulties, or because of the death of a spouse, or because of the indifference of children, or because of a chronic disability which requires them to depend more and more on other people. This group is not too anxious to live; they consider death as a relief from all their troubles. Old age is for them not a golden age but an unhappy period which, the sooner it finishes, the better.

The aged people who are shy and withdrawn as they were when younger and hardly had any social life, will be even more so as they get older. They are withdrawn because they are afraid of other people. They do not trust them. They do not want to show emotions even towards members of their own family. They are afraid of everything unknown, and therefore they have to be afraid of death, even if they do not show it.

On the other hand, we have manic people who have frequent emotional outbursts of crying or laughter, of happiness or grief, or of imaginary or true catastrophes. They are very much involved in their physical well-being. Even if they tell one that they do not care if they would have to die, they are very much scared of death and will try their best to avoid it by all means at their resources.

We have also the elderly who do not want to get old and die. They will not rest. They will work as before, even if they damage their health by it. They just cannot relax or do not want to relax; they want to enjoy life. They are outgoing. They have a rich social life. They will play all kinds of games. They will travel extensively, if they can afford it. If they are poor, they will join church or social groups, clubs or societies. And all this in order to avoid old age. They cheat themselves in the belief that they are still young and think that they cheated others too. Funny enough, they believe they can cheat death itself. Characteristic for that group was a patient of mine who managed his large factory at the age of 80 and more. When I asked him why he did not retire—after all, he had plenty of money and no obligations—he answered me jokingly. But underlying was a serious thought of his: "You see, I live in New York City; my factory is in New Jersey. The Angel of Death is looking for me in New York, where my address is; and as long as I spend most of my life in my factory in New Jersey, he will not find me. And besides, I rather prefer to die in my boots."

To sum up, there are different attitudes towards death among aged people. Some take it more philosophically; these are resigned. Some fight death as well as they can. Some consider death as a relief from misery. But, basically, all of them are afraid of death. The multitude of individual approaches to death is only an expression of a general common attitude as a common denominator: nobody wants to die, and everybody is afraid of death.

A problem different from the attitude towards death is the attitude towards dying. The first question in this respect is: should a physician tell a fatally-sick person that death is unavoidable—in short, that he or she is going to die? The answer is highly individual. One cannot say, "All critically-ill persons should be informed that they are on the verge of dying"; and one cannot say, "Nobody should be informed that he is going to die." It depends how a person would take such an information. Some will get so shocked that, instead of waiting for the death, they will rather commit suicide. Others will take it calmly as a matter of fact, as something which should be expected. Still others will be angry with the doctor that he gave them such information. They would try not to believe him, or they would expect him to be wrong—that by some miracle they will survive. Therefore, a doctor will have to be very careful in his decision whether to tell a patient of his or her impending death. Even if a patient requests such information, it does not automatically mean that he wants it. Frequently he wants a reassurance of his fears, a denial of impending death; and he tells the doctor "to tell him the truth," which he wants to be different from what he is afraid of. In other words, he wants the doctor to tell him that he is not dying.

The great majority of terminal patients want their family to be told of the impending death. The reason is a double one: if they surmise that they are going to die, they want the relatives to make all preparations for a proper funeral and settlement of all necessary formalities, obligations, etc. And then, if the family knows, they will pay more attention to them. The dying one will be in the position of a prisoner condemned to death who can expect some privileges ordinarily denied to him. Such a patient would expect to have more frequent and prolonged visits of relatives, maybe some gifts, some last wishes fulfilled; and maybe such a dying person wants to hear some lies that he or she is not going to die—lies which one in such condition is very eager to believe.

Just the same, some people have the courage to hear that they have to die. Most prefer to die without knowing that they are dying. But if the aged are asked theoretically how they would spend their time if they had only a restricted time—a year or so—to live, the answer (if they think it is just a hypothetical question) varies according to the personality of the person who is quizzed. The majority answer, "I would travel"—meaning, to spend the remaining time in catching up with the things which one always wanted to do, to see, or what one missed in life; especially if one did not travel extensively before.

In the TV series "Run for Your Life," such a hypothetical problem was serialized. The hero was told that he had an incurable disease which would end in death within 18 months to two years. He chooses traveling and adventure because he wants more of life than the sedentary, routine life as a lawyer; at the same time the traveling, the adventures, the meeting of many other new people somehow postpones the inevitable. One has hardly time to think of dying; it gives one also the advantage of not being anymore afraid of death in the various risky adventures, because after all one is dying anyway. And basically it is true to life, because the TV escapism is also the real escapism of a dying person who wants to escape the sentence.

Some answer the question how they would spend the remaining time by wanting to be more with the family, or continuing life as usual. In the first instance, the attachment of the family is the old desire of eternity—to live longer in the memory of the relatives by being closer and longer with them than usual. The other instance, to continue as usual, means the so-called ostrich policy—to bury the head in sand in order not to see the danger. By living as usual, the death in a year or two ceases to exist, and maybe will not materialize at all.

Still others have a guilt complex. Standing in front of the inevitable, knowing that they are dying, they repent in expectation to have to answer their Maker, and want to spend the remaining time by helping others, by making good, by prayer—just to have a good conscience that their life was not in vain. Very sick people regret, not their sins, but the opportunities which they missed in life.

Dying is a tough time for patients and doctors. The doctors who know that their patient is doomed and that they cannot help, have to learn to be comforters—and not only to the family who knows about the impending death of the relative, but also to be a comforter of the dying. It is a tough job of daily white lies if the patient does not know that he is dying, or making the best of it if he or she knows. In a way, it is a silent fight between two personalities—of the doctor and of the patient—in which the victor is only a third party: the death. Though it gives the doctor the feeling of the inadequacy of medical science in a case of an incurable disease, it is also uplifting from the moral point of view and shows the caliber of the personality of the doctor.

But it is also tough for the dying one, whether he or she clings to life or not. If the dying is connected with a lot of pain, it is just waiting either for relief by the injection of the sedative, or waiting for when the medicine wears off and the pain reappears. In such cases, there is a limit to the degree of suffering. Not rare are the cases when a patient finds that he or she cannot take it any longer and commits suicide, thus making a premature end ot the dying process.

In cases like terminal heart disease, when the pain is insignificant or not existent at all, it is easier to induce hope in a sick person. Hope for improvement should not be withheld from the patient, even if he can hardly breathe or move. It is important to alleviate the discomfort of the dying, to make it at all costs easier to bear, and to sustain life and hope.

Death-expectation and dying in old age are trying times and show the real character of a person. The close cooperation between patient, doctor and family can bring a harmony which brings a bright light to that sad and dark period of human life.

CHAPTER XXXI

SLEEP IN OLD AGE

Most doctors and laymen seem to take it for granted that elderly people sleep less and need less sleep than young adults. In some textbooks you can find a statement that older people require only 5-7 hours of sleep, contrary to younger adults who need 7-9 hours. However, though the problem of sleep and its meaning for the health and well-being of people is now being investigated more than ever, the results are not only controversial but still not based on a very large number of subjects, in order to come to definite scientific conclusions. In most cases, the published reports are based on what the subjects under investigation tell the doctor, and therefore have to be considered as subjective and not objective findings. One has to understand that investigation of sleep is much more difficult than, for instance, the investigation of the function of the heart or of the kidneys. There is even no consensus of opinion whether sleep means rest or activity of the brain. While some think that the brain rests in sleep, just as the other organs of the body do, other research workers are of the opinion that in sleep there is a higher activity of the parts of the brain which are responsible for intelligence and higher cerebral functions. In other words, the brain does not rest under normal conditions of life when all the organs are in good shape.

With all these contradictions of findings regarding sleep in elderly people, there are certain points which can be considered as definite pertaining to almost all persons of old age. It has to be emphasized that, like all other functions of a human being, sleep is also highly individual, and what is abnormal for one, can be normal for another. The investigations which are done for sleep patterns are based on volunteers who were brought to a sleep laboratory. They were connected by wires with machinery, such as an electroencephalogram, which measures pulse and the movement of the eyes during sleep (so called REM, that is, "rapid eye movement"), and so on. In this way, the number of volunteers was obviously small. The number of nights when they were under observation attached to the machinery was also small. And therefore the conclusions do not necessarily apply to all people. More reliable is the observation of sleep of elderly subjects compared with younger ones, in institutions such as hospitals, nursing homes, mental hospitals, homes for the aged, and so on. The least reliable are the reports of the subjects themselves. They tend to exaggerate, and for some reasons in order to show off, they give smaller figures for actual sleep hours. Unless they are real insomniacs and sleep very poorly and suffer from it, older persons consider the fact that they can function with less sleep as a sign of vigor and youth. They apparently do not know that younger people need a lot of sleep in order to be able to function well.

It is definite that, regardless of whether the brain is active or not during sleep, an elderly person does require at least as much sleep as a younger one, and possibly, even likely, more. The story that in old age you do not require much sleep is a fallacy. What is true, and found by all investigators and known by the subjects themselves, is the fact that an elderly person rarely sleeps 8 hours through. A younger one also wakes up, but the number of periods of awakening is much smaller in younger than in older persons. And the time of being awake from sleep is much longer in an elderly than in a younger one. Even if an elderly person is a good sleeper, if he or she wakes up during sleep, it takes quite a while—at least double as much as in a younger one—to fall asleep again. There is also another difference: a younger person falls asleep almost immediately, while an older one needs a lot of time to fall asleep, and usually only with the help of all kinds of devices—such as reading or drinking beer or watching television, listening to the radio, taking a long walk, etc.

And even then, the sleep is restless and leads to the above-mentioned intervals of wakening.

One has to remember that many old-age persons take a nap of an hour or more during the day or in the early evening. Even if they sleep less during the night, the number of sleep hours during the 24-hour period may total the required number of 7-9 hours sleep. There is also the fact that, contrary to another fallacy, if one takes a nap in the daytime, he or she sleeps more and better during the night, not less or worse. Apparently the nap is a relaxation and counteracts the tension which impedes normal sleep.

Apart from actual sleeping-time there is a question whether an elderly person should spend more time in bed resting, asleep or awake. The answer is yes. It is better for an elderly person to stay in bed longer. Many old people complain of fatigue, tension and apprehension. If they have an increased bed rest, their sleep increases too, to at least 8 hours or more. The tension and apprehension either disappeared or became much less pronounced; from severe or moderate it went to mild or negligible. There are, of course, a lot of elderly persons who are used from the time of their former active years to get up early in the morning, sometimes even at 6 a.m. and earlier, without knowing what to do with themselves after 10 a.m. They have to either relearn to start the day later, or to have a program of what to do in their free time—which is a different problem, of retirement, not of sleep. That brings us to the problem when to go to bed, even if we accept the proposition that old people also need 8 to 9 hours of sleep.

Basically, regarding the body functions, it makes no difference when, or at what time of the 24-hour period, the 8 hours of sleep are taken. However, it is not that simple. Our body mechanism is adjusted to a certain routine. This is easily seen in the function of the bowel movement. If a person is used to have a bowel movement shortly after arising, or the bowels are trained to move after a meal, then any change of the routine schedule, such as a vacation or a journey can cause constipation when one cannot adhere to the normal routine schedule.

The same applies to sleep. Some people go to bed at the same time, day after day, and wake up at the same time, weekend or vacation or whatever it is. After retirement, if one has no obligation to go to bed at a certain time or to get up at a given hour, it is difficult to find oneself to be a boss of his time, to get up, to eat, to sleep whenever one desires. And that causes a kind of revolution in the body. We can see it in daily life in two instances: a woman who comes into change of life not only loses her menstrual period, but also notices (or her friends or relatives notice) a change in her psychological behavior; she gets more nervous, more moody, and maybe she gets depressed. In another instance, we see difficulties arising from the fact of the speed of transportation. By jet plane we are in no time transferred not only to a different climate and a different sea level to which we have to adjust ourselves, but suddenly due to time changes we leave at night and arrive in another place within a few hours—not in the morning, but either in the afternoon at the place of our destination or even earlier than at the time of our departure; or, according to the clock, only one or two hours later, and that after actual flying time of 7 or 8 hours. That means that we were (if not asleep in the air) 16 hours awake. And though it is, for example, only 4 p.m., according to our body it should be 10-11 p.m.—that is, night and sleeping time. This problem is now considered serious for aircraft crews—pilots, hostesses, etc.—who have the discrepancy between body function and time all the time.

Ordinarily, a person who has no travel occupation does not have this problem—only on vacation. But older people, if they retire, have the same problem, though not as crass as pilots or air hostesses. Just the same, sleep is a very important problem in old age.

We have, apart from the difficulty of adjustment for all old-age people, definite "insomniacs" that is, people who just sleep poorly. I would say that they probably slept poorly even as young people. The number of such people seem to be not small, considering the fact that we have night shows which start about 11:30 p.m. on almost all national TV channels, late and late-

late shows of films, some of them starting at 1:30 p.m., and also radio shows the whole night long. After all, all these are commercial shows sponsored by firms which would not pay for them if they would not be watched or listened to by large crowds of watchers and listeners. Their number cannot be compared with the number of TV watchers in the so-called prime evening hours—between 7:30 and 10 p.m. but they must be in the millions, if one counts the watchers of the TV shows and films which start at 11:30 p.m. and the radio shows, all of them going on for hours, sometimes the whole night long. One can safely say that these night owls are not youngsters, but elderly people with maybe a sprinkle of middle-aged.

The question arises of what to do with these people—what kind of influence the insomnia, which is the basic reason for watching and listening, has on the organism of the person in question. We gave the answer beforehand on previous pages. If the insomniac can catch up later with the required 8 to 9 hours' sleep, it does not matter whether he or she makes a day out of the night, and vice versa. This is meant for retired people who can afford to participate in late shows and to rest and sleep in daytime. We have to remember the large group of entertainers who are used by the nature of their occupation to keep late hours—to have dinner or supper maybe at 2 a.m. and to go to bed at 3 or 4 a.m. But this group can usually afford to sleep late in the day, to wake up at 1 p.m. and to start the working day at 4 p.m. or even later. In this way, they still get their 8 hours' sleep; and by that kind of routine their body gets adjusted to such peculiar (for an ordinary citizen) hours and functions quite well. Interesting for that group of entertainers is that they keep their accustomed routine and hours even when they are "at liberty"—that is, without engagement, and very often even after retirement from active life. That this routine is not deleterious to life and health is proven by the fact that very many entertainers—comedians, singers, actors— live a very long life, and some even still entertain at the age of 70 or 80. The reason is just adjustment to a certain mode of life, and keeping to it.

In a way it also applies to our elderly insomniacs if they make a habit out of it and keep to a certain schedule. One has to emphasize again that they have the opportunity to catch up with lost sleep by taking naps and sleeping in other periods of the day. It is worse if for any reason whatsoever they do not catch up—in other words, if they lack the needed 8 hours. In such a case, especially if people do not sleep and do not watch television and do not listen to the radio and are not interested in reading, we find that lying in bed and waiting for the sleep which does not come makes such elderly insomniacs nervous, apprehensive, and tense. It is more difficult for them to cope with daily life, as insignificant it may be. Some of the old-age insomniacs are desperate, and try everything to get sleep.

They have to be helped because their mental behavior frequently leads to depression and occasionally to suicide. The answer is devices to achieve sleep, which can be simple or complicated or even peculiar. Each insomniac has his own method. Frequently, it is a purely psychological reason for sleeplessness. On the whole, insomnia, except for very rare cases, is not an organic but a psychological problem. Some do not sleep because they are afraid to sleep. They are afraid not to wake up —to die in their sleep. Some do not sleep because, in old age, they are afraid to lose the remaining precious days and hours before they die. But the majority do not sleep because they do not get tired by physical work in daytime, which they do not do anymore; and because of that they have too much time to think. In daytime, the ordinary tasks of washing, of eating, of cleaning, of dressing, of shopping, of walking, of talking to other people is a kind of occupation which does not leave too much time for thinking. At night, in bed, one is not disturbed, and can consider many things, and most of them are unpleasant. One can easily say that a happy person does not suffer from insomnia. Lack of sleep is due primarily to worry. One can worry about health, about financial difficulties, about children or any other family problems, about life and death. There are plenty of reasons for worry, if one is a worrying type. It is not even necessary to be unable to sleep because of real trouble.

Some have a very lively imagination and worry, not about what happens, but what might happen. Or, if they start thinking, they think about opportunities which they missed in the past, or of sins or mistakes, or of foolish things which they did many years ago, and which leave a guilt complex or a regret; in any case, something which preys upon their mind and does not let them sleep.

The simplest way to fight insomnia is to take a sleeping pill. It does not have to be a barbiturate or a tranquilizer. It can be an aspirin tablet or any other tablet. If we speak about habit-forming, one can say that any device which is necessary to induce sleep is habit-forming. One can get the habit of drinking milk in order to fall asleep, or of taking an aspirin tablet or a hot bath. The main thing is that without such a device the person cannot fall asleep. Some, even many, people take tablets for sleep. Not rarely, they fall asleep even before the tablet can exercise any effect on the body, when it is not yet digested or absorbed. It is enough to have the psychological effect that one will sleep because something was done to induce sleep.

I remember a patient of mine who imagined that he could not sleep without taking an aspirin tablet. Once, when he finished watching a late-late show and decided to go to bed, he noticed to his disappointment that he was out of aspirin. It was very late; the drugstores in the neighborhood were all closed. Just the same, he dressed and walked about 15 blocks to a drugstore which he knew used to be open late at night. He actually got his aspirin tablets and, not finding a bus or a cab, he walked home. Then he put the tablets with a glass of water on his night table and fell asleep before taking his habitual aspirin. This true story shows only one thing: not that he was tired from walking 30 blocks and therefore fell asleep, but the fact that in many cases the addiction to sleeping drugs is not a real one but lies in the imagination of not being able to sleep without them.

On the other hand, under changed environment such as confinement to a hospital, or even sleeping in a strange bed in a motel or at friend's home, can cause insomnia in people who usually fall asleep easily without any drugs or any other sleeping devices. Just the same, if people get used to sleeping drugs, the drugs do become habit-forming; and it does not make any difference whether they contain barbiturates or any other chemicals. The question arises, especially in the aged: supposing they do suffer from insomnia for this or that reason, should they take a sleeping tablet, or should they rather lie sleepless the whole night long? In my opinion, they should take a tablet and sleep, rather than toss around and become more and more nervous—and after a sleepless night to have to confront a day with a kind of nervous hangover, and to become even more jittery by the thought that they will have to undergo again the ordeal of another sleepless night. Of course, there is a limit to the number of hours which a person can endure without sleep; and sooner or later such a person will either go crazy if not allowed to sleep, or will fall asleep, as was found in several experiments by various investigators. The question, however, is—is it worthwhile to endure the torture of insomnia for the doubtful price of having fallen asleep without a drug? In the case of an elderly person, it is definitely not worthwhile. In evaluation of the effect of a sleeping pill on the body compared with the effect of sleepless nights on the general condition of the subject, the answer is that the tablet, even a habit-forming one (and all of them are sooner or later habit-forming) is the better solution of the problem of insomnia. The trouble is not that the effect of the tablet wears off and one may be obliged to take more to achieve the same result, but that the tablet does not solve the basic problem of why a person does not sleep. In other words, if the cause of insomnia is worries or a depression, anxiety or fear, these psychological causes will remain and poison the mind of the sleepless patient, and cause an early awakening even with the most potent drugs.

So, in short, sleep or insomnia depend on happiness and contentment, or unhappiness and dissatisfaction; and that applies to old age more than to any other period of human life.

Connected with the problem of sleep in old age is the problem of *dreams*. We have now an indicator of a period of sleep during which a person dreams, namely, the period of "REM"—that is, of *rapid eye movement,* which is considered as the period during which a sleeping person dreams. It is proven that if a person is awakened during the time of the rapid eye movement, he will on questioning tell that he was dreaming, and often will be able to tell the contents of the dream. Of course, nobody dreams all the time without interruption. Rather, there are stages of sleep with dreams and stages without dreaming. Whether an older person dreams more or less than a younger one is a moot question, not definitely decided by investigators; the results of their research is not conclusive and often contradictory. Generally, it can be said that the amount of dreaming in *all* ages depends on emotion and imagination. If a person is highly emotional and has a lively imagination, he or she will dream more and livelier. If we consider that an elderly person has a lower level of emotion and imagination, then we can expect that such a person will dream less. However, that is highly individual and depends on the personality of the subject under observation. There are 80 to 90-year-olds who have a very emotional life and participate as much as possible in all possible activities; on the other hand, persons who never excelled intellectually will do that even less in older age, even if they do not become what is called "vegetables"—interested only in pure vegetation activities, without any mental effort. It is said that elderly people have a lesser recall of dreams. That might be the case when there is a general impairment of memory; in such a case, there will be a deficiency of dream recall. But, again, it is highly individual, and the number of subjects under scientific investigation by various researchers is too pitifully small to come to definite conclusions. So let us say in general that dreams and their recall or lack of ability to recall on awakening depend on the intellectual capacity of the elderly person. It is not necessarily a sign of senility if an old-age person does not know whether he or she dreamt, and what about.

We spoke about the theory that in sleep the brain shows not a rest but even an increased activity. If dreams are to be considered as signs of activity of the subconscious mind which comes to the fore when the consciousness is eliminated during the sleep, then we have to accept that the brain activity exists during sleep and finds its expression in dreams.

It would go too far to go into details regarding the meaning of dreams. The best explanation is still given in Sigmund Freud's *The Interpretation of Dreams*. In short, one can say that interpretation of dreams is not too difficult for a psychologically-trained person, and that dreams are on the whole a conversion of daily happenings and thoughts into images which are often frightening, become nighmares, and cause awakening with fears and anxieties. This is especially the case in older people who are easily emotionally upset or are suffering from anxiety depression. That does not mean that elderly people have only bad dreams. On the contrary, some dreams of the elderly are a dreamy realization of desires which were not fulfilled in life; and in their dreams the wishes and the desires become happy realities. Often when such an elderly person awakens and finds that all this was only a dream, he or she is bound to be disappointed and depressed. They would wish not to waken at all, to continue the pleasant dreams in eternity. Sometimes, if the dream sequence occurs after having taken a sedative or tranquilizer, such an elderly person would take the same drug in order to achieve the same result of a nice dream. However, there is the interval of brutal reality of the day, and the next night might show a completely different dream picture. Whatever it may be, dreams are a part of our night-life in sleep. They occur and exist whether we like them or not, and whether we recall them or not. Old age has no effect on the intensity of the dreams or on their nature. Dreaming is only the mirror, though a distorted one, of our mind and its working in the daily reality of life.

Part III

LIFE IN THE "GOLDEN" OLD AGE

CHAPTER XXXII

OCCUPATIONS IN OLD AGE

What kind of occupation one has in old age depends on many factors. If we consider old age as starting at 65, the age of retirement, Social Security, and Medicare, then the occupation which one has after that age is reached depends on the following possibilities. If the retirement is not mandatory, if the company for which one works does not mind continuation in the same job, in the same capacity, then the occupation which one has continues as before, as long as one can, or wants to work. I mean *can*. That is, the problem is only of capability or of possible disability. If we ask, does one *want* to continue in the occupation which one had most of his life, we have to admit that this is a very individual question. There are plenty of people who would like to forget that they are 65 and entitled to Social Security and Medicare benefits, and who desire to continue as long as their health allows it. On the other hand, there are also many people who look forward to the time of retirement with the hope of living a leisurely life, to enjoy doing nothing, and not to have any obligations to get up early, to travel to a place of work, and to have aggravations as they occur in every job. Generally speaking, these are the people who work for a living in an occupation which they do not like and which they would like to get rid of. In such a case, the problem is not of an occupation but of a voluntary retirement.

We have also to deal with people who work in an organization, corporation or even in a hospital where there is a policy of mandatory retirement at the age of 65, whether the employee likes it or not. In most cases the bitter pill is sweetened by a pension plan which is supplementary to Social Security benefits, so as to enable the retirement employee to live, if not in comfort, then at least modestly. Here the occupation which a person had cannot be continued, whether it was in banking or insurance or as a railroad employee. It is highly unlikely, if not impossible, to start in the same capacity with another firm, even if the new firm did not have the rigid policy of mandatory retirement. Who will take up an employee of 65 or more? Even with all the experience of such a person, there is a risk of sickness, disability, etc.—which can, of course, occur also in younger people, but chances are that it would sooner happen to old ones. Therefore, if one is compulsorily retired he or she should think either of life as a retired person, or look for a part-time job where age does not play any role—and which, on the one hand, augments the Social Security benefits, and on the other gives one an occupation which gives an outlet to the still-existing energy which is wasted in a case of mandatory retirement.

We have to remember that, among people over 65, we have also a large reservoir of self-employed persons where the cessation of work at the age of 65 depends solely on two conditions: financial independence which would allow one to retire, if one so desires, and health, which can easily compel one to give up his or her occupation. It does not even always mean very bad health or invalidism; it is just too much. The health might be good enough for daily life but not good to take up the daily routine of dealing with customers in a shop or a beauty parlor, for example. The same applies to lawyers, certified accountants, dentists, chiropractors, optometrists, and doctors. It is rare for self-employed workers in these fields to give up practice at the age of 65, unless they are very rich and at the same time have hobbies to which they want to devote all their time. Wealth alone is not enough; the majority of rich, self-employed persons continue in their profession or occupation until very old age and/or disability, unless they have a passion for a hobby and want to spend the remaining years of their life in the pursuit and satisfaction of their hobby, which is more their life than the profession or occupation which they exercised all their adult life.

In this way, we actually do not have to consider all groups of people over 65 in regard to occupation. The self-employed will either continue in their work as before, or they will retire when they have had enough and would not like to continue any more. The persons who can continue in their occupation after they reached the age of 65 will do so in the greatest majority of cases. So we have to deal only with the group who will be mandatorily retired. The problem of their occupation after retirement will depend on their financial resources. If they have savings, some dividends from stocks and bonds, Social Security and pension benefits—in short, if they can make ends meet—their new chosen occupation will not have to depend on what it will bring in financially. If the benefits are not large enough and one has to get some additional money, and considering the impossibility of returning to the previous occupation, a resourceful person will nevertheless find additional income which may be from something completely different, but might come up to the 125 dollars monthly which a person under Social Security is entitled to earn additionally. Among my patients, if they did not consider it beneath their dignity, some got jobs as night-watchmen or as part-time doormen in apartment houses, especially if they did not mind taking a night-doorman's job; others worked as messenger men for the Western Union or for a flower shop. Another patient of mine who was a CPA in a big firm became a bookkeeper on an hourly basis for a garage. Another CPA, mandatorily retired, got his own small clientele as a tax accountant, at least for preparation of tax returns for some small businessmen and for keeping of their books. As far as I could judge, as soon as they made up their mind that the old life was over, and that they needed additional revenue without consideration of previous achievement in other, similar or dissimilar fields of work, and if they put aside their pride, they found work, usually part-time, and were quite happy in it. The women had it even easier. They went as baby-sitters, as mother-substitutes for working mothers, as companions to ailing old ladies, as nurse-aids, as alteration and repair seamstresses if they could sew and shorten or lengthen dresses, as part-time cooks or cake-bakers for parties, as manuscript typists if they used to be secretaries in younger age, as salesladies before Xmas, and so on. Resourceful people could always find ways and means to make an additional honest penny.

What to do in all the time suddenly more than available, if there is no financial need for a real occupation, is a basic problem of retirement, not of occupation, and has to be discussed in a separate chapter.

CHAPTER XXXIII

HOBBIES IN OLD AGE

A hobby is not something which arises in old age after retirement. In a way, it starts in childhood and is connected with the character of the person, and also with the influence of the environment in which the child, later the adolescent and the grown-up, lives. In general, hobbies can be divided into two groups: hoarding hobbies and creative hobbies. A child who in old age has a hoarding hobby had to have the opportunity to observe in his parental home a respect for objects, whether there are pieces of furniture which are preserved for the longest possible time, or clothing, or china, or any other utensils of daily life. This has not necessarily anything to do with poverty, which compels one to keep things as long as possible because one has no money to buy new ones. The best proof is the observation of the behavior of welfare recipients. While some make ends meet on the scanty allowance given to them by the welfare department, and even succeed in buying some pieces of attire from the few dollars, there are plenty of other welfare clients who squander the allowance on expensive food or on liquor, and are broke and in need of additional money a few days after having received the allowance check. In homes where there should be a budget of how to spend the earned money, frequently due to either husband's or wife's extravagance or just because of poor judgement there are debts and difficulties to meet ends, which should not exist. A child is often a victim of such a situation; and if not (the extravagance sometimes results in exorbitant expenses for toys, etc.), he is an observer with two possible results. Either the child and later the teenager and the adult copies the behavior of the parents and becomes a spendthrift, or a reaction arises in his mind and he wants to live a life completedly different from that of his parents—to be economical, to live with a budget, to save money, in order to avoid the difficulties and possibly deprivations which he saw at home.

In still other homes, there is budgeting and respect for acquired values. The child who imitates his parents will also be economical, will also accumulate values, and will try not to spoil whatever he possesses, whether toys or clothing or any other belongings of his. On the other hand, a reaction can occur here too. By continuous reproaching a child regarding wasting food, or clothing, etc., the child may consciously or subconsciously rebel against the restriction imposed by the parents, and as an adult will become a spendthrift without any respect for the value of objects.

In the cases when a child learns to have respect for values and is reluctant to give up what he possesses, an instinct for hoarding develops. As an adult such a person will stick to an old suit or slippers; or, in fear of deprivation of possessions, he will buy more than he needs in order to make sure that he will always have what he wants. This leads to hoarding. It starts with necessary items and ends with hoarding even of useless things of no value whatsoever. It can develop into being a miser, as described by the French writer Moliere or by the Russian Gogol, to quote two classical examples in literature, but it can also become a harmless hoarding hobby. People become collectors, which is only another word for hoarding. One collects pictures (if he can afford it), another sculptures, still another one stamps or coins, or books of matches or ash trays, Bibles or nature books; still others collect china or crystals, or records, and so on, and so on. It is usual for teenagers to collect stamps. When they grow up, they acquire new interest in life and lose the interest in stamp collection. It is rare for a young or middle-aged man to collect stamps. The adolescent, when he loses interest, gives away his stamp collection to a younger relative without a second thought. However, when he gets old, when the scope of his interests shrinks and when he retires, he regrets his generosity as a youngster and the loss of his collection; and he starts, if he is the hoarding type, to collect stamps again. It is sometimes fascinating and it takes up a lot of time, which is heavy on his hands. The same, of course, happens to any other collector, though usually they start collecting things as an adult or even as an elderly person who can devote his time to that hobby.

It is interesting to note that women rarely collect the same things as men. They are hardly ever interested in collection of stamps, coins or butterflies. They hoard and/or collect china, crystals, household articles, antique furniture or antique home utensils. They too develop, for the same psychological reasons as men, the hobby in older age. Usually they start it around the period of menopause, when the children are grown up or married, or when they are childless. As they get older, they get even more interested in their hobby, which occupies a great part of their life. One has to remember that a hobby of collection is a kind of adventure. You have to look for the things which you collect. You have to go to auctions. You have to read about what you want to collect and where to find it, and the adventure of seeking and discovering the hidden treasure is exciting and gives a meaning to life.

The other type of hobby is the creative one. The human mind is basically creative. Without the desire to create, we would not have all the achievements of culture, civilization and technology. In addition, a human being has the urge to create art, which has no utilitarian value but satisfies the inborn wish to create something of beauty, something pleasant to behold. That explains the pictures found in caves drawn by prehistoric man. There exists also an instinct of preservation of happenings, a kind of history instinct; therefore description of old wars, of cataclysms, of everything which was unusual and worthwhile to preserve it in the memory of future generations. It was done by word of mouth, as in the example of Homer; or in writing, as in the Bible and Egyptian hieroglyphics or Chinese scrolls. These instincts of creation of works of arts, of invention of new hitherto-unknown gadgets and technological innovations, start in childhood and remain as long as a person lives and his mind functions. In adult life, not infrequently, many of the talents do not come to the fore because of the need to make a living; and only a few of the talented ones can make a living from their creative and/or artistic talents. If the talents are not in the utilitarian direction, or are not big enough to allow the artist or the inventor to make a living out of his talents, then the daily life buries them, and the earnings and jobs have nothing to do with the hidden capabilities. That is one of the reasons why some people want to retire—to wait for the retirement in order to devote their life after retirement to the creation of what they think they were able to do but could not do because of the pressure of jobs, family life, raising of children, and so on.

Now, after retirement, when one has plenty of time and leisure, an elderly person enjoys life by devotion to the hobby. If he could and loved to do carpenter's and cabinet-maker's work, now he indulges in the creation of chairs and tables which he always wanted to make. Maybe he did the carpenter's work on weekends but, of course, he had to interrupt that hobby work, and occasionally he told himself that the real big work he will do when he retires. The same applies to any other creative hobby—painting, sculpting, putting a ship into a bottle, weaving, and so on and so on. The women knit, sew, make rugs or blankets, pullovers, pillows; occasionally they take up painting like, for instance, Grandma Moses. There is from time to time in New York an exhibition of work done by old-age people, and one marvels at what they are capable of doing with immense patience and ingenuity. Most of the exhibition work is done by people far above the age of 65, in the high seventies and eighties. It is clear that they always had the necessary talent to do these things; however, in younger age they did not have the time needed for the creation of these items, which may be objects of beauty but are of little commercial value. However, it serves to satisfy the inherent desire to create, which is not only not extinguished by age, but in contrary—freed from other obligations—now blooms and flourishes.

It is not important that most of the items done in old age

are imitative and rarely are they something new, not done or not known before. Even famous artists, world-known, and I could name a dozen, did not create any new trend in their old age; they only continued the work or the direction or the style or the trend which they started in younger years. The same applies to inventors whose basic inventions stem from the time when they were young. You can find the same in science. Even such a giant as Albert Einstein, published his epoch-making theory of relativity at the age of 28. And the medical discoveries were done mainly by young physicians and scientists. The reason is that somehow a young mind, not cluttered by disappointments, bad experiences, derision, and the pessimism of elder contemporaries, and full of enthusiasm, hope and confidence, is more creative and inventive than an old one. Therefore we do not expect that the old-age hobbies will be revolutionary and will add a lot to our inventory of art and science.

But the enthusiasm of the elderly is there, and their patience is greater than of the youngsters. It helps their health; it prolongs a useful and satisfactory life. Therefore, one can only say to the old-age hobbyists, "More power to you and Godspeed. Amen!"

CHAPTER XXXIV

SPORT AND PHYSICAL ACTIVITIES IN OLD AGE

Some of the sports in which elderly people participate belong to the category of hobbies. Or let us say they are partly a sport which can develop into a hobby. To name only a few; golf, fishing, boating, hunting and bowling. Each of them can be considered as a sport activity. But sometimes, and not rarely, these sports fill the center of interest in elderly people. One could say they live for these sports, and everything else in life becomes secondary. In such a case, one has to define the sport as a hobby.

In which hobby category has one to include the above-mentioned sports? They are neither in the hoarding nor in the creative category, and therefore they do not quite fit the definition of a hobby. I would call them a filling of an emptiness in life and a fulfillment of a dream.

It is impossible even for an intellectual to spend all his days in reading, whether a book or a paper or a magazine. It is in the long run tiring and even boring, unless one is a writer or a thinker; and even a prolific writer will not spend 10 to 12 hours daily on writing or reading. He too will need recreation, because to him the reading and/or writing is either a must, an occupation, or again a hobby—a pleasure in which one can indulge from his own choice. Now, in order to variegate the day's occupation or activities, one turns to a sport which is a pleasure, harmless, and gives one also a feeling of accomplishment and/or a victory over a competitor. And that gives the satisfaction of superiority which most people desire.

With the advent of technology on the one hand and unionism on the other, we live in more comfort and have more leisure. Even a fully employed person usually does not work more than 40 hours per week, and at least 48 hours are all of his own, which he can spend as he wants it. Considering that reading and participation in other cultural activities, such as listening to music or going to a theater or concert, is a recreation of only 10-15% of the population, sport becomes a major occupation at leisure time, and all equipment for leisure and sport is a billion-dollar business. In younger age, most people try to be active in the sport of their choice, such as baseball or football in the United States. In Europe it is primarily soccer. With age, many of the sport activities of younger age, such as baseball or football, are out of the question, and elderly people can be only spectators. However, elderly people indulge even more in the sports mentioned in the beginning of this chapter. Golf is still rarely a youngster's sport for several reasons: it is slow; it requires a lot of time if one wants to play at least one game of 18 holes; it is also expensive and time-consuming in regard to traveling to and from the golf course. All these obstacles do not appeal to younger people, and they therefore prefer to play baseball or football. The same obstacles do not apply to old people who have plenty of time, who enjoy the slowness of the golf game, who walk after the ball—or, if even that is too much for health reasons, drive around in a golf cart. If the golf equipment is too heavy, they have a caddy who carries it. And finally, they have also more money to indulge in such a sport. It does not mean that you have to be 65 years old to play golf; usually people take it up in the forties, when playing golf is a sign of a status, of economic achievement. It is not a sport of the socioeconomic lower classes. But at the age of 40 or 50 it is an occasional recreation; for the elderly it is a part of his life—and nowadays also, a minor part, but a part, of *her* life. A wife who does not want to become a golf-widow prefers, even if she is not keen as her husband, to go with him to the golf course in order to play a bit and be with him. Occasionally she even excels in golf more than the husband, and he definitely does not like it.

    Hunting is a sport, an outdoor activity which cannot be pursued at one's whim. We have hunting seasons, and one can indulge in it only in certain months of the year. Many people, mostly country-dwellers, not city slickers, go hunting periodically. This is a man's sport and satisfies his inborn instinct for adventure and for violence which can be satisfied peacefully—that is, within the framework of the law; again it is also a satisfactory feeling of some achievement. After all, you have to have some marksmanship in order to shoot a deer, a rabbit or a bird, which are all moving targets. It is also a sport of middle age which can be continued in old age if health permits. The older one becomes, the less frequent will be his participation in hunting because it is a strenuous sport. One has to get up very early; one has to spend many hours stalking a deer, to walk many miles, to be exposed to change of weather and temperatures. Therefore, hunting as sport activity is rarely a sport of old age. Just the same, if one is used to it since younger years, one will go hunting even at the age of 70 or more.

Fishing is different. It is a leisurely sport. One sits for hours, smokes a pipe or even reads a paper, and waits for the fish to bite. If one fishes in the ocean, it is practically the same —only, instead of sitting on the edge of the water in the river or lake, one sits in a boat. It is not dangerous, as hunting occasionally becomes (not a few people are shot by mistake by fellow hunters). It soothes the nerves, it gives time for reflection and idle thinking, and again it gives the satisfaction of accomplishment and a proof of a certain skill. Therefore, even if fishing is indulged in by almost all age groups, even by children, it gives a special happiness to elderly people, and it is even a desirable sport from the medical point of view.

Boating and bowling belong to a different category of sports for elderly people. Both are strenuous from the purely physical point of view. Boating is either sailing or using a motorboat. Now sailing requires a great skill, in order to be able to maneuver the sailboat in all kinds of weather. After all, if there is no wind, there is no sailing. And the velocity of the wind changes, and one has to use sometimes a lot of physical strength in order to bring the boat to the place of destination.

Here again as in hunting, if one sails all his life, sailing in old age is not a particular problem, though a wise sailor will try to get a younger companion even in a small boat, just for the sake of security. Nevertheless, we saw the old man Sir Francis Chichester sailing all by himself around the world to Plymouth in England; and, after all, the professional fishermen go boating and fishing in very old age. So, if the health is satisfactory, one can participate in old age in that sport.

A motorboat, of course, is easier to handle than a sailboat. Basically, if one can drive a car, one can drive a motorboat too. And, out of town, where public transportation is neither frequent nor reaches all residences, one has to drive a car if one does not want to become a recluse and to depend on the good will of neighbors or shopkeepers. Accordingly, you can see, more than in cities, very old people driving cars, even if they are somehow handicapped. Of course, the traffic on the roads is not hectic, therefore more manageable. And the same applies to traffic on a lake or river. Therefore, one can consider motorboating for elderly people in general as a pleasant and not too strenuous sport. Again, as in driving a car, one expects that an elderly person who takes to motorboating as a sport will do it only if used to doing it since young or middle age, and will not start for the first time at the age of 65 or more. After all, if not strength, a proper function of nerve-reflexes is needed for driving a car or a motorboat, and that is a training by using the car in younger age, until in old age it becomes an automatic function.

Finally, bowling. It used to be a German national sport, connected with beer drinking—rarely or hardly ever indulged in by the women; and considered as a sport which does not require a lot of strength. It was just the proper sport for middle-aged men with plenty of fat and beer bellies who looked for the day of *"Kegeln,"* as bowling is called in German, as the day of getting rid of family obligations, of relaxation by a mild physical activity and plenty of beer and sausages.

All this is different in the United States. By promotion, skilled advertising and plentiful construction of bowling alleys with automatic pinsetting in every district of the country, it becomes not only a lucrative business with refreshment stands, etc., but also a center for gathering of young people, a meeting place for dates. And so bowling became a sport of youngsters. However, the youngsters grew up, married the girls with whom they bowled and necked, and after marriage they continued to frequent the bowling alleys. And when children arrived they also were taken to the bowling alleys. Thus, bowling became a family affair for all ages, and there was no reason why the elderly should be excluded. On the other hand, for obvious sociological reasons, there is a division between old and young; the youngsters prefer to go to other bowling alleys than the older family people, just as they frequent other dancing halls than the older people, their parents.

There is also, partly for commercial promotional reasons, a competition and contests of bowling teams with awards, trophies, etc. Again, you would not expect older people to participate in this type of bowling games. Normally, bowling for older people can be relaxing and not too strenuous, but it depends on their health. With a heart condition or hypertension, or chronic bronchitis or arthritis, you can hardly expect old people to participate in bowling. And if such patients do it, as I experienced it in my practice, it is done at the peril of their health and even life. Heart attacks, heart failure, shortness of breath due to emphysema are not uncommon occurrences in bowling alleys frequented by old people. It can be recommended for all sports that, before active participation in any sport, an elderly person should be examined by a doctor of his choice, and get his O.K.

I do not mention other sports. One can ask, what about tennis in old age, or rowing or bicycling, and so on? The answer is simple: it all depends, first of all, on the general health of the aged. And secondly, when one starts to participate in a sport not as a spectator but actively. If the health condition is satisfactory and if one is active in any sport since a young age, there is no reason why he should give up the sport—such as tennis, which is strenuous, or any other sport which requires physical exertion—if one does not overdo it and takes it easy. But, I repeat, a regular checkup is advisable even in cases when one is used to those kinds of sports; and the same applies to skiing or skating, and so on.

A question which I am often asked is: "Supposing I retire. I would like to have some physical activity which is healthy for old age. Which one should I choose?" My answer is: there are four physical activities in which an elderly person can indulge, provided that his general health is satisfactory. The simplest, cheapest and most effective is walking—just walking on a level ground, not uphill or downhill, which is a different type of exertion. How far and how long one should walk depends on the condition of his heart and the arteries of the legs. If both are in good shape, one should start with ½ mile and slowly increase up to five miles daily. In a city like New York, it means 100 blocks daily, because 20 blocks correspond to one mile. One can, of course, rest if he feels tired in between, but not too much. 50 blocks equal 2½ miles in one direction; a rest of half an hour, and 50 blocks for the return home is absolutely safe—good for the arteries of the legs, for the muscles and for the metabolism of the body. People who are used to their daily walk live longer, are healthier, do not accumulate cholesterol in their arteries, and do not get fat, which is detrimental to their health. I have a patient who is 89 years old and walks five miles every single day. He is under my observation for several years, and as far as I can judge, he is healthier now than years ago.

Of course, there are obstacles to the walk. The heart can impede the walking, if one has heart failure or frequent chest pain. The arteries in the legs can be narrowed by hardening and do not supply enough oxygen and blood for walking. However, even the walking of such patients can be improved, especially if the heart is still quite good. The arteries get good exercise from walking, and by persistence, a person who could walk only half a block little by little will learn to walk longer distances.

There are three other physical activities which are appropriate in old age. After walking, bicycling is a good exercise, and something which nowadays in America is left only to teenagers or children. And even teenagers prefer to ride in or drive a car. In Europe there are plenty of cars, but bicycling is still popular. Queen Juliana in Holland indulges in bicycling daily, and you can see thousands of bicycles on all streets of Dutch cities and, of course, in the villages. When I was a few years ago in Holland, I was shown magnificent residences of very rich people. While passing one of them, the guide remarked that the owner of the house was not at home. When we asked him how he knew, he answered that he knew it by the fact that the Cadillac of the rich man was parked next to his house, but his bicycle was not there. Apparently, he had taken it for a ride. The same picture of the bicycling you can see also in the Scandinavian countries; but one sees it also in our neighboring Canada, though not to the same extent.

Swimming is also a good physical exercise for old people who are used to swimming, though I would not recommend diving into the water, or competitive swimming—neither surfing nor water skiing; because these require too much exertion. The same applies to prolonged or long distances in swimming; because contrary to walking or cycling, one cannot rest if he or she is in the ocean or on a lake, and it is always possible to get tired and to exhaust the normal capacity of the heart and of the lungs.

These are practically all generally safe physical activities for old age. I do not talk about the physical activities of housewives, which are not insignificant. One has to remember that an average housewife does plenty of walking in her apartment or house, even if the rooms are small enough. If she works in the garden, if she tries to keep it in shape, it requires a lot of energy expenditure, even if the lawnmowing is done by other people. Lifting blankets and pillows, making and unmaking of the beds is heavy work. The same applies to laundering, even with a washing machine on hand. The mopping of the floor and its waxing is not easy either. The same goes for carrying groceries and some other domestic work. If an elderly lady has to perform all these chores, she can easily get exhausted, even if she does not have to climb stairs 10 times daily when she lives in a country home. It is only due to the stamina of the women that they can continue at old age with this kind of work. But, even so, they get worn out, and some of the above-mentioned chores are just too much for the old ladies. For the sake of the prolongation of their health and life, they need a relief. The modern gadgets are only a very poor substitute for real help. Here we come from physical activities to the general problem of life conditions in old age, and that we shall discuss in the following chapters.

On the whole, one can say regarding physical activities in old age: slow down, take it easy, and take your time. Do not live on a *strict schedule,* and do not hurry.

CHAPTER XXXV

MARRIAGE AND RE-MARRIAGE, SEPARATION AND DIVORCE IN OLD AGE

One should not think that a couple who has the good luck to live together in marriage after the age of 65 are automatically happy and contented. If we consider that on the average people in the United States married at the age of about 25, it means that such an elderly couple are married 40 years or more. One should expect that they are sufficiently used to each other with all the good and bad sides of the character of the mate, and that this should be a guarantee for a happy marital old-age life. However, it is by far not always the case. Very often people live together, but not in the meaning of "togetherness"; actually, they share the mutual life without having mutual interests. The question arises: if that is the case, why do they live together? Very often for three reasons: first, they have mutual financial interests. Even, if it is not true that two people can live on almost the same amount of money as one, nevertheless in old age it make a difference whether a person lives on his or her Social Security benefit plus small savings, or if a couple has a combined income, pays only one rent and other fixed expenses, and by spending it together can make ends meet better. One has to remember that old age usually brings a diminution of income, especially after retirement, and that in many cases people have to live on 3,000 dollars' yearly income or less. So, the finances play a great role in an old-age marital life. The second reason is children and grandchildren who are the common binding interest, and who would not understand a sudden end to a marriage of their beloved parents and grandparents. And the third reason, maybe the most powerful one, is the fear of loneliness, of not having anybody even to quarrel with or to talk to. It is an old saying, and I hear it not rarely in my practice, "Better a bad husband than no husband at all." In plain English, it means that, if a couple live together, they have a home, and that is the most important unit in human life and human society.

Of course, one has to emphasize that there are very many old-age happy couples. The fact alone that both are still alive after 40 or more years of marital life should make them happy. After all, we have in the United States about 7 million widows to one million of widowers. Considering that an average family consists of four or five members—parents and children—it means that widowhood, male or female, befalls and concerns about 40 millions of our population, that is, around 20%; and this has a tremendous effect on the family life, as will be discussed in the following chapters.

Leon Tolstoy, in his famous novel *Anna Karenina,* says in the first chapter, "All happy families look alike. The unhappy ones are each differently unhappy in their own way." This applies to any couple, but it is more so in old age. The happy old couple is well adjusted, in the meaning that each mate knows the other's faults, habits and idiosyncrasies, tries to make the best of it, and accepts even things which one does not like. But if one is smart, one knows that it is impossible to change in old age, and one has to live even with things which one never liked and still does not like. In order to be happy and contented, one has to look at the unpleasant sides of the mate benevolently and with a sense of humor. Without humor, it is difficult to go through life with all its vicissitudes anyway; so it is simpler to take it easy and to try not to see and not to hear things which one does not like.

However, not everybody is endowed with a sense of humor, or indulgence and benevolence. One has also to remember that in old age a character does not change; and, even without influence of senility, the main characteristics of a person are more pronounced and therefore sometimes also less tolerable. The same applies to both mates in an elderly couple, and it can easily lead to a breaking point. It depends on the domineering character of the male or female, which one will sooner reach the breaking point. There is an old joke which is not quite a joke but the truth: "A couple who celebrated their golden wedding anniversary were asked by a reporter whether they ever quarreled. The answer was: hardly ever, but now and then one wanted to kill his or her mate." Just in old age, when one has no more obligations, the children are happily married, one does not have to rush to work to make a living and has plenty of time to observe the doings of the mate and to think, a breaking point arrives when one does not want to continue the same life in the last remaining years. If the husband or the wife objects to the change of mode of life, then it can lead to separation and divorce. The family courts and the marriage counselors deal not only with young people. Separation and divorce are not rare among elderly couples. Not infrequently, the separation or divorce are prevented by the children or by professional counselors. However, this is not always the case. One has enough of the kind of treatment meted out by the marriage partner, and wants out, wants a different and independent life. Not long ago one could see a mild film comedy *The Shameless Old Lady*. There, the little old lady, after the death of her husband, instead of spending the last years of her life as a dignified old mother and grandmother, sells all her possessions and leads an adventurous bohemian life, to the despair and embarrassment of her family. It is not important that she does it only after having become a widow. The basic idea is that the old lady fulfills the dreams of her life, which she had to forget in the sober realities of her daily life with her husband and children.

The same can and does happen occasionally in real life, and not necessarily when a woman becomes a widow. As said before, when the responsibilities towards the nearest family members do not exist anymore, one—husband or wife—decides that now there is the last chance to live a life which corresponds to the hidden desires, such as playing cards or an instrument, going to the theater or joining a club. And, if in such a moment of decision, the husband opposes and objects, or vice versa and the wife is the opponent, the strong-willed partner declares independence even at the risk of a separation or divorce.

It does not necessarily have to be the desire to lead a more active life. Often, the wife or the husband says—"Enough is enough. I don't have to tolerate the obnoxious ways of my mate any more. I want to live my own life, and just as I, and not he or she, want it."

If one reads the proceedings of the family courts, one finds the psychological reasons which lead a partner in such a marriage to go to court, to sue a husband or a wife. Very often, and I would say in most cases, the judge or judges try to bring about a reconciliation, and usually they do succeed in doing it. The success is not due to the persuasion powers of the family judge or of the marriage counselor to whom such cases are often referred by the court, but to the fact that the rebellion is a weak and tired one, not as vigorous as it is in younger cases. After all, the plaintiff is more or less of the same age as the defendant—elderly, tired, with an undermined health from the wear and tear of the daily life-struggle; the rebellion is just a flare-up when one cannot stand it any more, or thinks that it is impossible to go on like that forever. On the other hand, one is afraid of the possible sudden change, even of the sudden freedom and of the need to cater for himself. While one dreams of liberty and independence, underlying is the fear whether after so many years one will be able to live alone and whether one will be happy in the new ways of life. Therefore, after the first step of forcing the marriage partner to attend the court action or to go to a marriage counselor, one gets second thoughts and resigns oneself to the continuation of the old life, with all the resentments and psychological aggravations produced by the marriage partner. It was always my impression that the fact alone of giving vent to the accumulated grievances by speaking to the judge or counselor gives the offended party a relief, and a hope against hope that the interference and the advice of strangers in authority will change the behavior of the husband or wife. Of course, it does not change, or only for a short while—because basically the character does not change.

Some do mellow with age, some get worse; the reason for the mellowing lies not in a change of the character but in the feeling of need for help, in the feeling of inadequacy connected with aging. The mellowing is a feeble attempt to make amends in order not to lose the helping hand of the mate.

In cases when the partner gets worse than before, there is, apart from possible signs of senility which causes it, also a more egotistical attitude. In old age the scope of interest, with some exceptions, narrows, and with the lack of wide interests there grows more interest in oneself, to the exclusion of the mate and of children or of grandchildren. The all-embracing concern is for oneself, which leads to negligence in regard to the needs of the marriage partner; and that results in the worsening of the character, with increasing grievances of the opposite party in this partnership. Of course, it all depends on the character of the marriage partners. Some are so subdued that they would accept anything from the domineering husband or wife in old age, because they accepted it all their marital life and they would not expect anything else. But, if the characters are more or less equal in strength, old age can lead to divorce or at least separation.

One has to remember that egotistical tendencies and narrowing of interests works equally for both partners. They both look for their own advantage, which is not necessarily the same for both of them. Here I have to say that, though by far not always, women usually are the sufferers, the victims, and the ones who give in and do not go away from their husbands, even if they have ample reason to do so. The reason is the eternal maternal instinct, connected with pity, which causes them to endure the frequent cruelty of the husband, usually mental cruelty, because the husbands at that age are no more strong enough to inflict physical cruelty in addition to the mental one. And words can be a more bitter cruelty than any physical punishment. I know of cases of men in their early seventies who could bring the wife to such an exasperation and despair that she left her husband, only to return in a day or two after hearing a perfunctory apology of her husband; and the only reason for her return was just pity that the poor man will not be able to cater for himself and will be too lonely.

There are exceptions: I remember a woman who had to endure frequent infidelities of her husband and negligent treatment for years and years until he became seriously ill, and she was praying for his death. And when he died, she was admired for how heroically she behaved through his last illness—admired not only by doctors and nurses at the hospital, but also by her acquaintances who should know better, knowing the marital life the couple had. Only I, as family physician, who knew both of them intimately, knew of her death-wish for her husband, and of her relief and feeling of a fulfilled revenge when he finally died. One reads from time to time of a wife who poisoned her husband, and not when he was young and desirable. And not always such a poisoning is recognized as such, and a wife gets away with murder and gets rid of a husband who is no more desirable. And the cause is by far not frequently greed; it is more often a feeling that death would be the only escape. Murder is not frequent, but suicide is also an escape from an intolerable situation.

I do not try to paint the frictions between husband and wife too darkly. But such tragedies exist; there is no use to close the eyes to reality, even if we cautiously accept that the majority of old couples are happy.

But supposing, we find that such incompatibility exists. Should an old couple in such a situation be separated or get a divorce? In my opinion, the answer is yes. It is much better to live separately, lonely but happily, than to endure unhappiness in the last years or decades of life. There are, after all, compensations: children or grandchildren, old buddies, golden age or other clubs, and sometimes living, instead of with an obnoxious husband or wife, with an old friend who has the same inclinations or interests.

And here we come to the problem of re-marriage. Usually, people think that re-marriage in old age is only a problem for widows or widowers. As for the old women, divorced or widowed, who will marry them? There is no rule about that.

It is true that we have seven widows to one widower, who in this way has a wide selection, while the widow's re-marriage is a very remote chance. Even less chance has an elderly divorcee. However, in reality it does not work in this way. It is surprising to find that one woman is wooed by many men, not infrequently younger than she is, while others can be in a society of many men, and none would pay any attention to them. The reason is simply the same as in younger age. One woman looks feminine and sexy even at the age of 65, while the other looks drab and not attractive even in younger age. And surprisingly, it is not the glamorous lady with plenty of paint and the dyed hair who attracts the men, but the woman who is high spirited, does not conceal her age, has a sense of humor and a maternal, feminine instinct; who pays attention to her looks so as to look clean, fresh and wholesome. She is the one who will always have men, and who can choose a new spouse. This applies to widows as well as divorcees. In the case of divorcees, the feeling of freedom, of independence gives them sometimes a new vigor, a new liveliness and loveliness. Divorcees are supposed to be an easy prey for men for psychological reasons, because the divorcees have an inferiority complex that they could not make a go of their marriage; and by having another man, boy friend or husband, they want to prove to themselves that they are attractive and desirable. This does not apply to elderly divorcees. They are just happy in their newly-won freedom and independence; they don't want to exchange one slavery for another. Therefore, they will be more critical of prospective candidates. They have also more experience than the young divorcee. There is also a feeling of bitterness that so many years were wasted, and a regret that one endured it so long and unnecessarily. Therefore, a re-marriage in elderly divorcees is comparatively rare.

What are the prospects, as we say in medicine, the prognosis, in a re-marriage of elderly people?

There is an old saying that, for people who lived in a happy marriage, when one partner dies and the remaining spouse remarries, the second marriage will be also a happy one. On the whole, the saying is correct, and for psychological reasons. A happy marriage is a marriage of compatibility and adjustment. If people had the common sense to marry a compatible person, one can expect that in re-marriage they will also look for a compatible mate who has the same or similar qualities of character which were so attractive in the deceased spouse. Therefore, in such a case one can expect a good second marriage. However, not every marriage which looked so happy to the outsider was actually so happy. The incompatibilities were not so gross as to lead to divorce, but there might have been a great discrepancy in character and interest. In such a case, after the death of the spouse, one looks for a completely different person; and the result of such a second marriage is very poor, and that after a very short time. There is no blindness of sex and infatuation as in young couples, only poor judgement of character of the person whom one wooes. Soon after the second marriage one discovers, in such a case, the mistake, the greed, the stinginess, the overcriticism, the egotism, or the desire to get everything and not give anything in return. This type of re-marriage in old age does not always lead to a speedy divorce. People are ashamed to show their poor judgment of character, to admit the mistake; and they go on living, being unhappy and cursing the day when they decided to re-marry. These are frequently the cases who appear in family courts, asking for adjustment or separation or divorce. Then they try again, and cool calculation of gain and loss in case of divorce usually gives some respite—some improvement in marital relations—though not always.

There is also frequently the clash of not only personalities but of family interests. His children and her children, his friends and her friends, his mode of life and her mode fo life. Very often one group does not accept the other. Children are in principle against re-marriage of a parent; women friends are jealous; men friends compare the first wife with the second and find the latter wanting. In the case of the widow who marries again, the same happens. There is always the comparison of the first spouse with the second.

And the same goes on in the marital life itself. He or she will compare characters, habits, inclinations up to smallest details.

But again, it is a question of character. In short, the prospects of re-marriage whether it will be happy or not happy, are 50-50. Basically happy, well-adjusted people will have a happy second marriage. Unhappy, insecure people will not be happy in remarriage. Old age is neither a guarantee for a happy second marriage, nor is it a barrier. In principle, a remarriage is a solution to loneliness if this, as often happens, is hard to endure.

CHAPTER XXXVI

CHILDREN, GRANDCHILDREN AND RELATIVES IN OLD AGE

The problem of the relations between elderly people and their children, grandchildren and other relatives is of primary importance, because it colors the life of the aged and, in a way, decides the well-being of such a person.

First of all, let us consider the aged who have no children and therefore also no grandchildren. If they are lucky, they usually have brothers and sisters who either live in their neighboodhood or far away, maybe even in another country. There is also a question of how attached they are one to another. Some are very close, maintain an intimate relation, and are a help in need and a substitute for a family of one's own. If the brothers or sisters are widowers or widows, they feel a greater affinity to brothers or sisters who are in the same position. There is, however, always the priority of one's own children and grandchildren, as is understandable. In other words, if a person has the choice between visiting with a child and/or grandchild, or with a brother or sister, there will always come the decision to leave the brother or sister and go or take care of, or assist or help or babysit for, a child who is a chosen relative. That will happen, even if the brother or sister needs more help than the child; unless the child (and mind you, they are grown-up people) waives his or her priority and asks the father or the mother to take care of the uncle or aunt. This should be clearly understood by old people who expect more interest and more care from their brothers and sisters; and if they do not get it, they are not only disappointed but angry and mad. Occasionally, the relation between siblings is broken off for that reason.

The question of distance between residences of old relatives is of greater importance than in younger people. Sometimes, the distance of one mile can be an insurmountable obstacle to a closer contact. Aged people are not keen on traveling (with some exceptions). They are often frail and vegetate in a routine life which saves their diminished reserves of strength and energy. Therefore, if the contact with brothers and sisters demands traveling, whether by bus, subway, train or plane, it is being broken off and maintained only by infrequent letters or telephone calls. Even in this way there are handicaps like poor vision, or a shaking hand due to old-age Parkinson, or bad hearing, which also makes telephone conversation difficult.

Ideally, it would solve the problem and make things all-around easier if such siblings would live together. However, even if there are no financial obstacles, very often it does not work for two reasons: a difference of characters and their changes due to aging—very often brothers and sisters are completely different persons who do not agree on anything—and the degree of deterioration by aging, in other words, the degree of the health condition. The difference in age may be only a few years, but while one is comparatively healthy and spry, the other is frail or even a semi-invalid who needs physical help in order to maintain an ordinary routine life.

Therefore, we rarely see aged brothers and sisters living together, unless we deal with a bachelor and a spinster, or two bachelors or two spinsters, rarely three, who have no closer relatives, combine their financial resources, and spend the rest of their life together. In most cases, each brother or sister lives separately and, if health permits, they visit each other more or less frequently. The mutual affection and relation is very individual. I know elderly brothers and sisters who spend a lot of their time together, have at least one meal per week together; on the other hand, some just don't like each other, as they did not like them in younger age, and, even without any handicap, are more or less strangers to each other, and may not see each other for months or even years while living in the same city. It also depends on upbringing and difference in age. In some ethnic minorities, like the Italians, the Greeks, the Jews, or the Puerto-Ricans, there is a closer relationship between family members. And in poor families an older child had to play the role of a substitute mother or father, if the parents were working and the younger children had to be taken care of by the older ones. In old age, the relation frequently remains the same; namely, the older sibling feels a kind of duty and obligation towards the much younger one, even if the younger is 65 and the older 72 or 75. The maternal or paternal instinct goes to the younger brother or sister.

There exists also a substitute or vicarious fatherhood or motherhood. You can find it in childless couples or in a childless widow or widower. It is similar to the godfather or godmother institution. And very often these elderly people *are* godfathers or godmothers. In any case, the childless couple, or widow or widower, takes an extraordinary interest in the life of the lucky sibling who has children and grandchildren. Not only are they interested in all that pertains to the life of the brothers or sisters, but they, so to say, adopt the children, become participants in all birthdays, anniversaries and all joys and sorrows of the family. Sometimes such an adoptive attitude is appreciated, sometimes it is resented. Not everybody has the psychological training to understand the motivation of the behavior of an aunt or uncle. Not infrequently, even when receiving gifts, the overzealous desire to help in every respect is considered as an intrusion not only on privacy but also on the relation between parents and children; especially, if they are foolish enough to comment on the behavior of a parent or of the child, and/or take the side of one or the other. A smart childless couple or a single uncle or aunt will do the duty of a relative. But otherwise, even if the life of the close family fills the void which exists in one's life, they would wait until asked for help or advice. The letters, published in all papers, addressed to psychologists or professional advisers very often touch the above-mentioned problems. The letters themselves show the interference of the aunts and uncles in the life of their "adoptive" nephews and nieces, and the resentment on both sides. One side complains of lack of gratitude; the other complains of too much meddling. Not infrequently, there is also a complaint of wrong upbringing of the children by the real parents. It sounds silly, but it is something which happens frequently. One has to understand that aged people are also very sensitive. They have the correct or incorrect feeling that they are not wanted, even with their love, their wisdom, their experience, and even with their money, if it is given with expectation of gratitude. Therefore, they bitterly complain if their being not wanted is shown by close relatives.

The relation between elderly people and their grown-up children is definitely not uniformly the same. It depends on upbringing and, let us be frank, on luck. This latter was recognized already 2,000 years ago by the wise philosophers of old. You can try everything, and under the same circumstances, the result can be completely different. There is the known fact that children brought up under the same circumstances in the same environment, in the same schools on the Lower East Side of New York, grew up to become judges, scientists, famous doctors, successful businessmen, and gangsters and robbers and thieves and murderers. The same applies to the upbringing of children in a family. You can try the permissive way and spoil them outrageously and they become good children towards their parents and also the worst possible in this respect. Or, vice versa, you can use the harshest discipline, be very strict to imbue respect for the parental orders, and, when the children grow up, they are either obedient and respectful as they were as little children; or the resentment which they harbored in the time when they had to obey, contrary to their desires and will, shows now, when they are on their own and live a life free from parental interference. They do not care for the old parents, and whatever obligations they still have are performed perfunctorily and not readily.

Here again, it is not only the relation between particular parents and particular children which influences the attitude of the children, but the environment in which they were brought up. Again, the traditions of ethnic groups play a significant role as long as they are not completely broken down by the equalizing effect of modern civilization. In Chinese families, the respect for elderly people, not even parents, is a part of the upbringing and even of the religion. You can find the same respect for parents among the Jews (after all, it is the 5th Commandment) among the Italians and all Spanish-speaking nations. In New York, not infrequently, the parents of the Puerto-Ricans stayed in their native town, while the children emigrated to the United States. It is touching to see how close are the relations; how money is saved in order to fly over and to visit the parents; especially in case of sickness; and how the whole family, all the brothers and sisters, travel for the funeral in case of death of the father or of the mother—and in most cases, they can hardly afford the costs of the journey. The same happens when a parent visits a son or a daughter, and all the expenses are borne by the children, including the best possible medical care (which they themselves cannot afford). In a way, the same happens in Italian and Greek families, though the travel is out of the question because of the time and the money involved; besides, very often the children were born here and the parents are also here, contrary to the Puerto-Ricans, who are practically new immigrants. The same applies to the Jews, if and when they are still Orthodox, religious, and keep to the tenets of the Jewish religion. You can find the same among the members of the Amish sect as long as they keep to their tradition.

In short, love in all these cases is an individual thing; but respect for the parents, and whenever possible, obedience, is a natural tradition, imbued since childhood. And it is not to be questioned, even if one thinks that it is not right or is overdone.

If we speak of the American family in general, and not of ethnic groups or minorities—in other words, when we take the population of the United States as a whole and the relation of an older generation to the younger one, and vice versa—we come to the following observations. On the whole, the influence of the Judeo-Christian religions and traditions plus the influence of the Bible still play a great role in that relationship. A complete estrangement between parents and children is very rare, and rather an exception than a rule. In all layers of the American society there exists a degree of respect for elderly people as such and for old parents in particular. This shows in the fact that in the great majority of cases, the aged parents are supported financially to the best of the ability of the children, at least as long as there is a need on one hand and an ability to help on the other hand. The cases when an old parent has to apply for welfare assistance are not rare, but they are due to the fact that the grown-up children are themselves on the welfare rolls. But if there's a possibility, the old parents are being helped financially and visited. There is at the welfare departments of the cities a special category of old-age assistance where a part of the money needed for that purpose is given by the children of the assisted elderly people.

To be frank, it is not always love which motivates the children to give help or partial help. Frequently, in small towns where everybody knows everything about everybody, it is shameful to let the old parents live on welfare assistance by the town or city while one can afford to give money for support. In the big cities, there is a certain legal obligation which allows the welfare authorities to force the children to give at least some money for support of the parents. Then, there is the guilt complex which originated in the upbringing in religious beliefs, the Bible, and respect inculcated by the parents in childhood. All this together causes the majority of the children to give financial support to the aged parents. Of course, there are many cases when the shoe is on the other foot. The old parents are financially independent and often even able to support children and grandchildren who are not so well off as the old people. In such a case, there may be love which causes attachment—and maybe just greed, with a hope for a fat inheritance.

However, financial relation between old parents and grown-up children does not exhaust the whole problem. The problem is primarily one of sentiment and understanding of the generations. Each generation was brought up in a different environment and even in a different world. It is not only that many old people were still born in the old country of origin and brought with them different traditions and views of life, while the younger generation was already born in this country; all the ideas of the old country and of the old generation are completely alien and even incomprehensible to the generation to whom the American way of life is the only known and natural behavior. Even if the old parents come here as little children or were born here, there is still a chasm of a different time in which one or the other generation was brought up.

For example, the Great Depression of 1929, about 42 years ago, which molded the life of that generation for 12 years (as most people know, the Depression ended about 1941 when the U.S.A. entered the Second World War) is ancient history to people who were born in those 12 awful years. The impact of the Depression caused a psychological scare for the future, with the resulting obsession of obtaining security, Social Security, pension, savings—anything which would insure the avoidance of the still-remembered times of deprivation, unemployment and hunger of the Depression years. The younger generation is more interested in the enjoyment of daily life's pleasures and luxuries: cars, dishwashers, refrigerators, television, movies, bowling, ballgames and so on. Most of these pleasures of life are bought on installment plans; and though people still save, if they can, the problem is primarily to meet the dates of installment payments and to calculate which new item can be bought on a new installment plan or credit card. In other words, while the older generation is interested in security, in being sure that one will not starve, the younger generation is interested in raises of wages and salaries for greater enjoyment of daily life. Unavoidably, any discussion of aims and goals leads frequently to clashes, to a lack of communication and understanding between the generations. Each goes his own way, lives his own life; and the best way is small talk about daily occurrences and nothing about basic problems, thus avoiding clashes.

Under such circumstances there is little likelihood of the two generations wanting and being able to live together under one roof. It is interesting to observe that grandparents and grandchildren often understand each other better than old parents with their children. And I mean teenagers with their grandparents, not only small grandchildren. The reason is obvious. There is a clash between the ideas of how life should be conducted between the teenagers and their parents, as it always was, is and will be between two generations. The grandparents are out of it. They are not participants, they have nothing to decide in the controversy between parents and children. On the other hand, there is a certain amount of tenderness between grandparents and grandchildren; not only generosity, financial and otherwise, but an affinity between the idea of the old and the very young—and even if not an affinity, then at least understanding and lenience towards the aims, goals and desires of the very young. I would say they are nearer to each other than in the relation between parents and children. You can see that sometimes when there is an estrangement between old parents and their children, it does not extend to the grandchildren and their grandparents, where there is love and attachment on both sides. That can be seen in cases of intermarriage when the parents violently object, while the grandparents, if they do not condone, are at least more lenient and understanding. The same applies to choice of occupation by the youngsters.

On the whole, the relation between elderly people and their relatives—children, grandchildren, brothers and sisters—did not change the pattern as evolved in thousands of years of civilization. The pattern of living is nowadays different and requires a separate chapter.

CHAPTER XXXVII

LIFE EXPECTANCY AND LONGEVITY IN OLD AGE

In pre-war China, where great age implied great prestige, a son often showed his respect for an elderly parent by making him a birthday present of a longevity robe. The gown, made of expensive silk, was embroidered with the Chinese characters for "long life."

Longevity and life expectancy was always and still is the desire, the dream of humanity over the ages. In all nations and in all religions there are stories of people who attained very old age, to give only the example of Methuselah in the Bible. The idea of reincarnation, which we find in most religions, is psychologically built on the premise that, if you cannot live eternally and if you die in old age or prematurely as a young person, you can come back to life either by appearing in a different form of life, such as an animal, or as a new human being who is a reincarnation of the person who already spent some time on earth. The idea of resurrection of the dead when the Messiah will come, which exists in the Jewish religion, is a kind of consolation that the death is only temporary, and that after a time the dead will be again alive. The same applies to the idea of Heaven and life after death, which is common to the Jewish, Christian and Islamic religions. It is, apart from the religious tenets, also the realization of the dream of human beings of eternal life. People just love to live, even with all the possible miseries, aggravations and vicissitudes, and know very well that death is the end of all hopes, of all aspirations, of everything. And after all, medical science is directed towards one aim—to prolong the life of human beings by fighting diseases, by research into the reasons for decay and wear and tear of the organism, and by searching for the fountain of youth; how to turn the time-clock back; how to make people younger and therefore to expect to live longer.

Young people are not so much attached to life as old ones, and therefore the problem of longevity and life expectancy is more important in old age. The reason why young people are not so much attached to life is simply because they cannot imagine themselves old. And the question who is old depends on who asks and answers the question. For a boy of 10, a most beautiful woman of 25 seems to be old. For a man of 45 the same woman would be a most desirable young girl, while for a man of 65 she would be a kind of spring chicken.

In old age one knows that the years which one has yet to live are numbered. It can be a year, five, ten or even twenty; but in any case the years are measured, and very precious. We have to distinguish between life expectancy and longevity.

Life expectancy depends on external factors, such as climate, epidemics, diseases which are prevalent in a given environment and in a given age; it depends on nutrition, on the type of food, on social and economic conditions. In a social class which is financially better situated, life expectancy will be higher by better and more food, by more sanitary conditions, by a possibility of evasion of diseases which are primarily connected with food, sanitation and housing. It was not always so, due to the fact that medicine was not on a high level and science did not understand the reason for mortality from diseases. Diseases and epidemics were considered as bad vapors, as supernatural evil influences, and so on. That better sanitary conditions could improve the health of the population and diminish epidemics was not even considered, and if anyone timidly gave such a suggestion, he was ridiculed.

The ignorance, the lack of rudimentary hygiene and sanitary rules, greatly diminished life expectancy. It was very low in the poor sectors of the population, but it was low enough also among the rich. Out of 10 children, maybe two or three survived to adult life. One hundred years ago, a man of 40 was considered as an elderly person; if he was at the end of the twenties, he was middle-aged. In one of the novels of the famous Russian novelist Turgenyev, there is a sentence "A middle-aged man of about 28 entered the room." The life expectancy was low because of mortality from diseases in childhood, such as measles, diphtheria, summer diarrhea, pneumonia, smallpox, polio. Tuberculosis was rampant, and epidemics of cholera, of the plague and other pestilences occurred from time to time. It was, until the most recent decades, the question of survival of the fittest, of the healthiest, of the most resistant who could overcome all the diseases, including the poor sanitary and nutritional conditions.

With the advent of modern medicine, of better housing, better and more food, of less overcrowding, of less work and of work in better sanitary conditions, the chances for survival became much better. Even a delicate child had a good chance to attain adulthood; especially since we started to vaccinate children against all kinds of diseases, thus eradicating their occurrence. Accordingly, the chances that a newborn child in the U.S.A. will reach the age of 65 now are: 66 per cent for boys, and 15 percent higher for a newborn white girl. If we go by the reliable statistics of the Metropolitan Life Insurance Company, females have steadily increased their margin of survival over males. It is the same all over the world, and also in the animal world; and it always was. The basic reason is the fact that females are more needed for the survival of the species, in which the males play only an incidental and rather transient role. The ratio of survival of females increased even in the last decade. The difference of survival over males was 10.5 percent in 1940, while it is 15 percent now. However, the chances of surviving to the age of 65 have remained practically unchanged during the past decade for males and have improved only slightly for females. The explanation, as far as I can judge, is in the fact that we reached a certain summit in prevention of diseases, with only a slight modification of prevention of serious diseases, such as the new vaccination against measles. On the other hand, there are still diseases for which we have neither cure nor prevention. And as long as we do not know how to fight them, they will take a certain toll of the population, and the life expectation will remain the same in childhood and adult life.

One has to mention that the statistics of the Metropolitan Life Insurance Company pertain primarily to the white population of the United States. The reason is not discrimination, but because the statistics are based on life insurance policy-holders and the proportion of Negro policy-holders is too small to allow for a correct statistic. The life expectancy among Negroes is, of course, lower because of a lower standard of living, greater overcrowding in the ghettoes, poor nutrition conditions, less education, more ignorance of the sanitary needs, and therefore more spreading of diseases. The Negro children are, of course, just as much vaccinated as the white ones; but parasites, tuberculosis, and syphilis are more prevalent among the colored population, and therefore life expectancy is lower. Just the same, on the whole, the life expectancy in the United States, due to union collective bargaining contracts and the welfare programs, does not differ very much in the white or colored population; the more so because in case of illness the achievements of medicine are accessible to white and colored, poor or rich, more or less in the same way.

Now, at the age of 65 which interests us in this book, the expectation of life among white men gradually rose from 11.5 years in the years 1900-1902 to 12.8 in 1949-1951, again according to the statistical analysis of the Metropolitan Life Insurance Company. It has changed very little since then. Altogether the gain in 65 years was only 1.4 years. However, life expectancy at the age of 65 among white women increased from 12.2 years in 1900-1902 to 15.0 years in 1949-1951 and to 16 years in 1962. That means that the total gain for females since 1900 was 3.8 years—more than double that for men.

Today, about 20 percent of white men reaching the age of 65 can reasonably expect to be alive at the age of 85. One third of white women who reach 65 now can expect to survive to the age of 85. On the whole, progress has been made during the past 25 years in improving survivorship after the age of 65.

White men at that age can now expect to live an additional 3 years, or about one year more than in 1940. Life expectation of white women at the age of 65 now is 16.3—an increase of 2.7 years since 1940.

The reason for the improvement of the life expectancy in old age is largely the significant advances in public health and medicine, as well as marked improvement in nutrition and living standards. As a result, as the Metropolitan Life Insurance Company reports, the mortality from tuberculosis, pneumonia, and other infectious diseases has been greatly reduced, and accident fatalities lessened. Future gains, however, in regard to mortality control will depend for the most part on advances in the fight against the degenerative diseases. The report says further that, for example, a 10 percent decrease in the death rate from all causes at age 65 and over would add one year to the average remaining lifetime. The gain would be greater for men than for women.

Most important in the outlook for gains in longevity at the older ages would be a possible reduction in deaths from cardiovascular and renal diseases—that is, diseases of the heart, of the arteries and of the kidneys. A 10% decline in mortality from these conditions would add almost 2/3 of a year to the average life span of aging people. A 30% reduction in such deaths would increase life expectancy by about two years.

Control of cancer is the second largest source for increase in average longevity after the age of 65. However, a reduction of as much as 10% in mortality from cancer would yield only a slight gain of less than two and a half months; and a 30% reduction in the cancer deaths would add only about ½ year to life expectancy of white men and women at the age of 65. Decrease in the death rates from other major causes of death in later age—such as accidents and pneumonia—would have an even lesser effect on the longevity of older people.

All this is the problem of life expectancy in old age. It is not the same as the general problem of longevity. Supposing one escaped all the diseases of childhood which threaten the life of an infant, a child or adolescent, either by having had the diseases or not having contracted them. The first question is, how one did it to survive, especially, if one is now 65 or more —which means that he or she was born around the beginning of the 20th Century, when all the great achievements of medicine and science did not exist yet. The second question is: in what condition did one arrive at the age of 65 or more? And the third question: if 20% of men or 33⅓% of women over 65 have a life expectancy of 20 years more, how does one know whether one belongs to that lucky percentage and not to the unlucky remaining percentage of men and women?

The three questions are parts of one entity, namely, that of a person who happens to belong to the group of people who live long, and longer than the average. I say the average, because after all 80% of men and 66⅔% of women do not attain the age of 85 or more, if and when they come to the age of 65. There must be some special reasons why one group of people lives longer and the other not.

In my practice I see a lot of old people: and when I am asked (not infrequently) what to do in order to prolong life, I answer jokingly: first of all, you have to choose the proper parents. Though it sounds silly and like a joke, it is not quite a joke. Actually, people who live long have also parents who attained a very old age. In other words, barring accidents, there are families where very old age is habitual in many generations. There are several explanations for that phenomenon. One theory is that of natural selection and survival of the strongest, of the most resistant specimens. The other theory is the genetic makeup, that is, something in the genes, in the inheritance, in the blood which makes some individuals more resistant to infections, to diseases, and gives them the little extra which is necessary for survival. The speakers at the 7th International Congress of Gerontology (the science of old-age diseases) in 1966 came to the conclusion that human longevity is predetermined not only by the genetic makeup, but is also influenced by a great complex of physiological, psychological, social and environmental factors. In an effort to find a common denominator for longevity, mass studies of long-living populations are under way in several nations. The first findings of investigators in the United States, Great Britain and the Soviet Union were reported.

Professor Pitskelauri of the Tbilisi University in the Republic of Georgia of the U.S.S.R. stated that there were over 21,000 persons aged 100 and older in Russia, and that Soviet Georgia alone has 51 centenarians per 100,000 residents. The scientists examined about 15,000 individuals over 80 in Georgia, and established a number of factors which positively influenced human longevity, namely: (1) 85% of these aged resided at altitudes of 500 to 1500 meters (1600 to 4500 feet) above sea level, and longevity was higher in a humid, subtropical climate. (2) Some 70% of the parents, siblings and other close relatives of the subjects under investigation lived to a ripe old age. (3) Nearly all of the aged were married, indicating a favorable effect of family life on longevity. Over 90% of the women had wed before age of 25, and became mothers before 30. Large families were the rule—as many as 18 children. (4) About 60% of these old still worked on farms, in orchards, etc. They enjoyed horseback riding and hunting, remained socially active, spent a major part of each day in the open, and did a considerable amount of walking. (5) About 55% were quite healthy and had no physical complaints. Many were examined by a doctor for this study for the first time in their life. More than 50% had a normal sight and hearing. (6) Their diet was of mixed food, with strong seasoning and plenty of vegetables and fruits. (7) As a rule they did not smoke or drink alcohol to an excess; they did drink at their meals small quantities of home-made natural wines, similar to the peasants of Italy, or Spain, or France. In short—the Russian professor concluded—favorable social conditions, life in the country at a temperate climate, suitable, not excessive, physical work and exercise up to old age, family life, high female fecundity, diet, moderation in smoking and drinking of alcohol—all these factors promote longevity. According to the Russian medical theories based on Marxism and less on accepted medical research, he did not add the inheritance factor, what we call the genetic makeup, to the list of things needed for promotion of longevity; though he did mention that all close relations of the subjects under research investigation also lived to a ripe old age.

Interesting was the report from England. After all, the climate there, the social conditions, the food, the habits and occupations are completely different from those in Soviet Georgia. The report was given by Dr. Hall and Miss Croft of Newcastle General Hospital in Newcastle-upon-Tyne, based on investigation of 100 consecutive admissions at the Geriatric Unit—41 males (average age 88) and 59 females (average age 90). Surprisingly, the results of the investigation hardly differed from the Russian results. Again: most led an extremely healthy life before admission; 50% of the females and 33% of the males had never been admitted to a hospital before. The family—parents and other close relatives—tended to live above the life expectancy at their time. They usually came from large families. They were born when their parents were young. The vast majority came from the lower middle class. They had more formal education than the general education at that time: and the English investigators thought that, maybe because of that, the subjects were better prepared to adapt to changes in later life. Considering the first awful conditions, especially in industry, in England about 70 years ago, it may have played a certain role in survival, though it was not clear whether the old people spent their childhood and youth in a rural or urban environment. The other factors in the English research work were also similar to those in Russia, namely: a long period of happy married life, with about 75% of the old people having celebrated their 50th wedding anniversary; they all worked longer than others before retirement, and some were still working at age 86 or 90. And even after retirement, about 75% had hobbies which kept them occupied.

At the same Congress an American study was presented by Dr. Belle Boone Beard of the University of Georgia in the United States. She was interested in the mental and psychological functioning of the very old people. On the basis of interviews, questionnaires and psychological tests, she came to the following conclusions: one trait of survival of these subjects is a lifelong habit of elimination from consideration of unimportant material, and the ability to concentrate on problems relating to living or jobs. Their memory (100 men and women from 100 to 123 years) is still very good for recall and stored memory tests (such as reciting the alphabet or naming Presidents). They retained intelligence in situations which demanded an evaluation of knowledge and a choice of decision based on new evidence. This involves adjustment in thinking, modification, acceptance and adaptation of new knowledge. They showed ability to make decisions and to accept a change in daily life. About 80% of the subjects under investigation still selected their own clothes; 40% did their own shopping. Nine men still had and worked in their businesses; a 100-year-old judge still presided in court; others still made decisions of importance in their businesses.

An interesting observation was that the very old people had a keen sense of humor; they told and invented jokes. This sense of humor seemed to be an important weapon in the life fight for survival, to be able to see everything from a humorous point of view—even bad news, vicissitudes of life and unwanted changes in the routine pattern of life.

Most centenarians were still active mentally and as much as possible physically. Poor hearing and/or poor vision, did not impair their mental abilities or interests.

If we try to paint the image of a person who has succeeded in reaching a very old age of 90, 100 or more years, we can easily do it on the basis of the three investigations which were done in three so different countries as Russia, England and the United States. If one adds one's own experiences, the picture of such a person becomes quite clear, and gives a clue to the problem of longevity. These are the qualifications for a long life, and one has to make the proviso in advance that there are plenty of exceptions to the qualifications.

One exception is striking because you find it in all countries: namely, the world of performers and of artists. That comprises actors and actresses, singers, comedians, dancers, musicians, painters, sculptors, and writers of all kinds—novelists, biographers, historians, columnists, theater critics and so on. Many of these people achieve very old age and are mentally alert and not infrequently physically quite fit at the age of 80 or 90. The amazing thing about this group is that all of them do not lead a healthy routine life which is supposed to be contributory to longevity. They go to bed very late, usually at two or three a.m. They get up late, rarely before noon. On the other hand, some of them, like film and television performers, have to get up very, very early, at 5 a.m. and often they do it after having slept only a few hours. They sometimes work for 10 to 12 hours almost without interruption and certainly without a proper intermission for a good meal. Accordingly, their meals are irregular and haphazard. If they are performers, they have to watch their diet, and as women are often semi-starved in order to keep their figure and not to lose their job. The male performers are not in a better situation regarding nutrition. The life vacillates between feast and famine. Tension, aggravation is a part of their daily life. In a way, the same applies to the people who work for newspapers and magazines as reporters, columnists, cartoonists or editors. Writers, too, cannot lead a normal life, especially if they have to meet a deadline. Even poets or painters have to get an inspiration by mixing with others, by participating in a social life—which means also overdrinking of alcohol and taking too many sleeping pills or stimulants.

Such a life, which in many cases also means a lot of traveling with even greater irregularity of food, sleep and rest, with frequent changes of climate, should by all rules lead to a shortening of the life-span and acquisition of all kinds of psychosomatic diseases, such as ulcers, colitis, heart trouble, etc. It works this way; and many of the artists, to use one noun for all people connected with art, die young or earlier than they should.

But it does not always work in this way. We know many people connected with art, actors and actresses, opera singers, writers, poets, painters, comedians and so on whose life was by far not exemplary in almost every respect and who just the same lived or still live to a long, ripe age—mentally still alert, or alert to the last day of their life, and quite often also physically doing not too badly.

I have often considered what is the explanation of this exception, which after all defies all the rules which we specify for a good, healthy, long life. It is difficult to come up with a complete answer, but personally I believe that this phenomenon is due to two factors. One is in the American study which I just quoted—namely, elimination from consideration of unimportant material. In other words, an artist is so engrossed in his art that he is not interested and does not pay attention to anything else. Just being devoted to his art—whatever it may be—helps him to survive. As Dr. Boone Beard said, this in itself is a survival trait. And this attitude towards life eliminates frictions, aggravations, tensions. Even if the artist hurts others, he or she does not hurt himself or herself. This egotistic attitude is an act of self-preservation, though despicable from the humanitarian point of view. It is healthy for the artistic individual and allows to overcome the tensions of the artistic life, because they are limited and therefore self-effacing. It is well-known that it is difficult to be a spouse of an artist, mainly because the artist is self-centered, limited in interests, and egocentrically oriented.

The second reason for survival and long life may be the metabolism and glandular condition of the organism of a true artist. Primarily, it is the thyroid gland which by its hormone adds a little more pep to the functioning of the individual. It does not have to be too much overfunction. If that happens and such a person suffers from Grave's disease, it is definitely detrimental to one's health and shortens the life-span. But just a little more than usual works like a pinch of salt in the dish, and enhances the vitality, allowing the person to overcome unpleasant and tough times.

I would like to stress that the theories which I give as an explanation for the miraculous survival and long life of many artists who lived or still live contrary to all health rules are presumptions; and it would require a deep investigation of each medical biography of an artist who lived to a ripe old age, in order to come to a final scientific conclusion. At present, we have to accept the fact that they are exceptions to a rule.

In returning to the rules which govern survival and longevity, it is comparatively easy to state the conditions which are auspicious for a long life. We have to find the common denominator for the studies in three completely different countries as given above, and we can in this way describe the characteristics of a person who will most likely live to a ripe old age. Here they are:

1. The person has to be a member of a long-lived family, where several generations and close relatives lived to a very old age.

2. He or she (more often she than he) is one of a big family, one of 8 or 10 siblings. The explanation for that fact probably is that in a big family there is little coddling and spoiling, and early beginning of some work at home or on a farm.

3. The subject in question is or was invariably married, and usually happily married for many decades. There is hardly a bachelor or a spinster among the people over 85 or 90 and more. Apparently, married routine life is conducive to longevity.

4. The person has to be very healthy at all times and has very rarely to require hospitalization or doctor's care.

5. He has to be moderate in his habits regarding food, drinking of alcohol and smoking; though, he does not have to be a teetotaller, or non-smoker.

6. Working and physical exercise as long as possible, also daily walking of long distances—all this not in excess—prolongs life.

7. In case of retirement, a hobby which occupies most of the time is a good substitute for work. If the hobby is not connected with physical exercise, walking—a daily constitutional—is imperative.

8. Social activity, participation in community life, belong-

ing to clubs, conversation with other people, discussion, going to the movies or to television shows help a lot. Being a recluse, and loneliness, shorten the life-span.

9. And finally, one has to have an interest in life and the daily happenings; in other words, one should not retire from human society but be an active member of it, whether by participation or, if being an onlooker due to poor health, an interested one.

One more item has to be stressed in enumeration of conditions for longevity. Though senile symptoms are to be expected in very old age, just the same, complete senility, turning into a vegetable, does not prolong life. Even when such a person has no troubles, financial or otherwise—eating, drinking, elimination and sleep—it is not enough to sustain life for a long period of time. Lack of mental activity causes a diminution of resistance to external dangers, such as colds, pneumonia, accidents and so on, and these external factors kill such persons in no time.

If one over 65 asks how to achieve a very old age, the answer lies in the points mentioned above. While some are beyond the power of an individual, others are possible and can be done by turning the course of life in the proper direction. The will to live is a very strong instinct which still exists in mentally alert people of any age who are interested in life, and in what it brings now and will bring in the future.

CHAPTER XXXVIII

THE PROBLEM OF RETIREMENT

The age of 65 has become the fixed date of the period of retirement. This is the age when a person becomes an old man or an old woman and should think about giving up the usual work, whether an occupation or profession. Very often one does not have to think about retirement; it is being done for him by compulsory mandatory retirement, whether the person likes it or not. In view of the fact that we live in our decade especially with an accent on youth, whether in fashion, dress, movies, television or music, it is not surprising that in a great number of enterprises—corporations, banks, industrial complexes and even in professions—the age of 65 becomes the time of a mandatory retirement. In order to facilitate the change from a productive life to a long period of idleness, many corporations and unions have instituted pension plans which should augment the meager Social Security monthly allowance which is due at the age of 65. We see the same nowadays in the pension plans of municipal and state workers. Also there are voluntary pension plans promoted by the insurance companies with big advertisements—"How I retired with 300 dollars monthly income for the rest of my life." Apart from the financial problem of retirement, the mandatory retirement at age of 65, and sometimes even only 60, is now in force also in professions. Some hospitals have a mandatory retirement age of 65 for physicians, even if they are unpaid attending physicians. The general idea is everywhere the same: give room and opportunity for younger people. "You are stale and cannot conform with the new ideas, new inventions, new gadgets and the new approaches." It does not matter that by this mandatory retirement you throw away an experience acquired slowly in the course of many years of trial and errors, and the skill which is needed in the occupations and professions.

There is, of course, something logical in this mandatory retirement. On the one hand, it gives the young man an opportunity to show his mettle, to prove in real life his ideas, if he has any, and lets the corporation or the hospital benefit from his new approach to the daily problems. On the other hand, from one day to another it throws into the garbage can the experience of maybe 40 years. In the medical profession, in the case of an attending physician or chief of a department, it is particularly pathetic: one is being retired mandatorily and becomes an honorary consultant—which title means nothing and usually does not lead to consultations with younger doctors, but at best leads to concentration on private practice without practical participation in the daily life of the hospital. In the industry, when there is a mandatory retirement, it gives the executives a bonus, an excellent pension, maybe additional shares, but it implies a complete retirement from the activities of the corporation. The rank and file in case of retirement is just fired and has to live on Social Security and on a pension, either from the corporation or from the union, if any.

Where does the mandatory age of 65 come from? Funny enough, and hardly known, it was suggested by the German Chancellor Bismarck in 1879. At that time, longevity was much lower than nowadays. 65 was a very old age, maybe corresponding to 75-80 of today. Somehow, the age 65 suggested by Bismarck in his Social Security plan, which was the first in the world of today, got fixed in the minds of people, and it stayed fixed after 90 years, notwithstanding all the changes which occurred in the century.

Fortunately, 65 is not everywhere mandatory, and many people, not only self-employed, work longer and sometimes to a very old age, high in the 80's. If I say fortunately, it is, because there are many medical and psychological, and also financial, reasons why there should be objections to compulsory retirement at the age of 65.

To start with financial reasons. We have to remember that the population of the United States ages. We have now in 1971 about 26 millon people over 65. By 1980 the statisticians consider the probability of 30 million over 65 as likely, maybe even more. That means more than 10% of our population. The Social Security and pension plans, the Medicare and Medicaid plans, will have to be paid by the part of the population who make a living from salary and wages. The more people retire at the age of 65, the greater will be the burden of the wage earners to pay for all these retirement plans. On the other hand, if a person works after the age of 65, he or she contributes to these plans by deduction from the salary or wages.

One has also to remember that retirement in almost every case means a reduction of income. The savings of the average retiree are small, sometimes no more than a few thousands of dollars or less. The cost of living is rising, and the pension granted by the union as an addition to the Social Security allowance (which, by the way, is ridiculous compared with the money paid in as a deduction in the 30 years or more of its existence), is only a pittance. In short, the retired person, in the great majority of cases, has to count every penny and is a minor consumer, though just the same a consumer, and has no productive life of his own.

So, as matters stand at present, from the financial point of view, retirement is a disadvantage, a loss, a monetary degradation, a source of aggravation. Financially, apart from few exceptions, the golden age is not golden, hardly silvery—rather a tinfoil age. According to statistics, poorer people are the great majority of the old; after 65, one in five has an income of under $1000 a year, and half of our aged families has less than $3000. Regarding savings, two out of five have liquid assets of under $200. Few old people own a substantial amount of property, though 2/3 own their own houses; but the value is small. Retirement is difficult economically. Most older people have less than the Federal Government estimates to be a minimum adequate budget for an elderly couple in good health.

From the medical point of view there is no such thing as a mandatory retirement age. One can be old at the age of 55, another person is still full of pep and vigor at the age of 75 or 80. It depends primarily on the condition of the organs; if the heart and the circulatory system are intact, if the mind is not impaired, the chronological age is of little importance. Important is the evaluation of the biological age and of the functional capacity in terms of the job requirements. If this capacity does not correspond to the requirement of the job, then one can talk of a medical need for retirement. This incapacitation may occur in younger age, not necessarily at the age of 65, because of illness, or a heart attack, or a premature aging with arteriosclerosis. It also depends on the type of work. A bookkeeper, a stenotypist, a filing clerk will and should be able to continue such an occupation longer than a machinist, toolmaker, or even a female operator of a sewing machine where speed and accuracy are essential.

And it is little known, that our aging population is, generally, sound of body and mind. No more than three to five percent of persons of over 65 are in institutions of any kind. And another five to ten percent of old people are disabled at home and are cared for by relatives; but even these could live a more active life with better home care and more occupational therapy.

All this leaves us with the problem that we have about 26 million people of 65 and over who are capable of work to a lesser or greater degree, and whose abilities are wasted, not utilized. This can be considered as a great loss to the economy and the progress of the country.

Here we come to the psychological impact of retirement on the old-age people.

One wonders, why should a person retire? Of course, we do not speak of the medical need for retirement, about the invalids and the physically and/or mentally incapacitated. But, as even mentioned, we have about 26 million people who are able to work after 65. When and why should they retire? To begin with, there is a percentage of people who look forward to retirement, to get rid of the daily routine, and to be able and have the leisure to do what they always wanted to do. But even those people who have longed to retire get disillusioned after 6 months of retirement. It is fine to be able to wake up and not to have to rush to work. But, after a time of leisure, one gets bored and has the problem of filling the tremendous amount of time on hand. We spoke in a previous chapter about the hobbies and occupations in old age. But, apart from that, psychologically there is the problem of a feeling of having been discarded and marked as a useless man. What should be the meaning of the retirement, and in which way will it make a person happy? The result of idleness is that a retired person is disturbed, neurotic and depressed. One wonders why he should retire at all. Would it not be better to follow the word of God, "In the sweat of thy face thou shalt eat bread till thou return unto the ground?" It is usual for the rural section of the population (which, by the way, diminishes more and more due to agricultural machinery and its efficiency) to continue working as long as strength is left, regardless of chronological age. A farmer cuts down the work which becomes too hard for him, leaves it to the son or a hired hand, but does not give up his farm until he dies. Among the industrial workers the pension plan does not appeal to many who are entitled to it. This is the experience of the union of miners and of the ladies' garment industry. Not a few who refuse the pension and continue working, do it not for financial reasons but because they would miss the work, the environment, the feeling of belonging to a useful community, and, last but not least, the desire to have an obligation to go to work and to come home with a feeling of fulfillment and of the right to rest.

Three instances can well illustrate the psychological need for work, and it shows that the urge to do a useful work applies to all segments of the population. It is not necessarily restricted to the uneducated workers who would not know what to do with their time without work and without hobbies, and without any participation in the cultural world such as reading, theater, concerts, music etc.

One approach to the problem of retirement work was done in England. The owner of an engineering works at Garlaston in England was asked by the retired employees that they should be allowed to go on working. He gave them tools, a separate building in his factory, and also equipped it with easy chairs, games and a radio. There was no foreman, no supervisor; they could work or play as they wished. They were paid piece-work for all machine parts which they produced at the same rate as the younger workers.

To the surprise of everybody, the old people put in a full day's work. Absenteeism was low, the production high. With their pension, many of the elderly workers now had more money than before the retirement. Instead of operating at a loss, the work of the old people had returned a profit. Some old workers invented new methods which increased the productivity ten times.

Another example of utilization of old-age people was done in the United States. The Hasting College of Law in the University of California has a faculty which includes some of the most distinguished law scholars and teachers. All of them are 65 and over (average age 73). According to the Dean Emeritus of the Harvard Law School, this is the strongest law faculty in the country. They were all invited to teach in California after reaching the mandatory age of retirement at other law schools.

In another instance, thousands of mandatorily retired executives in the United States decided to prolong their creative years by helping organizations which are related to their professions and training. They created an organization called "Score," which means the initials of "Service Core of Retired Executives." This organization is connected with the Federal Small Business Administration. The "Score" has established 180 branches all over America and helps primarily with help, advice, knowledge and small loans to businessmen whose business has less than 25 employees. The "Score" sends a consultant to such a business which needs help. He is a former executive who spends a few months with the business in question, finds out what is the trouble, and on his recommendation the way of improvement is found, or the application of the small businessman is rejected. The businessman pays only the administrative expenses of "Score" connected with the straightening out of his problem. The retired executive does not get paid. He is satisfied that his experience and knowledge are utilized and not wasted because of his mandatory retirement.

All the examples prove one thing, and they can be multiplied in every way of life and in any profession or occupation, namely: as long as the mind of a person works, as long as his body does not fail, a human being has a creative urge and a desire to utilize his or her faculties. Retirement as such, and especially a mandatory one, is a fallacy and a dangerous one. It creates a wasteland, a prospective graveyard, and causes a tremendous loss of human resources.

It does not mean that retirement is not needed. Wrong is a mandatory retirement, because it does not take into consideration that each person is individual. What should be done is a check-up at the age of 65—a physical, psychological and mental in order to ascertain whether the person can continue in his or her work as before. If the answer is in the affirmative, one has to be asked whether he or she wants to continue working or prefers to retire. Some will gladly retire, especially if they would be financially secure. Others, and probably a great majority, will choose to continue working: maybe part-time, if that would be possible in the prevailing circumstances.

In any case, retirement, as it is practiced nowadays, is arbitrary and unjust. The greatest injustice is the restriction of the working capacity of a person receiving Social Security allowance to an earning of $1700 per year after the age of 65, while giving him or her an allowance which is a pittance and not commensurate with cost of living and a generally decent life in the "golden age." Completely ridiculous is the provision that, at the age of 72, one can earn as much as he or she can without losing the Social Security allowance. In this respect I heartily agree with Dr. Irving Wright, the former President of the College of Physicians, that the earning restriction for people between 65 and 72 should be abolished. After all, the Social Security allowance, now in action since 1935, is not a welfare measure, but an insurance for which a person paid for a long time a premium which was withdrawn from his or her earnings. One should not be punished for receiving what is only due him and her.

This abolition of the restriction in earnings alone would help the financial status of the retired old people, would help to build a bigger consumer population, would help the economy and lift the morale of the old-age people. And the money earned in this way would by taxation also increase the Social Security fund.

To paraphrase the famous words of Bernard Shaw, "Youth is wasted on young people," one can say, "Retirement is wasted on old people." They do not appreciate it, they do not want it in the majority of cases, they do not enjoy it and do not know how to enjoy the retirement; and if the retirement is mandatory, they are apprehensive. The old people cannot enjoy the age of retirement under the best of circumstances because of aging; they just don't have the strength and the stamina for long and strenuous journeys, for lively entertainment, even for the theater and concert parties which easily exhaust them. They prefer to stay at home and to lead a routine life.

A young engineer, in conversation about retirement, gave not a practical but a good theoretical solution of the problem. "Let people retire for 20 years at the age of 30, and then return to work and stay working to the end. In these 20 years they will be able to enjoy life, and then they will come back to work with additional vigor." But, of course, this is a brilliant but fantastic idea.

Retirement is a complicated and difficult problem. If tackled by economists, sociologists, psychologists and physicians, the problem can be solved to everybody's satisfaction.

CHAPTER XXXIX

WHERE TO LIVE IN OLD AGE?

The best place to live for an elderly person is at home, and preferably with the close relatives such as children, or brothers or sisters, if there are no children. This is the ideal solution for the problem of residence of old people; but, as all ideals, they cannot always be realized, and for several reasons. First of all, there are a great number of children who do not want their parents to live with them; sometimes because of lack of accommodation, there is just no spare room for the parents or for a widowed mother or father. In this respect the old saying is still valid: "A mother has room for 10 children, but the 10 children have no room for the old mother"—and there goes the fight over who should take the mother or the parents in residence. The fight usually does not go on because each of them wants the parent, but on the contrary, because every one of the children thinks that the other should take up the "burden" of caring for the parent. It is, of course, not always the case. There are some loving children who cherish the idea of having the mother or the father, or both, at their home. In some countries it is understood that generations live together. So is the case in Puerto Rico. So it is in Greece, where it is considered as a moral crime not to take care of one's old parents—and such a neglect is punishable by fine and imprisonment. The same applies to India, where there are always some relatives who take aged people into their own homes. It is very common in Italy; and even in the United States the Italians live together very often as a closely-knit family, with two or three generations under one roof. It used to be the case in the first generation of Jews and Irish who immigrated into the United States.

However, all this is nowadays here rather an exception than the rule. On the other hand, there are many old people who for usually psychological reasons do not want to live with the children, who want to preserve their independence and also do not want to interfere in the life of the children, or to be the bone of contention.

The fact is that, at least in the United States in the urban areas (it might be different on the farms), the problem of residence of old people in the great majority is not solved by family ties and living together with the young generation.

If we accept this fact, the next question for old people is: what is the best solution? Where should they live in order to preserve their physical and mental health and to lead a happy and contented life?

One has to understand that this is not a short-term but a long-term problem. As I mentioned in a previous chapter, the total number of disabled old people does not amount (according to statistics) to more than 10%. If we accept that in 1970 we had about 26 million people over 65 in the United States, there is still a problem of over 2 million disabled to various degrees, and the solution for them is not simple. Definitely even more difficult is to find a solution for proper living quarters for the over 20 million who are quite healthy and have the intention and the prospect to live many years to come, while their number multiplies, and is predicted by the statisticians to reach 30 million in 1980.

In order to give some answers to the problem of housing of old people, we have to divide them into groups. There are, first of all, the disabled, who have to be subdivided into:

a. totally disabled and dependent completely on somebody else's help,
b. needing some personal care and domestic help,
c. independent in personal care but needing considerable domestic assistance,
d. independent in personal care but requiring some help services.

Among these 4 categories of disabled there is also a group of temporary totally disabled by an acute illness or accident who, after a while, will come into the above-mentioned categories, but might under favorable circumstances return to the large group of old healthy people.

Regarding the disabled, it is clear that the subdivision of those who are totally disabled and dependent completely on somebody else's help, need custodial care in an institution or hospital for chronic diseases. Not always is such a disabled person beyond rehabilitation. With doctors specializing in rehabilitation, physical and mental, in charge of a hospital for chronic diseases, it is possible to improve the condition of such patients—if an institution considers itself as a *therapeutic* unit where every inmate is not someone to look after his or her material daily needs, but as a patient who requires daily treatment and, if possible, daily examination and daily physiotherapy. Not infrequently, an old person is considered and treated as incontinent because there is nobody to give a bedpan or help to the bathroom in time. The same applies to daily exercise in walking, whether with a walker or with a cane; which means the difference between being confined to a wheelchair or becoming independent by learning to walk after a hip fracture or a stroke.

The second group of old people needing some personal care and domestic help are actually only in need of a partial nursing, and that can be provided in their own home by visiting nurses, Catholic sisters, family service volunteers, and so on.

The third group of disabled who are independent in personal care but needing considerable domestic assistance are actually candidates for a home for the aged, unless they can afford to pay for domestic help—such as a day maid who will clean and cook and leave enough food for the hours when the disabled will be on his or her own.

And the fourth group of disabled who are independent in personal care but require *some* home help services is definitely not a group of candidates for a nursing home; they need a part-time cleaning woman, and/or some help from relatives.

(a) *Nursing Homes*

If that is so, the question arises, who needs a nursing home? The answer is: by far less people than those who populate the existing nursing homes. The general idea of a nursing home is to be a custodial institution, and that is where the nursing home is wrong. In almost every case the nursing home is considered as adequate if it is clean, if the food is sufficient and palatable, if there is a bit of static entertainment such as television and radio, and when occasionally it is visited by an occupational therapist. For the rest, the nursing home, into which the old people are packed away, is a waiting room for death to come. Those waiting for death are the old people inside, and the relatives outside who have to visit and to pay, if the welfare department does not take over the expenses.

Inside the nursing home there is no segregation in more or less disabled groups of inmates. Except for some of the better-type nursing homes, food is brought on a tray to the bed. The patient is either perpetually in bed or sits in a chair next to his bed. In some nursing homes there is a dining room for more mobile patients; occasionally there is a room for watching television. And that is all. The doctor comes for a few minutes once a month to order medication, or is called in an emergency to call an ambulance for acute illnesses when the patient is sent to a hospital. Not infrequently while he is at the hospital, his bed is taken over by a new admission; and on discharge from the hospital the old man or woman is taken over by another nursing home, and has to start anew to find new friends, to get accustomed to another environment, to new faces, to new nurses and new doctors.

The nursing home is here to stay as long as two conditions are not fulfilled. First, our home aid program is awfully inadequate, far behind any other civilized country. In England, over 300,000 old people now receive home aid; in Sweden, 50,000. But in the entire U.S.A. at the end of 1963 this home aid went to only 1,205 old persons. In both England and Sweden, at least 500 of every 100,000 of the total population get home aid. In the U.S.A. the ratio is less than 5 per 100,000 population. The second condition is the conversion of the custodial type of nursing home into a full therapeutic nursing home where an inmate gets, as in a hospital, daily examination and daily treatment. That is, we shall have to consider the nursing home as the third part of the treatment of a sick person who cannot return to his or her home. If I say the third part, it is because I expect that we shall soon, due to Medicare, have the new European style of hospital—as is, for instance, the case in the Cantonal Hospital in Geneva, Switzerland, or the Oxford Cowley Road Hospital in England, to cite only a few examples. This second part is a halfway house where patients are treated before being discharged either home or to a convalescent home. The patient is transferred to such a halfway house when he recovers from an operation or heart condition or any other disease, does not need any more daily or hourly care, and can take care, at least partly, of himself by eating in a dining room, by dressing and washing himself without help—while still needing and being under observation and treatment by the same doctor who took care of him while being in the first house, the real hospital.

The third house would be the nursing home, to which would be confined the incurables, the chronic, the patients who need a long-term treatment—*treatment,* not custodial care.

In the meantime, before we get the ideal conditions, we have in the U.S.A. close to 8,000 of these nursing homes, of which 87 percent are operated for profit. Less than 8 percent are sponsored by private philanthropy, and only 5 percent are under government management. The average number of residents in proprietary homes is about 30-35, in philanthropic homes about 70, in government homes, about 110. About 70 percent of all persons needing nursing homes are in proprietary homes. There is little or no professional control of these homes. The licensing standards in many states are scanty and confined largely to safety, fire hazards, sanitation and overcrowding. The safeguards, as they are in general hospitals, are rare in long-term institutions.

By the same token, one has to know that the majority of

the inmates of these nursing homes are welfare recipients, and that therefore the bills paid for the nursing home care are paid by taxpayers, and occasionally by voluntary funds if such a home is under control of a denominational charity. In this way we are confronted by the fact that the great majority of our old, infirm poor are given away for care until death, to a person or a corporation with a manager who, in order to stay in business, must make a profit out of the misery of those unhappy old people, even if he has lofty humanitarian impulses or principles. The profit can come only at the expense of the inmates by saving on food and by offering a bare minimum of facilities which can pass a government or city inspection.

The medical care is also provided by the city or county which foots doctors' bills by accepting welfare physicians who are willing to treat the patients in the nursing homes for a minimal fee. They do it because of the volume and as an addition to their work at their offices with private patients.

In short, we have a nursing home industry with nursing homes bought and sold for profit, which often is considerable. The homes belong to businessmen who have no idea about medicine, medical and nursing care. They put in an office manager, a supervisor, and nurses as the law requires. Because of scarcity of nursing personnel there is usually one registered nurse, or maybe two in larger institutions, and the rest are practical nurses and nurse-aids on whose shoulders lies the burden of running the daily routine of the institution, and on whose benevolent attitude depends the daily life of the old, infirm people.

As long as nursing homes are not treated at least in the same way as hospitals for chronic diseases, but remain profit-making businesses and a dumping place for indigent, sick old people, we shall have the conditions as they prevail in most of the "homes." The motto for improvement should be "A nursing home is for treatment of chronically-ill persons, not for custodial care."

(b) *Homes for the Aged*

A home for the aged is not a nursing home but is meant for people who are not bedridden, who can dress and feed themselves, but who cannot live by themselves because they are frail; they cannot do any domestic work or cook, and cannot afford private help or companion who is healthier, more mentally alert, and able to perform the daily routine which is too much for the aged in question.

The difficulty of the maintenance of a home for the aged lies in the fact that the borderline between a person who needs a nursing home and one who is fit for a home for the aged is a very thin one, and an oldster can easily cross over the borderline by his mental and physical condition very fast in one or the other direction. The inmate of the home for the aged can deteriorate and has to be brought into the nursing home; or, vice versa, an inmate of the nursing home can by skillful treatment improve so much as to be eligible for admission to the home for the aged. The ideal would be where both types of accommodation are available, so that a patient does not have to be shuttled to another environment, but could be just shifted from one floor or one room or one building on the same premises to another, as the need arises. That such an arrangement is possible can be demonstrated by the example of the Hebrew Home for the Aged in New York, which combines it even with an infirmary for acute cases. Such co-ordinated geriatric services exist in several countries in Europe. In Copenhagen, Denmark exists the well-known complex of De Gamles By (Old People Town) which combines a hospital for old-age chronic diseases with a home. There are 1600 beds, out of which 450 are at the hospital (for acute and chronic cases), 500 beds in the nursing-home section with 4 homes for 125 people each, and 8 homes with 650 beds for ambulatory aged. Similar is the co-ordinated service in the town of Gavle in Sweden. In the Sodertull Hospital a special geriatric unit of 75 beds works in collaboration with the general hospital: 374 beds are available for chronic cases, and 600 places in homes for the aged. On the grounds of the main hospital within 100 yards are three annexes totalling 170 beds: one for physically disabled, one for chronic psychiatric patients, and one for mentally deranged. In addition, there are 100 beds in homes for frail elderly persons, and a block of apartments for 150 independent old people. And all this range of old-age care is under a single administration.

The ambulatory aged who live in the homes have individual rooms with an individual toilet, and mostly also with their own shower (which is preferred to a bathtub because it does not cause accidents as easily as a bathtub). The resident furnishes the room himself except for beds and curtains, and is even encouraged to do so in order to create a home atmosphere. It does not matter that the rooms are sometimes crowded with chairs, sofas, tables, the walls are covered with family pictures. This is as the elderly one had it in his or her home, and it gives individuality to his residence, thus avoiding institutional flavor. The name of the resident is on the door, just as it was in his former residence.

In some homes, eating in small groups is encouraged; there are large rooms for occupational therapy; there are beauty parlors and barber shops with hairdressing equipment and driers to encourage the care for good, clean looks of the men and women who reside in the homes for aged.

With all this wonderful arrangement of the care for old age, there is plenty of criticism, and some objections are justified. One could see it long ago on our national television when a little drama with the title "Do Not Go Gentle into That Good Night" was performed, with the subject of an old carpenter winding up in a home for the aged, and how he resents being treated as if he were senile or crippled. And after all, as he says, and what is unfortunately true, doing nothing and staying in a home for the aged is waiting for death to come. It is a sometimes luxurious, sometimes less so, waiting room, but away from normal daily life. One can understand the rebellion of the old carpenter who prefers to return home even if he is not wanted by his children; but, of course, it is not a solution for everyone, because many are unable to work any more, and others have no more a home to return to.

There is also a criticism that the homes for the aged are not near the district with which the old people are familiar, and they object to disruption of their local and community relationship. Also, the isolation of the aged, segregation with other old people, loss of contact wtih their adult children, even if the aged wished to live alone or separate from them, were objections noticed in Scandinavia as well as in North Dakota— as documented, for instance, in the study of Dr. Hawkinson, lecturer in sociology at the University of Minnesota. And that brings us to the problem of residence for the 90% of our aging population who are sound in body and mind and do not require hospitals and nursing homes, or at least no more than the younger sector of the population.

(c) *Residences of Old-Age People*

At a meeting of the American Psychological Association in New York in 1966, a 5-year study of the psychological effects of retirement housing, based on interviews with aged residents in several different types of retirement, was presented by Misses Sherman and Dodds and Messrs. Magnum Jr. and Wilner, all of the School for Public Health of the University of California at Los Angeles. I have the impression that their investigation, based on a census of 299 licensed and 330 non-licensed facilities, showed findings which correspond to findings in several other states of the U.S.A. and in Western Europe.

The authors investigated 5 different types of residency, which can be found almost everywhere, namely:

1. A retirement hotel in downtown Los Angeles which provided rooms and meals at the total cost of $103-145 per month.

2. A low-cost suburban retirement village in central California, offering apartments at a rental of $75-$101 per month.

3. A high-rise apartment building in the downtown section of a city in southern California, where rentals ranged from $66 to $111 per month.

4. A middle-income retirement village in a desert area in southern California, with houses in the $13,990 to $27,290 price range.

5. An upper middle-class retirement village in northern California, selling cooperative apartments for $21,000 to $32,000.

6. A life-care facility in a college town near Los Angeles, licensed by the state and offering rooms, apartments and cottages at an initial investment of $5,000 to $25,000 plus maintenance of $175-$700 per month.

If you are interested in the subject and look around, you will find the 6 different facilities everywhere—in Florida, in the state and city of New York, in Atlantic City or Asbury Park, New Jersey, in Philadelphia, or in the Middle West, or any other state of the Union. The price range may differ. In some places the facilities will be cheaper, in some others more expensive. But characteristic is the fact that business, private enterprise as well as communities, started to realize that old-age people represent a huge market for real estate investment, and that with their savings and Social Security benefits and the other income which they might have, the oldsters can be a source for smart manipulators' big profits. This profit is often justified; occasionally the old people are gypped out of their savings and money. In any case, in pamphlets and advertisements one has to draw a rosy picture of a blissful life in the respective accommodation. There must be emphasized also some special attraction. The old people want a warm climate in order not to be exposed to the rigors of a severe winter which takes a toll of their energy reserves; therefore, the attraction of California, Arizona and Florida. They have to count their pennies, therefore the price range has to be modest. They don't like to drive, or have no money for the upkeep of a car, therefore the house or apartment has to be near public transportation. And finally, there should be a kind of community life in which one could participate, make friends, be active in mild sports such as bowling, or shuffleboard, or golfing.

If the operator of a real estate can give the old people the above-mentioned conditions, he can count on finding customers for his accommodation.

Whether the customers will be happy in these residences is a different matter. The above-mentioned authors investigated the status of the elderly residents. The findings were not surprising and corresponded to observations made by other investigators in various states and countries, and also seen by physicians specializing in old-age diseases. It corresponded, more or less, even to my own observations, which were confined to the practice in the city of New York.

It is clear that poor old persons are not classified in the 6 categories given by the Californians. The poor elderly are mostly on welfare assistance. They live, if healthy, in broken-down hotels or rooms in rooming houses, at a rent defined by the welfare authorities. In some cases, they continue to live in their own rooms or apartments which they had for decades when they did not belong yet to the old-age group, and had some income from work. Now, they try to keep the room on Social Security benefits, some savings and some assistance from welfare authorities, if they are eligible.

The six categories' range is from lower middle class to upper middle class or rich. The categories 5 and 6, with investment of $21,000 to $32,000 and a corresponding maintenance per month of 125 and more dollars, is beyond the financial capacity of an average old person, though a small percentage can afford it. This percentage is comprised of retired businessmen, executives, lawyers and physicians.

The accommodations, with a rental per month of 75 to 110 dollars, could be considered as an average; very often it is below the rent paid in the larger cities such as New York, Los Angeles or Chicago. The lower rent would attract the elderly people whose income after retirement would be sharply reduced. The so-called retirement hotels—or, as they are advertised, "Senior Citizens' Residences"—are mostly for single people: widows, widowers, and bachelors and old spinsters. The California authors found it in their study; I can confirm it for New York City, and I shall include the nursing homes in that category regarding the marital status. Of course, the new apartments and houses for retired people are taken over by couples; it would be too much work and too much loneliness for an old retired person to buy or to rent a house or an apartment in a retirement housing project where he or she has to make new friends and to start alone a new mode of life.

The education level is also the same everywhere, whether in California or Florida or New York or New Jersey or Illinois. It corresponds to the price range of the rented facilities. A laborer, a blue-collar worker, could not save enough money to afford a high-rent apartment or a more expensive house. By the same token, he started working after elementary school or after junior high school. Therefore, college education is rare among the residents in the lower-class residences. The old people with college education also prefer residency in a town or city where they can continue their cultural interests, such as theater, concerts, lectures, have good libraries, and on the whole be able to participate in the intellectual life of a community. To have a peaceful life without worries is not enough for them. They need some food not only for the stomach, but also for thought.

The whole problem of where to live in old age cannot be solved by financial considerations only. In this respect the California study, though it gave a lot of interesting facts, did not touch the sector of old people who live in their own apartments, nor the ones who live with children or siblings or other relatives, and whose rental problem differs from the persons mentioned in the six categories. There are two main problems connected with housing of old people which have little to do with rentals, namely: (a) Is it advisable to create old-age ghettos by promoting "senior citizens' hotels," "retirement villages" or "retirement apartment houses"? (b) What is the relation of the housing to contact with children and other relatives?

We do not have to discuss the problem of housing of old people who live with children or brothers or sisters. In their case nothing has changed since they reached the age of 65 and became even officially Medicare patients. Whatever personal problems they had or have, these are highly individual and have to do with character traits, family happenings, etc., but not with old age. I would consider them as happy as they can be.

If one does not have the good luck to live as an older family member with the second and even the third generation—so to say, as patriarch or matriarch—and the great majority do not live with children or brothers and sisters, the two main problems of ghettos for old people and the relation to children are interwoven.

First, do old people want to live with other old people of more or less the same age, or not? According to the California study, about 38 percent said they have friends less than 40 years old. Only one third wanted to have greater contact with youth. Sixty percent denied that having young people around would be more fun. But only 38 percent said that they actually enjoyed living apart from young people, and only 36 percent said that they had moved to the retirement site primarily to be with their own age group.

The problem of advisability of building of housing for aged only is discussed everywhere, in the U.S.A. as well as in Western Europe. Scandinavian countries, as the most progressive ones, started expressing doubts about continuing to build houses for the aged, because the elderly objected to being segregated with other old people.

It corresponds to my experience and that of other physicians. Whenever I broach the subject of entering a home for the aged or to live with old people, I get an answer, even from persons who are not well and have orthopedic or cardiac ailments which impede their functioning at home, "What? I don't want to live with old people. I am not yet senile." And in most cases I get that reply from people in the high seventies who just don't want to accept that they too are old; maybe the others are, but not they. For a person whose mental capabilities are not impaired, life with other old people is somehow, in their imagination, connected with living with senile persons, and therefore in most cases not acceptable yet. The attitude of old people towards children and youth in general is a double one of love and hatred at the same time. They realize that there is a difference between modern cultural values, interests, and activities, and those which prevailed when the old were young. In a way, they are attracted by the new trends and are jealous that they cannot be young again and take part in the activities of the young. On the other hand, because of the discrepancy of views, they prefer to be with people of their own generation. But they do not want to be completely isolated, and it expresses itself in the wish of aged parents for more frequent and intimate contact with their adult children. Whatever town, city, state or country you compare—California, New York, North Dakota, Amsterdam, Copenhagen or England—you find one common denominator in all the studies of the attitude of the aged. They prefer not to be isolated from the community, from the younger ones; they do not want to live in old-age residences, unless they are forced by external circumstances to do so; they do not want to live with their adult children, unless they did it always by tradition or family ties; and at the same time they want to have a close contact with their children by frequent visits, if the children live nearby; they want more affection and intimacy while maintaining their independence.

What is the solution of the problem of housing for the old people? There is no general solution for all of them. Each case is individual, and what is good for one is terrible for another.

One might be happy in a home for the aged, as I know one whose happiest day in the last 20 years was the day when she was informed that, after a waiting period of two years, she was admitted to the home—and, though she had only a small Social Security benefit and no savings, was even given a room for herself. I have rarely seen an expression of such happiness in the eyes of a lonely woman of 80 who had no relatives whatsoever, having come to the U.S.A. from Russia. I saw the same expression of happiness in the eyes of a colored woman of 75 whom I helped to obtain a two-room apartment in one of the city's integrated "projects" on the Lower East Side. As she told me, "Imagine me having an apartment on the 14th floor with a kitchen and a bathroom, all for myself, and that after not having had a bathroom for myself ever in my life." But I also saw unhappiness when a patient of mine left New York for sunny California with a good amount of savings, bought a house there in one of the retirement villages, lived there with his wife unhappily ever after, and finally sold the house and returned to live in Los Angeles, in the hustle and bustle of a big city. I saw a happy retired couple who alternate between New York and Florida, where they have a co-operative apartment, and have apparently the best of two worlds; in New York they see the children and grandchildren, in Florida during the winter they enjoy the sunshine and escape the dreary climate of New York in wintertime. I saw and see the unhappy old bachelors and spinsters, widows and widowers who live in the residential hotels of Manhattan, and spend most of their time lingering for hours over a dreary luncheon (they cannot afford a dinner) in the cheaper restaurants, and then either sitting for hours on the benches of Broadway or, in bad weather, in the lounges of their hotels, hoping for an opportunity to exchange some gossip about neighbors, or food, or the manager. And I know dozens of the lonely men and women, each of them cooped up in his or her room in a rooming house or apartment, and considering how to kill the time, and how to make ends meet and what one can afford to buy in the supermarket. And I know many lonely old people who are not lonely anymore because they became volunteer workers of all kinds—nurse's aides, book and magazine distributors, letter writers, file clerks and so on, in hospitals, Red Cross, institutions for the blind and found themselves suddenly wanted and valuable.

There are some common trends which apply to most of the old people. First, they want to keep their privacy and independence as long as they can. The private room or apartment may be as dreary, old, and slummy as possible, but it is their own, filled with memories. And it is something they can go back to, a space which belongs to them and where they are the boss, where they can do whatever they want. Secondly, they are all afraid of not having help if they get sick or disabled, and should lose in this way their privacy and independence, should they be obliged to give up their apartment or room and go to a nursing home or a home for the aged. They are also afraid that they might get sick, be unable to call for help, and die without anybody knowing about that.

In my own experience I have several times seen things like that happening. The patients died and were lying dead in their apartments for several days before anybody noticed that something was wrong. Not infrequently, lonely patients had an accident, broke a hip, or became unconscious and were lying for many hours on the floor before they were found in this condition, occasionally by pure chance.

The old people with only distant relatives, or even with children living thousands of miles away, dread such a possibility. Even in the villages they are not sure that the neighbors will miss them and will come asking about their welfare.

Nevertheless, it is my definite impression, and I know that I am not the only one, that the desire of elderly people to keep their independence and privacy as long as possible by sticking to their own apartment or room is a legitimate one and should be encouraged. Old people should not be pushed out of society by putting them in a nursing home or a home for the aged, as long as it is by some means possible not to. We can save their private residences if we would only organize *more home aid* for the partly disabled or the weak, who are, just the same, not complete invalids. There is an untapped source of home aid by one old person helping another one. The same hospital volunteers could be re-directed into helping not-so-fortunate oldsters with some domestic chores, with doing some shopping for them, or going with them for a walk or to the movies, or just being companions for a few hours and relieving the duties of a relative who can attend to some business or job at that time. Very often such home helper can get paid and augment his or her income.

The emphasis on homes for the aged is on the way out. The houses, the villages, the apartment buildings all designed for the old people only, is a wrong idea. As previously mentioned, the majority do not want to be segregated and to live in a kind of old-age ghetto. They do not want the younger generation to interfere in their activities, but they want to be in the center of daily life, to participate in all social, political and cultural events. The recent construction in Copenhagen, Amsterdam, and Stockholm, where there is always an advanced sociological understanding of geriatric problems, has taken into consideration the wishes of old people; and accordingly in the new houses, 10 to 15 percent of the space includes apartments allocated for the elderly, with government subsidies to encourage the builders.

To sum up: the problem of where to live in old age is very individual, but can be grouped as follows:

1. Complete invalids and chronically-ill old people have to be in nursing homes; these have to be managed as institutions for constant treatment, not for custodial care.

2. Whenever possible, an old person should live with close relatives, children, brothers and/or sisters.

3. If not possible—and in the majority of cases it will not be possible—they should stay in their own apartments or rooms as long as feasible.

4. The semi-invalids should get home aid as outlined.

5. Homes for the aged are needed whenever an old person cannot take care of himself anymore.

6. The solution of having apartment houses with a mixture of younger with 10-15% old tenants is the best, contrary to retirement residences, whether in hotels, villages or high-rise apartment houses.

POSTSCRIPT

This book, *The Old Age Story*, was written for the elderly men and women who at the age of 65 and more were confronted with many problems which they did not have in younger age. These problems are of a financial, sociological, economic, physical, psychological, and even mental nature. Some of the problems are due to their own aging; some are interrelated with their own family and with the community in which they live.

The multitude of the problems of old age cannot be completely discussed in one book, and not even in a series of books, because they are too many and too variegated. Therefore, we have a section of medical science which deals with them—at least, from the medical point of view; and it is called geriatrics or gerontology.

My book tries to give an answer to the many questions which old-age patients ask doctors in general practice, specialists in their fields, and sociologists who deal with the relations of old-age people with the community in which the elderly live.

From the medical point of view, as I have stressed several times in various chapters of my book, the old-age people have many ailments and, not infrequently, they have multiple ailments, physical, psychological and mental. The significance and importance of these ailments are discussed in the appropriate chapters. Not omitted are the serious sicknesses which threaten the well-being of the elderly and their life.

This book is meant as a reference book for the elderly, who can find an answer to the signs and symptoms which he or she notices and which annoy and cause a sometimes justified and sometimes unnecessary anxiety. It does not substitute for the need to see a physician and to obtain a proper treatment. On the contrary, in a way, it shows when to visit a doctor and to receive as early as possible the proper treatment, and thus escape the possible dire consequences of the discomfort which he or she might feel.

Though the book is primarily written for the elderly, it is also intended as a guide for the younger one, in a double capacity. Namely, it tries to show which diseases are due to the aging process and do not occur in younger age; and also it tries to be a guide for the younger-generation members who are concerned with the phenomena of old age which they observe in their parents, relatives and friends, and the importance or insignificance of which they do not understand and cannot evaluate.

While my book deals primarily with the organic, mental and psychological diseases of old age, it is just as important to stress that, according to statistics and research, only about 10% of our aging population can be considered as chronically, physically or mentally (or both) ill and in need of constant treatment. In view of the fact that we have in the United States already 26 million persons over 65, and that we expect to have 30 million by 1980, the 10% is still a multitude of, at present, over two million sick people; and it is a major task for the communities and government to find the proper way to handle this problem.

On the other hand, we still have 20 million elderly persons over 65 who are sound of body and mind, apart from ailments, accidents and acute sicknesses which can befall them just as it happens to younger people. These 20 million healthy oldsters represent already one-third of our voting population, and therefore can play a very significant role in the formation of the destiny of our country. But, though they are a power in themselves, they, by the nature of the aging process, do not realize that they could influence the medical care and sociological and even economic decisions made on their behalf, and not necessarily with their own participation.

The fact that we have Medicare and Medicaid assistance and insurance is a proof that our country is waking up to the need to do something to improve the lot of our elderly senior citizens. I do not doubt that we are also heading in the direction of improving our nursing care for old people. And the trend is also that changes will occur in respect to the ability to improve the working and earning capacity of our elderly people. This will be a boon to the economy and a blessing to the healthy old-age retired persons. With this will go an improvement of housing for them; and instead of segregation will come a restoration of the just, deserved and dignified place in the daily active life of the community in which they live.

ACKNOWLEDGEMENTS

I wish to acknowledge with thanks the help given to my research by the wealth of statistical material and medical reports in several issues of the monthly digest magazine *Geriatric Focus,* published by the Knoll Pharmaceutical Company, and by some of the material of the weekly magazine, *The Medical Tribune.*

NOTES ABOUT THE AUTHOR

Leon Merkin, M.D., is an Attending Physician at the Medical Clinic of the Roosevelt Hospital, Associate Physician and Chief (ret.) of the Gastro-enterological Service of the Sydenham Hospital, in New York. He is also an Associate Fellow of the American College of Cardiology, and a Fellow of the American Geriatrics Society.

For several years he was assistant editor of the *American OSE Review*, the medical journal of the Jewish World Health Organization, of which he is still a member of the Board of Directors. He was also, as long as it was published, the chief editor of the yearly Health Almanac for the laity.

During the war he was in London, England and worked as Medical Director of the Refugees Fund, which was created in order to take care of the refugees who escaped after the Nazi invasion of France, Belgium and Holland.

Dr. Merkin graduated from the Medical Faculty of the University in Berlin, Germany. He was, in addition to his private practice as specialist for internal diseases, an Assistant at the Medical Clinic and Polyclinic of the University Hospital Charité in Berlin, in preparation for a research and teaching career. The Nazi regime forced his dismissal from the University. Dr. Merkin published medical papers in his speciality in Europe, and also in New York while an Associate Physician at the Cardiac Clinic of the City Hospital, and later. Dr. Merkin was elected for 1971 as President of the Federation of five American-European Medical Societies which comprise about 1500 members, physicians practicing in New York City, and some of them teaching in medical schools and colleges of the New York Metropolitan area.

Dr. Merkin continues practising as specialist for internal diseases in New York City.